EQUIPPING SPACE CADETS

Children's Literature Association Series

EQUIPPING SPACE CADETS

PRIMARY SCIENCE FICTION FOR YOUNG CHILDREN

EMILY MIDKIFF

University Press of Mississippi / Jackson

The University Press of Mississippi is the scholarly publishing agency of
the Mississippi Institutions of Higher Learning: Alcorn State University,
Delta State University, Jackson State University, Mississippi State University,
Mississippi University for Women, Mississippi Valley State University,
University of Mississippi, and University of Southern Mississippi.

www.upress.state.ms.us

The University Press of Mississippi is a member of
the Association of University Presses.

First printing 2022
∞

Library of Congress Control Number: 2022930230
Harback ISBN 978-1-4968-3902-2
Trade paperback ISBN 978-1-4968-3901-5
Epub single ISBN 978-1-4968-3900-8
Epub institutional ISBN 978-1-4968-3899-5
PDF single ISBN 978-1-4968-3898-8
PDF institutional ISBN 978-1-4968-3897-1

British Library Cataloging-in-Publication Data available

For Aleister—
I hope that by the time you can read,
you have a galaxy of choices.

CONTENTS

ACKNOWLEDGMENTS

Many people deserve my gratitude for helping this book come into being. At the top of the list, I want to express my love and thanks to Chris Clark for your R wizardry and baby-distracting and picturebook-hauling, on top of your usual support—this project would have been literally impossible without you! I am also grateful to my family, who fostered my love of reading and the creativity that led to this theory of mine, which is my theory that I have, that is to say, which is mine.

Marek Oziewicz, Megan McDonald Van Deventer, Sara Sterner, Laura Lemanski, and Bonnie Laabs were there when this project first leapt into being, and their continued support, emotional and academic, was a cornerstone for those first drafts. Thanks are also due to Joe Sutliff Sanders for giving me the confidence and writing tips to turn this project into a full-fledged book, and to Farah Mendlesohn for laying the groundwork for this study and encouraging me to proudly display my results, even if statistics are not to everyone's liking.

Finally, I am endlessly grateful for the schools, librarians, and children who participated in my studies, and especially the assistance of Brendan McCaffrey, who helped me get my first taste of real data.

Thanks to everyone for all your encouragement!

EQUIPPING SPACE CADETS

INTRODUCTION

When Jon Scieszka was writing the first book in his *Frank Einstein* series of middle grade novels, his publisher tried to discourage him from including too much science in this science fiction (sf) series. The editors thought the robots were great but believed that the scientific explanations for how the robots worked would bore or intimidate children. Scieszka included the science anyway, and it plays an important part in the quality of the story—especially as an example of sf for children.

Scieszka's book offers an interesting example of how sf is dismissed when children are the audience, even though the genre can be just as complex. In book 1, *Frank Einstein and the Antimatter Motor* (2014), the titular character tries to invent a robot that can teach itself. The first chapter immediately shows Frank attempting to bring his SmartBot to "life" in a scene that evokes James Whale's 1931 *Frankenstein* film. The full-page picture, illustrated by Brian Biggs, shows a limp robot being cranked toward the ceiling in a Radio Flyer wagon while Frank grips an electrical knife switch. The text gives a vague explanation that Frank needs to "supercharge" the robot with "lightning power."

In a different book, this mad scientist scene and ambiguous explanation might have been the extent of the science. Instead, Scieszka's story includes the sort of plausible explanations found in sf for adults. Shortly after that lightning scene, we see Frank explain to his Grampa Al how he might achieve the processes required for a learning robot. Frank says that "human brain cells are arranged in a network, like this . . ." and draws an image on his refrigerator (27). At that point in the book, an image of Frank's sketch interrupts the text. Frank continues: "But computers make yes or no decisions following rules. More in a long, straight line, like this. . . . So that kind of robot brain can't learn the way we do. It can only do what it's programmed to do. But what if I made the robot brain like this—" (28). Each time Frank says "like this," the text is paused for an image of Frank's drawing.

In this passage from *Frank Einstein*, the pictures are simple diagrams comparing interconnected neural pathways to the yes/no paths of computer logic. In Grampa Al's words, Frank is "using a biophysical model from human neuroscience" (27). This book is not a how-to manual for programming, but the concept is plausible and specific. Consider its similarity to the dialogue between the robot experts in Isaac Asimov's classic short story "Robot Dreams":

> Finally Calvin said, "What is it you have done, Rash?"
> Linda said, a little abashed, "I made use of fractal geometry."
> "I gathered that. But why?"
> "It had never been done. I thought it would produce a brain pattern with added complexity, possibly closer to that of the human." (92)

This is all the scientific explanation that Asimov offers. Scieszka and Biggs use illustrations instead of a phrase like "fractal geometry" to think about the same kind of robot brain complexity. It is no coincidence that Frank is reading a copy of *I, Robot* when Grampa Al asks to know what he is working on. Like Asimov, Scieszka uses a tiny piece of science to extrapolate new possibilities.

Of course, sf is more than just stuffing as much science as possible into a story. In the original version of Frankenstein, Mary Shelley's 1818 *Franken-stein; or, the Modern Prometheus*, the science is actually fairly light. Shelley never really explains the scientific breakthrough that allows Frankenstein to create the monster, under the framing pretense that the repentant scientist does not want anyone to re-create his experiment. Shelley only implies that Frankenstein may have used his interests in electricity and galvanism to animate the monster. The lightning storm scene was added for Whale's 1931 film, solidifying Shelley's implications about electricity and—perhaps more importantly—offering a dramatic visual spectacle of science that super-sedes any explanations of galvanism or what it is actually capable of doing. Similarly, Scieszka also never explains why Frank needs lightning to jump-start the SmartBot. In this scene the flashy, visual performance of science coexists with the specific scientific explanations. Both Shelley's book and Whale's classic *Frankenstein* film focus on the consequences of making the monster rather than the plausibility of the science that enables it. Likewise, Scieszka's tale is mostly about what happens as a result. *Frank Einstein* draws on many traditions of the sf genre, from the scientific extrapolation to the wondrous spectacle.

That Scieszka's editors wanted to cut down on the science indicates that they wanted the spectacle and the adventure, not a story about the consequences of scientific experimentation. Fortunately, Scieszka insisted that the science stay in, and, with help from Biggs's illustrations, he filled *Frank Einstein and the Anti-Matter Motor* with complex yet accessible concepts that highlight the science.[1] Yet children apparently did not run screaming. They did not even yawn off to sleep. In fact, it seems that they *liked* it. With six books in total, the series has been well received despite all that science in the fiction.

Sf for preadolescent children, like the *Frank Einstein* books, is often approached with the belief, demonstrated here by Scieszka's editors, that scientific extrapolation and speculation in fiction are beyond most children's abilities or interests. This belief is not exclusive to editors; it manifests among even the most well-meaning of teachers, librarians, teacher educators, and scholars. As a result, children's sf books are often ignored or considered fantasy rather than "true sf." Meanwhile, no one questions that the book and the 1931 film of *Frankenstein* are part of the sf genre. No one would doubt that Asimov's robot stories are sf. The *Frank Einstein* series demonstrates the same features as these iconic sf texts. Scieszka even uses intertextual references to point new readers to authors like Shelley and Asimov. *Frank Einstein* is sf, regardless of its audience.

I use the term "primary sf" in this book to refer to sf for readers under twelve, in reference to both the primary school age group and how these books often operate as children's first, foundational encounters with sf literature. The following chapters demonstrate that primary sf certainly exists, some of it is high quality and embraces the best radical messages of sf, and the whole category deserves recognition as a valuable type of literature. The dismissal of primary sf is fueled by largely ungrounded beliefs about children, science, and genre. This haze of assumptions obscures the interests and abilities of real children and leads to fewer good primary sf books being circulated.

"But computers make yes or no decisions following rules. More in a long, straight line, like this.

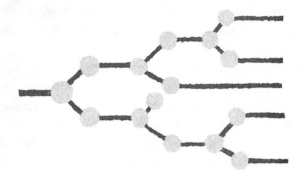

"So that kind of robot brain can't learn the way we do It can only do what it's programmed to do."

"Mmm-hmmm." Grampa Al nods.

Frank continues excitedly. "But what if I made the robot brain like this—"

Figure 1. Scieszka's text is filled in and expanded by Biggs's illustrations. From *Frank Einstein and the Antimatter Motor* by Jon Scieszka and Brian Biggs. Amulet Books, 2014.

This book is intended for those teachers, librarians, teacher educators, and scholars who are not convinced that sf for children is possible or worth the effort. I hope that by demonstrating how primary sf is feasible and beneficial, we can change the narrative around it. If the professionals who teach and recommend and study children's books select high-quality primary sf books for their libraries and classes and analyze these books in their articles and blogs, then we can collectively influence the publishing and production of these books and encourage more primary sf to be created and embraced.

In chapter 1, I offer an overview of relevant issues within children's literature and sf studies before defining primary sf and the debates that it inherits from those larger fields. The perception that primary sf is an impossible genre reflects traditional ideals of children as simple and natural and therefore the opposite of complex and technological sf. This contributes to the pervasive belief that sf is for ages twelve and up. Adult beliefs create and perpetuate this boundary through outdated developmental theories and genre stereotyping. The end of this chapter offers a straightforward list of criteria for high-quality primary sf, based on the literary aesthetics of the sf tradition and children's literature scholarship.

In chapter 2, I demonstrate how primary sf requires only slight modification for even the youngest audiences. While sf calls for knowledge of the genre intertext and special reading protocols, children's literacy training and the specialized formats of children's literature enable genre complexity in ways that many children are especially well equipped to understand. I refer to a sample set of 357 illustrated primary sf books as examples of how primary sf functions and flourishes in different formats for children like picturebooks, early readers, comic books, graphic novels, and hybridized middle grade novels.

In chapter 3, I consider whom primary sf represents, and how this may impact the accessibility of primary sf for a wide variety of readers. I compare the gender and diversity representation in primary sf to the fields of children's literature and sf at large. Exemplary primary sf books employ approaches from adult sf, such as the techniques of sf feminism, Afrofuturism, Indigenous Futurism, and Latin@futurism.

In chapter 4, I offer grounded evidence to combat the cycle of self-fulling prophecies around primary sf. I conducted three studies for this book, in order to build an interdisciplinary case describing primary sf. One study describes contemporary children's interest in sf through a national data set of school library lending during the 2016–17 school year. The second study describes the beliefs and habits of adult mentors regarding sf through a survey of teachers and librarians. Finally, the last study demonstrates children's reading skills with sf through recorded read-aloud sessions with primary school students.

The conclusion highlights how primary sf exists and persists despite the adult beliefs and interference demonstrated in the previous chapters. I show how one controversial but prevalent example of sf, the expansive *Star Wars* story-world, exemplifies the potency and pitfalls of the currently available sf for children. As the conclusion emphasizes, children make do with what they have, but adults could be fueling the genre and equipping young space cadets with the best of primary sf.

CHAPTER 1

DEFINITIONS AND EVALUATIONS

Children's literature and sf literature are both challenging categories to define, but the effort results in greater understanding of the purposes, goals, and beauties that are common to books in each. This chapter briefly explores both categories, where they overlap in primary sf, and how those books can celebrate the best of both—if given a fair chance. This chapter concludes with a guide for how to identify primary sf and evaluate its quality, and an extended example of it in practice.

WHAT IS CHILDREN'S LITERATURE?

"Children's literature," as one might expect, refers to books written and designed for children. In publishing standards, this means humans from birth through ages 12–14, depending upon the publisher. Beyond that, books are branded "young adult" (YA) until around 18,[1] when the relatively new category of "new adult" kicks in for ages 18–24, or even 18–30 for some publishers.

The idea that children can be a discrete audience for a particular category of books implies that they must be in some way different from adults. Aside from the differences necessitated by early literacy—discussed in the next chapter—children's books are also characterized by the absence of mature themes and complex ideas. These differences rely on persistent ideas that arose in the late eighteenth century that childhood is a time of innocence and simplicity. In 1762 Jean-Jacques Rousseau called for undisturbed, natural childhood in his treatise on education, *Emile*: "If the infant sprang at one bound from its mother's breast to the age of reason, the present type of education would be quite suitable, but its natural growth calls for quite a different training. The mind should be left undisturbed till its faculties have developed." Rousseau specifically claimed that reading was beyond childhood abilities and proudly declared of his ideal hypothetical child, "At twelve, Emile will hardly know what a book is." Rousseau's concept of the "natural" child and "the age of reason" has had a tenacious influence in popular concepts of children. While his idea of keeping books away from children clearly did not stick, he foresaw the modern obsession with dictating appropriate ages for children's reading materials.

Romantic authors eagerly took up Rousseau's concept of the natural child, and the Victorians famously followed suit to such a degree that they self-labeled their culture "the cult of the child." While it is tempting to point to the Victorians as the epitome of the belief in idyllic childhood innocence, this way of thinking about childhood may be even more potent today. In *Artful Dodgers: Reconceiving the Golden Age of Children's Literature*, Marah Gubar argues that Romantic and Victorian authors were more ambivalent about the notion of the natural, innocent child than scholars often claim they were. Instead, modern readers project onto the Victorians our own contemporary beliefs about the differences between childhood innocence and adult experience.

This is not to say that the Victorians were not moving toward that model of childhood, but it was not in the literature as much as in the culture around it. According to Gubar, it was the critics, rather than many of the Golden Age authors, who were most fervently pushing for children's books to align with the idea of the innocent and natural child. Nineteenth-century commentators called for simplistic children's books; those books that treated young readers as competent, worldly readers were declared unfit for or incomprehensible to children. This attitude derives from Rousseau and his portrayal of children as being unable to understand fiction until that "age of reason."

The belief that children's books are simple is often undermined by the field of children's literature research. Literary studies of children's texts make the argument, directly or indirectly, that children's books have artistic value on the same level as texts for adults, can be analyzed with the same tools, and produce similar cultural insights about the author, time period, and so forth. Research by educators and reading specialists reveals how children use complex techniques and rely on their worldly experiences to comprehend the content of their books.

Yet children's literature is generally not written, designed, or studied by children themselves. This key distinction has defined much of the more quarrelsome scholarship. The difference between the producers and consumers of children's literature means that analysis of these texts can reveal interesting insights about cultural concepts of childhood, but it also produces a sticky situation in which the scholars are all adults as well; the opinions of actual children end up ironically underrepresented in the whole body of children's literature studies.

Attempting to add real children into children's literature studies is a contentious affair, to say the least. Ever since Jacqueline Rose's infamous 1984 study *The Case of Peter Pan, or the Impossibility of Children's Fiction*, scholars have worried over the figure of the adult who looms large over children's texts. If, as Rose says, children's books are all about satisfying adult anxieties about childhood, then children's literature research can only be about finding the adult reflection. The "child" according to this theory is entirely ideological and symbolic, and the fact that children do actually read these books out in the real world is irrelevant. Karín Lesnik-Oberstein's *Children's Literature: Criticism and the Fictional Child* is similarly pessimistic about the lack of correlation between real children and children's literature. Many studies have subsequently examined the way that childhood is constructed by adults, such as landmark work by Perry Nodelman in his essay "The Other: Orientalism, Colonialism, and Children's Literature" and the book-length follow-up *The Hidden Adult: Defining Children's Literature*. These studies generally conclude that children's literature and the study thereof can never really be about real children.

However, there is pushback against this approach. Gubar's appropriately titled article "Risky Business: Talking about Children in Children's Literature Criticism" argues that while these scholars seek to rightfully point out the generational power imbalance and adult influence on children's literature, their discourse subscribes to what she calls the difference model of childhood, wherein children are seen as so *other* and different that they could not and should not be part of producing—or studying—children's literature. Gubar argues that this belief has, in turn, blinded scholars to how children

impact and influence children's literature or even contradict our understandings of it. Richard Flynn writes of Nodelman's work: "A once-useful hermeneutics of suspicion has devolved into a series of increasingly rote critical
gestures that border on the clichéd. I see these automatic critical gestures
implicated in an overemphasis on children's alterity, in a model of children
as helpless or even as victims, implying that children exercise little to no
agency in participating in and creating their culture" (255). Gubar and Flynn
insist that children do have agency, and scholars such as Robin Bernstein and
Karen Sánchez-Eppler agree that children may not have autonomy, but they
have agency within and around the scripts provided by adults. Victoria Ford
Smith argues that the history of children's literature is full of collaborative
authorship between children and adults, but scholars often do not recognize
these collaborations because they are too entrenched in the difference model.

As a solution Gubar proposes that scholars brave the risks and talk purposefully about children in children's literature studies, using what she calls
the kinship model: "that children and adults are akin to one another, which
means they are neither exactly the same nor radically dissimilar. The concept
of kinship indicates relatedness, connection, and similarity without implying
homogeneity, uniformity, and equality" ("Risky Business" 453). As opposed
to the difference model, as described above, and the deficit model, which
treats children as inferior to adults, Gubar's kinship model emphasizes "that
children and adults are separated by differences of degree, not of kind" (454).
Gubar acknowledges that children are limited by immaturity in a biological
sense but warns that "the moment we try to describe such limitations, we
risk setting into motion a disabling looping effect whereby we perpetuate,
contribute to, and even produce them" ("Hermeneutics" 299). The difference and deficit models both risk self-fulfilling prophecies about childhood
capability. However difficult it may be, Gubar advocates for talking about
real children anyway in an effort to include more than the conceptual child
in children's literature.

WHAT IS SCIENCE FICTION?

Meanwhile, sf hosts its own conflicts, starting immediately with its definition.
Genres are notoriously impossible to define to everyone's satisfaction, especially speculative genres like sf and fantasy. This is why flippant definitions

of sf, like Damon Knight's famous line that "science fiction is what we point to when we say it" are so appealing. Many try to define it anyway, for various purposes. Publishers and editors since Hugo Gernsback have demarcated what they want to see pitched as sf. Marketers apply and invent genre labels and, in turn, influence bookstore and library shelving practices. Academic books like Darko Suvin's foundational *Metamorphoses of Science Fiction: On the Poetics and History of a Literary Genre* outline complex theories about what sf is and why the definition matters.

Rather than quibble over the boundaries of rigid definitions, some have presented a shifting and culturally relevant concept of genre. Brian Attebery suggests that "all genres are what logicians call fuzzy sets: categories defined not by a clear boundary or any defining characteristic but by resemblance to a single core example or group of examples" (*Stories* 33). The fuzzy set approach allows for similarities, common tropes, and well-recognized stories to carry the greatest impact in categorizing a book. Andrew Milner empha-sizes that this core group of examples cannot be captured by a stagnant definition, because it is more like "a set of interested selections made in the present" (37). At any given time, an example of sf can be identified through its relationships to various other sf stories that are currently valorized in the sf tradition. Milner calls this a "selective tradition" and says that sf's selective tradition is always culturally decided and is a constantly evolving category. People try to reshape it all the time, for better or worse, by arguing what texts should be at the core.

Sf is also treated as a mode, which emphasizes the way that readers inter-act with it just as much as with the common traits of the stories. Veronica Hollinger says that as a mode, sf "serves not only as a narrative project finely attuned to the technocultural environment, but also as a kind of image bank through which to orient our lives in this environment" (1). Istvan Csicsery-Ronay Jr. argues that reading sf develops "a kind of awareness we might call *science-fictionality*, a mode of response that frames and tests experiences as if they were aspects of a work of science fiction" (2, emphasis in original). Sf teaches a way of thinking that is especially helpful in an age in which technol-ogy radically updates over the course of months. Csicsery-Ronay says that the core traits of sf lead to "the development of science-fictional habits of mind" (1). For instance, a 2019 survey by Linda A. Orthia found that many longtime viewers of *Doctor Who* were influenced by sustained exposure to the show to think more critically about science ethics and the role of science in society. A 2018 study by Kevin L. Young and Charli Carpenter showed that people with exposure to sf films had a significant difference in opinion about developing autonomous weapons than people with less sf exposure.

Thinking of sf as a mode allows for a very flexible idea of what is included. Csicsery-Ronay describes sf as a "constellation" of traits that draw readers: fictive neology (signs indicating other worlds), fictive novums (a new concept altering known history or reality), future history (the cause-and-effect connection between the past and the future), imaginary science (deviations from known science, wherein enters the fantastic), the science-fictional sublime (temporal, special, physical, American technological, and techno-scientific sources of awe and dread), the science-fictional grotesque (weakening or threat to significant ontological or identity categories), and the Technologiade (myth or fablelike qualities linking back to familiar reality) (5–7). The metaphor of a constellation means that an individual sf text can tap certain traits but not others. As a result, very different texts are included in the sf mode, but the focus is on the way that readers engage with and think about the stories.

To further complicate the matter of defining sf, Milner argues that people creating definitions often confuse the project of defining the genre with the project of evaluating its values and aesthetics. As a result, they get caught up in forging criteria for exclusion and inclusion that have more to do with what they want in the genre rather than what it generally contains (46). This effort to distinguish sf can take the form of painstakingly crafted definitions or histories of sf that conveniently include and exclude certain styles or subjects or even people. It is not uncommon to hear sf fans saying things like "That is *not* science fiction!" or "That's really just fantasy" in order to reject a story entirely at the level of definition.

Since defining sf is so often conflated with evaluating it, it is worthwhile to explore what is deemed good sf. Fortunately, the genre has several broad aesthetic ideals that can be used as a starting point. In Joan Gordon's "Literary Science Fiction" entry in *The Oxford Handbook of Science Fiction*, Gordon claims that sf strives for "scientific verisimilitude and plausibility, stimulating and innovative ideas, and that nebulous attribute, a sense of wonder" and should avoid "a lack of psychological depth or convincing characterization, clumsy or merely serviceable prose, wooden dialogue, awkward intrusions of information sometimes referred to as expository lumps or infodumps, and unlikely or wildly extravagant plots" (2). While Gordon's entry title adheres to traditional ideas that conflate "literary" with quality, it is a good starting point for considering in broad terms what is considered high quality within sf.

The very first item in Gordon's list, scientific plausibility, is at the heart of many disagreements about sf quality and is often framed through two sf concepts: extrapolation and speculation. Brooks Landon explains that "either explicitly or implicitly, all questions about extrapolation and speculation have somewhere in their background concerns with plausibility—its nature, its standards, and its degree of importance" (5). While extrapolation refers to "hard" sf with detailed and realistic science, speculation describes "soft" sf that emphasizes science-fictional thinking and the connections between sf and the fantastic. Fantasy literature is often grouped under the term "speculative fiction" too, and so "speculation" puts more weight on stimulating ideas than on plausible science. Robert A. Heinlein and John W. Campbell Jr. urged writers to stick to extrapolation based on clear, hard science. Isaac Asimov claimed there was value both in extrapolation from current technology and in speculation about future side effects of known or even distantly imaginable science.

Realistic science may not be necessary to achieve speculation or even extrapolation. As Brian W. Aldiss succinctly said, "Science fiction is no more written for scientists than ghost stories are written for ghosts" (1). Attebery argues that speculation and extrapolation do not require detailed science or realism and identifies several categories of the fantastic that serve the same genre goals:

> Natural Fantastic: the depiction of any natural process or product of technology in such a way as to strike us as extraordinary or astonishing. Second, there is the Rationalized Fantastic, in which an apparently impossible operation turns out to be explicable through some extrapolation of contemporary science (or, often, the application of scientific terminology in a way that looks like an explanation). Third, there is the Situated Fantastic: the imposition of alternative viewpoints upon a situation such that one character's magic is another's high tech. Fourth, there is fiction that places scientific materialism within a larger conceptual framework that includes the supernatural: the Dissensus Fantastic. In it, either the text or its writer dissents from the kind of commonsense, rationalist beliefs implied. (*Stories*, 3–4)

Attebery's categories highlight the "slipperiness" of sf and fantasy but also the value in that unclear boundary. Similarly, "imaginary science" appears in Csiscery-Ronay's constellation of sf traits, demonstrating the worth of stories that inspire awe and deliberation about science—including completely fake science. *Star Trek*, for instance, is a valued sf landmark that regularly features real science but also what fans fondly call "technobabble," or scientific-sounding nonsense. *Star Trek* has not been dismissed as fantasy, nor has it been shunned as poor-quality sf, because the plot often explores the science-fictional thinking of "what-if" questions, even when the science is imaginary.

In addition, evaluating sf on the criteria of plausible science becomes complicated when considering differences in what counts as "science" across cultures. Colin Scott demands that modern anthropology must ask, "How are logical/empirical and mystical/magical aspects of thought related, in all traditions?" (176). This question is very similar to Attebery's questions about the interconnected relationship between the fantastic and sf. Scott explains that Western science relies on the metaphors of myth and story; Western readers have merely become too familiar with them to notice (178). Consequently, it is all too easy for those Western readers to perceive science as unrelated to mythic stories, and fantastic storytelling as unscientific, but the very existence of sf reveals the draw of explicitly reuniting science and mythic fiction. Space operas and sf epics highlight this connection but are sometimes considered bad sf for emphasizing mythic resonance over scientific content.

Indigenous ways of knowing in particular challenge the boundaries of Western monolithic concepts of science.[2] In the introduction to *Walking the Clouds: An Anthology of Indigenous Science Fiction*, Grace L. Dillon writes that "many [Indigenous] cultures shared the pattern of disseminating scientific knowledge in everyday teachings. [. . .] Storytelling was the medium of choice for transmitting and preserving traditional knowledge" (8). In an essay for *Extrapolation*, Dillon explains the rising popularity of Indigenous sf by saying: "Western science has lost something vital by isolating itself from spiritual origins in a quest to achieve objectivity. When we look for sciences that model the inextricable union of the metaphysical and the measurable, Indigenous Futurisms offer new ways of reading our own ancient natures" (6). The topics of native storytelling, she explains, not only disseminate science but also share many core foci with what has been traditionally called sf, such as social awareness and Othering. Overemphasizing the plausibility of science asserts the European division between Enlightenment and Romantic ideals, rather than the rich place where they overlap.

WHAT IS PRIMARY SCIENCE FICTION?

Suffice to say, children's literature and sf literature inspire plenty of debates even beyond those detailed here. At the intersection of these two categories, primary sf combines the issues that I focus on above: the child/adult divide and the challenge of genre boundaries. Put together, the assumptions and debates from each field produce such a theoretical quagmire that the very possibility of primary sf has been called into question.

There are a handful of studies addressing sf specifically for children. Farah Mendlesohn's *The Intergalactic Playground: A Critical Study of Children's and Teens' Science Fiction*, Noga Applebaum's *Representations of Technology in Science Fiction for Young People*, and Karen Sands's and Marietta Frank's *Back in the Spaceship Again: Juvenile Science Fiction Series since 1945* offer many insights on sf for older children and adolescents. Yet the discussion of books for younger readers is limited, even in these focused projects. Sands and Frank include a few early readers in their survey, but no picturebooks.[3] Mendlesohn and Applebaum offer analysis of picturebooks, though in both cases this analysis is primarily allocated a small section at the end of their books. Mendlesohn explains that she had to reserve picturebooks for an appendix due to the relatively small number of sf picturebooks as compared to books for older readers, but she also says that this appendix "might be the most important section of the book, because it challenges the idea that we grow into science fiction" (8). Mendlesohn's point here is key; the existence of sf for young readers is a direct affront to the ways that adults often think about children.

When people talk about primary sf at all, they often evoke the difference or deficit models of childhood. With few exceptions the people who discuss sf for young people demarcate clearly between children and adults as potential sf readers, often focusing on one peculiarly rigid boundary between adults and children: the age of twelve. In the series introduction to Penguin's Galaxy editions of classic sf and fantasy, Neil Gaiman writes, "There is a saying that the golden age of science fiction is twelve." He then reflects that "there is truth in this," because he read five out of six of the collection's novels within a year of his twelfth birthday (ix). Like many who reference this saying about the golden age of twelve, Gaiman leaves it unattributed—as though it were a folk truth.

It is taken for granted that children will not discover sf until they reach adolescence, a time more commonly associated with reason and departures from childhood innocence and naturalness. Mendlesohn calls this "the argument common among sf fans and critics that one learns to read science fiction as one approaches the age of abstract thought" (*Intergalactic* 7) and, as I agree here, she attributes this idea to "unproven arguments about the nature of childhood" (7). Mendlesohn does not specifically mention the age of twelve in this context, but her reference to the age of abstract thought refers to the same phenomenon. The choice of age twelve, which was also Rousseau's "age of reason," reveals that this prediction has less to do with real children and more to do with developmental theories that are deeply embedded in our cultural conception of the child. The "Golden Age of SF" entry in the 1979 and 1993 editions of *The Encyclopedia of Science Fiction* goes so far as to cite age fourteen instead, but even that changed to twelve from the 2011 online version onward.

The catchy phrase about the golden age of twelve that Gaiman quotes started with the best of intentions but quickly became emblematic of the assumed boundary between child and adult readers and their ability and interest in reading sf. When it gets any citation, it is often David G. Hartwell's essay "The Golden Age of Science Fiction Is Twelve." Like Gaiman, Hartwell offers no source in the original 1984 edition. In the 1996 reprint, he attributes it to Peter Graham, editor of the 1950s fanzine *Void*. Even though the source remains ambiguous, Hartwell does not treat the saying as a natural truth about childhood capabilities and interests. He uses it for the pun. His point is to contrast the common literary concept of a genre's golden age with the "golden" moment that readers discover their passion for it. While Hartwell does describe an "intense immersion in written SF for at least six months around age twelve" (84), he does not claim that sf readership begins at that age.

Just as the Victorian critics and commentators were the ones who most loudly insisted that children could not read anything but simple books, contemporary critics and commentators are the ones writing that sf is suitable only for older children and teens. Some critics repeat Hartwell's saying about the golden age of twelve as though it were a literal starting point for sf readership. A. Waller Hastings's "Science Fiction" entry in *Keywords for Children's Literature* states that "most avid readers of the genre discover it around the age of twelve" (206). Hastings even puts "science fiction" in quotation marks when referring to books for readers under twelve, questioning the possibility of such books. Hastings attributes the age of twelve to Susan Fichtelberg's guide to teen speculative fiction. Fichtelberg in turn attributes it back to Hartwell (173). In *The Oxford Encyclopedia of Children's Literature*, Michael Levy acknowledges that Hartwell "was making a joke" but goes on to say that Hartwell was "also pointing to something very real. Twelve is the approximate age when children who will become lifelong readers of science fiction frequently begin to do so" (417). The age of twelve regularly returns to Hartwell but has lost both his joke and his point.

Sometimes, the age of twelve is implied through omission. The "Children's SF" entry in the 2020 edition of *The Encyclopedia of Science Fiction* admits, "In this encyclopedia, fiction seemingly designed for children eleven and under is covered very selectively; picture books—relatively few of them being sf—are generally ignored" (np). Books for the very young like picturebooks, early readers, and board books are rarely counted among sf texts or analyzed as key examples of the genre. For instance, only one essay in the edited collection *Science Fiction for Young Readers* examines a picturebook, but the essay's author, Millicent Lenz, says that it is a satirical picturebook and not really intended for children. The "young readers" in the collection's title would seem to mean teens. Similarly, histories of the genre's development usually mention juvenile sf, the sf publishing category for young adults and older children prior to the 1960s, but sf for younger children is not included. Only Milner's timeline of the genre stresses the significance of children's television in the development of American and Japanese sf traditions, but he does not mention any sf books for the younger set (51–52).

The common conception that sf is for older readers—and how commentators repeat it uncritically—is significant because these comments may create the conditions they seek to describe. Gubar argues that trying to describe childhood interests in definitive terms can result in self-fulfilling prophecies, using the following example of her deficit model:

Suppose that Richard Flynn, Joseph T. Thomas, Jr. , and other children's poetry experts began declaring on a regular basis to anyone who would listen—parents, teachers, curriculum designers—that children under the age of twelve could not possibly understand or appreciate poetry. You can easily imagine how this description could help cause the condition it claims only to describe, because it could lead adults to withhold poetry and poetry instruction until young people reach that age. After all, why share poetry with children if they cannot be expected to comprehend it? ("Risky Business" 451)

Gubar hypothesizes that it would take only a few experts following the deficit model to cause other adults to begin to align with this belief and act on it. Sf has already reached this point. Her choice of age twelve here emphasizes that age as a popular choice for those who subscribe to the deficit model.

The idea that sf is not for young children is reinforced by naturalist theories of childhood. The ideal, innocent childhood manifests in children's literature patterns, and Nodelman argues that as a result, there are "generic differences between SF and fiction intended for young reader" (294). Sf poses questions and supports change, he says, but children's literature is ambivalent about change and tends to conclude the story in the same place where it began. Sands and Frank similarly state that "science fiction may be the literature of the unknown, but children's series, which rely on the creation of a safe, comfortable, and known world, must work against this most basic tenet of science fiction literature" (28). Children's literature patterns and sf patterns would seem to be at odds. While Mendlesohn agrees that many children's and YA sf stories end at home in comfort and with none of the consequences important to sf, she claims that adults simply need to step up their expectations of what children can handle and create more sf for children with big questions and deep change. The difference here is between treating the perceived status of primary sf as evidence of the genre's impossibility, or as evidence that adult assumptions about children are getting in the way.

As Noga Applebaum argues, too many sf authors subscribe to the fear that young people subvert their own childhood "innocence" by accessing more knowledge than what adults see fit to give them. According to the natural child paradigm, children are simple, natural, and should be far removed from that which is complicated and technological. Applebaum describes the ideological content of sf for children ages seven to sixteen as:

> a manifestation of the enduring allure of the myth of childhood innocence and its relation to Romantic notions with regard to the role of nature in children's lives. The persistent attempts to hold on to such sentimental constructions of childhood are a form of resistance to the changing face of childhood and technology's contribution to this change. (15)

Adult authors infuse their stories with fears about children growing up in an age of swift technological advances, including the idea that children might use technological literacy to escape adult control. Applebaum focuses primarily on YA books but concludes that "fiction written for children, spe-cifically within the genre of science fiction (SF), engages with technology, yet in many of the works it is with the intention of 'exorcising' modern manifes-tations of the machine" (1) and acting as "socialisation agents in the service of the current adult-child power hierarchy" (15).

The natural child also necessarily disassociates children from the conse-quences and moral dilemmas of science. In the second half of the twentieth century, the icon of the child was even used to assuage growing public con-cerns about science. Rebecca Onion explains that popular science "had to remain apart from big questions about science and technology that troubled the 1970s and 1980s. Childhood 'curiosity' was a perfect balm for those ills" (164). Childhood was used to highlight the innocent joys of scientific dis-covery, without the sticky questions of consequences or fallout.

Accordingly, adults—in the US especially—want children to excel in the sciences, but only certain varieties of science. Onion notes that for the last half century, adults have been worrying about each new generation of children not engaging enough with science, but these concerns are often displaced worries about modern childhood and the erosion of children's "natural" interests, a direct echo of Rousseau's natural child. Adults may want children to be engaged in science, Onion writes, but only types of science considered productive for curbing negative childhood habits and leading toward future careers. To that end sf is acceptable if it promotes young people's interest in scientific professions.[4] In the 1950s "science fiction was cautiously, and then heartily, embraced by forward-thinking librarians and educators" but only if the books led to science and not just more fiction (Onion 118). Even Asimov was pleased to report, "I now have evidence that I occasionally help to win the initial victory and encourage a youngster to go into science who might otherwise not do so. Extrapolate this to science fiction in general and think of the many youths who are won silently and who do not bother to advertise the victory" (qtd. in Onion 27). Similarly, Sands and Frank's chapter on science in sf series implies that the genre is more valuable if it is teaching science or leading to a scientific career. When framed this way, sf is valuable only as a way of sneaking science to children.

The idea that sf must conceal otherwise boring science leads back again to the idea of that natural child, which assumes that children were not already interested in complicated or technological science. Mendlesohn lays the blame on constructivist science educators who prioritize entertainment over direct instruction and "seem to be operating from Rousseau's notion of the 'natural' child" when they avoid delivering information in favor of having children explore (*Intergalactic* 59). According to Mendlesohn, this attitude of treating science like a particularly unpleasant vegetable has no basis in real children: "where many adults see science as difficult and needing to be framed 'accessibly,' most children—at least until they are socialized into the same mindset in their teens—regard science and information about science as very exciting indeed" (50). This idea that children dislike science is commonplace and persistent. Onion describes "Heinlein's ongoing crusade to convince [Alice] Dalgliesh [his editor] that kids wanted more science" (131). As revealed in the introduction, Scieszka's editors required the same persuasion decades later.

Fortunately, education and literacy research has come to reflect that it is not the children who are avoiding the information density that typifies science texts, but rather the adults.[5] Panayota Mantzicopoulos and Helen Patrick's review of the research on teachers and informational science picturebooks describes teachers' nearly superstitious fear of science informational texts. The researchers list several reasons why teachers have avoided these texts in elementary school classrooms: the belief that children learn best from stories, that informational texts are too hard, that children are more interested in stories, that girls are less interested than boys, and that teachers are uncomfortable with science topics about which they know little. In the same publication, Mantzicopoulos and Patrick also review studies that show the inaccuracy of these assumptions about informational texts and young children. Then they go on to point out the unintentional ways that avoiding science books can cause other teachers and young children to propagate a negative conceptualization of what science is.[6]

When adults believe that children do not gravitate to scientific information, it is not surprising that children are far more likely to be associated with fantasy. Alan Richardson points out that Romantics championed fairy tales as the most natural reading material for children, paralleling their idea of the "natural, idealized vision of the child" (124). In Bud Foote's chapter for *Nursery Realms: Children in the Worlds of Science Fiction, Fantasy, and Horror*, he writes, "Fantasy is the typical literature of early childhood; science fiction, that of adolescence; and mainstream fiction, that of adulthood" (204). Foote emphasizes that he is not prescribing what different ages should read; as with the rest of this edited collection, he is interested in children for what they mean to adults rather than in the reading material of real children.[7] However, this association between children and fantasy has roots in those same persistent naturalist assumptions about children and their abilities. Foote displays the deficit model of childhood when he explains that children best represent fantasy because "everything is more or less magical" (204) to children and they have not "worked out the line between magic and technology" until they reach adolescence (205). Similarly, Hastings writes that "the difficulty in creating believable science fiction for the very young lies in the readers' inadequate knowledge of the world, which arguably does not permit them to distinguish adequately between fantasy and more plausible scientifically informed extrapolations" (207). Here again we see the idea that scientific complexities are simply not for young people. The odd implication behind this claim, though, is that children's supposed inability to distinguish between sf and fantasy somehow prevents the adult writers from making that distinction when writing the books.

Children cannot become familiar with that which is withheld from them, and no other genres are avoided on the argument that children cannot distinguish between them. Research indicates that children can be masters of genre from an early age, if they encounter the genre often. Literacy researchers as early as Jean Mandler and Nancy Johnson in 1977 and Nancy Stein and Christine Glenn in 1979 found that children recognize and utilize genre story grammar for creating and understanding narratives. In Deena Skolnick and Paul Bloom's 2006 study, children aged three to seven understood the rules of fantasy across media. Sf is rarely included in story grammar studies—a deficit that I hope this book inspires others to address. Nonetheless, these studies show that genre awareness is a reading skill that children pick up on early. Children deserve to develop an accurate idea of the sf genre, too. For this to work, the books need to actually represent the sf genre, including the full complexity of sf and its potentially fantastic components.

Especially since children are so often associated with fantasy, primary sf finds itself in the middle of the genre arguments that attempt to establish the "purity" of sf by shunning any fantastic incursions. When describing an example of sf for young children, Hastings says that "the trappings of the science fiction novel are used to frame a rather conventional story of adventure and active imagination" (206–07). He claims that sf for young children is often just fantasy in disguise. John Clute's entry for "Children's SF" in *The Encyclopedia of SF* makes a similar claim: "It might indeed be suggested that

Children's Sf might be defined as comprising multiply-sourced fictions with an sf coloration." Consider the similarity between "the trappings of science fiction" and the "sf coloration" in the quotes above with this argument from Donald E. Palumbo about why sf comic books are secretly fantasy:

> Comic books characteristically employ the trappings and concepts associated with science fiction to develop narratives and narrative worlds that are essentially fantastic. Their science fiction components are usually only a superficial guise for fantasy, as comic book narratives generally exhibit no interest in extrapolating from—or basing their worlds' divergences from reality upon—any sound, organized body of scientific knowledge or principle. (161)

This idea that sf is being used as a disguise for fantasy makes it seem as though primary sf stories—and comic books—are trying to get away with something devious, and besmirching the good name of sf in the process.

Any hint of fantasy is used to criticize primary sf. These books are expected to go to extra lengths in order to demonstrate distinct genres. Sands and Frank blame "science fantasy" for the lack of attention to sf for children: "Unlikely details frequently cause critics either to dismiss science fiction for children as being completely nonexistent or, at best, to label it science fantasy" (27). They write that when authors like Madeleine L'Engle refuse to clearly distinguish between sf and fantasy, this attitude "tends to ghettoize children's SF" in comparison to adult sf with equally unrealistic attributes (33). The authors fall prey to these higher expectations of sf for children, even as they point it out its unfairness. Their own judgment is apparent when they write that "true science fiction for the very young is rare; most of the series discussed here, for example, fall into the category of science fantasy—fiction that blends some scientific concepts or situations with fantastic elements that have no scientific base" (24). Their choice of the word "true" rather than "scientific" or "plausible" implies that science fantasy is "false" sf.

Insisting that primary sf distance itself from fantasy holds children's literature to different standards than adult literature. Refusing to acknowledge that children's books can be sf also reads like an attempt to construe the genre as mature and sophisticated. Acknowledging that children can read sf means that it is not the cerebral, highly complicated, and exclusive genre that some want it to be. Insisting that sf is not accessible for children is both a dismissive view of young people and an unnecessarily defensive view of sf. Sf is a huge genre with a varied history of space opera and silliness and pop culture shenanigans that can coexist in the same genre as high-concept experimental forms and hard sf brimming with terminology from theoretical physics and chemical engineering.

Despite genre purists, science fantasy is a valuable part of the sf genre and its history. Sands and Frank attribute the term "science fantasy" to education textbooks (33), but it has been in circulation much longer—at least since the 1950s UK magazine by that title. *The Encyclopedia of Science Fiction* entry "Science Fantasy" lists many important sf authors, including Edgar Rice Burroughs, Samuel R. Delany, Anne McCaffrey, Andre Norton, and Gene Wolfe. Yet that entry is not a list of shame among the other entries in the encyclopedia. Calling these books science fantasy is in no way an insult, or implying that they are "false" sf or really fantasy in disguise. To its credit, the *Encyclopedia*'s entry on "Children's SF" ends with this sentence: "The future of Children's Sf does not lie in the direction of purity." Genre purity is not necessary for quality. Just like adult books, children's books that mix genres are often improved, not undermined, by the combination of fantasy and sf components.[8]

In the end, it is important that primary sf is allowed to have the same nuance as adult sf. Hastings tries to resolve the tensions around genre purity by suggesting "that 'children's science fiction' and 'adult science fiction' may, in fact, constitute two related but distinct genres of equal validity" (205). However, this is just more of Gubar's difference model. While slightly different to accommodate new readers, it is crucial that sf for young readers be similar enough to adult sf that children recognize it as the same genre when they progress to titles for older readers. As Mendlesohn puts it, "the best science fiction for children has, as its hidden curriculum, the desire to persuade children to move into the adult genre" (*Intergalactic* 3). Mendlesohn emphasizes this point so much as to call it the "fundamental contention" of her book:

> The fundamental contention of this book is that children who are likely to want to read science fiction as adults should have access at all ages to science fiction that matches values with the genre as it is produced for adults. It is not enough to tell me that a certain book is popular with children and therefore *must* be good. If that book does not resemble the adult market, then the children it is popular with may well be the ones who are repelled by adult science fiction when they encounter it with its whole new set of values and structural expectations. Worse, if that book does not resemble the provision

of the adult market, then the children who might like science fiction may very well avoid it hereafter, because their first experience looked like science fiction, was packaged like science fiction, but adhered to a set of values quite other than science fiction. (5, emphasis in original)

A book may be good otherwise, Mendlesohn accepts, but if it is not accurately representing sf, then it is doing children a disservice in terms of their understanding of genre.

This approach requires faith that children have an interest in science and that they will be able to understand the difference between sf and fantasy. It requires theorizing children through Gubar's kinship model and avoiding conclusions based on the difference or deficit model. In keeping with the ideals of childhood studies, it is also important to hold primary sf to the same standards as sf for adults not only because of potential future readership, but also because high-quality primary sf can offer immediate benefits to young people. Primary sf that meets genre values teaches Csicsery-Ronay's concept of science-fictional thinking, offering young readers a skill that they can transfer to their technological world. This avoids treating children exclusively as future adults whose experiences are good only if they prepare them for adulthood. Primary sf can be expected to guide children toward advanced sf but should also benefit the child in the present.

In the end, allowing assumptions about the capabilities of young readers to go unchecked creates the impression that primary sf is "impossible," but the rare actual evidence indicates that the golden beginning of sf fandom happens before twelve and is possibly getting younger. Hartwell backs up his theory about the golden age of twelve with a survey conducted in the "early 1980s" by the semiprofessional sf newspaper *Locus*, wherein "almost every respondent" reported starting to read sf between ages ten and fourteen. Hartwell notes that this survey confirmed what "everyone in the SF field already knew, so no one has bothered to conduct another one since" (84). Two decades later, someone bothered. In appendix C of her book, Mendlesohn and Zara Baxter report a survey of 850 sf readers from fifteen to eighty-three years old. Of these responding sf fans, "over 90 percent had read sf by age 13" (212). The mean age of starting to read sf was nine years old; "the majority (55 percent) of readers started reading sf between the ages of 7 and 10" (212). Furthermore, 69 percent said that they read sf "written specifically for children" (212). Most of these participants claim to have become sf readers several years before turning twelve and did not jump immediately to adult books. Mendlesohn and Baxter express reasonable skepticism about the accuracy of this data, since it is based on recollection (204). A decade after Mendlesohn and Baxter's survey, I also bothered, and my results in chapter 4 show an even younger readership for sf.

Primary sf may have to contend with longstanding ideas about childhood and about genre, but operating under Gubar's kinship model of childhood opens up the possibility for us to examine primary sf flexibly and with nuance, just as we treat the genre for adults.

A GUIDE TO IDENTIFYING AND EVALUATING PRIMARY SCIENCE FICTION

In preparation for this book, I read all the children's books that I could find that were potentially sf in order to get a broad idea of the genre for children as it is currently available. In order to determine which books were sf, I borrowed Attebery's fuzzy-sets approach and Csicsery-Ronay's sf traits. I looked for proximity to core texts of both pop culture and classic renown, from *Star Wars* to the works of Robert A. Heinlein. I sought out tropes like time travel, rockets, and mad scientists, and traits like fictive neology and the science-fictional grotesque.

The resulting list, which can be found in appendix A, includes books that stricter definitions would reject for having too much fantasy or for prioritizing adventure over science. If a book included a few fantasy tropes or magical elements, that did not disqualify it. However, if a book had a greater resemblance to fantasy than sf, then it was not included, as this, in Attebery's terms, would place it further into the fantasy fuzzy set than the sf fuzzy set. Books that had an equivalent balance of fantasy and sf, those that might be called "science fantasy," were left in, and I made a note of them to see if they would influence my statistical results, but they did not.

However, just because I labeled these books as sf does not mean they are *good* sf. In this way, I distinguished between the projects of identifying and evaluating primary sf. Instead of categorically rejecting books that others may have left out, I included them and subjected them to the same standards of quality as sf for adults. I adopted the terms "speculation" and "extrapolation" as an effective shorthand for valued qualities of sf and evaluated each book in terms of whether it features either concept.

The concepts of extrapolation and speculation are not only related to plausibility, as described above, but are also an excellent way to check for many other qualities held up as desirable in sf without relying on concepts of childhood. In concluding her book, Mendlesohn produces a list of "core genre values" that she believes should be represented in children's and YA sf:

> an outward-bound trajectory; information density; emotional development grounded in a reaction to the world rather than a boy-meets-girl romance or other social networking skills; encouragement to analytical thinking, whether applied to political, social or scientific contexts; a questioning approach to the material of the text and to the built world; a moral or ethical ruthlessness that argues with the world rather than tritely positing one stance as innately good, another innately bad; a sense at the end both that one has learned something, and that there is something more to learn. (*Intergalactic* 183)

Many of these could be collected under the broader concepts of extrapolation or speculation. The emphasis on "analytical thinking" and "a questioning approach" is most obviously related to the "what if?" question of speculation. The value of having character development "grounded in a reaction to the world," a story that "argues with the world," and an ending where you "learned something" is based on extrapolation.

I would even argue that Mendlesohn's "outward-bound trajectory" is not possible without the impetus of the speculative or extrapolative plot point. After all, Mendlesohn comes to her conclusion about these core values after having spent the book analyzing the ideal sf plot structure. Mendlesohn modifies John Clute's concept of a "full fantasy" story to describe "the full sf story" in four stages (10). The first phase, "dissonance," results from the novum of the story that distinguishes it from realism, often established quickly through sf tropes. The second, "rupture," covers the cognitive estrangement when the reader experiences the difference of the imagined world because of the dissonance. The "resolution" phase is straightforward, but Mendlesohn contends that it *must* be followed by the "consequence" phase. Consequence refers to something in the story world that is different or changed, opening the ending of the story outward with possibilities, rather than closing it down as finished and contained—in other words, following through on the speculation or extrapolation of a story to answer the what-if question.

However, Levy and Hastings contend that Mendlesohn's criteria are too harsh. In a review of her book, Levy, who was often Mendlesohn's close collaborator, says, "My disagreements concern only her tendency to (in my view) undervalue specific works that do not fit her definition of 'full' science fiction and her insistence that books that 'aren't about the impact of technology' are by definition not science fiction" (411). Levy's comments point out that Mendlesohn's approach risks conflating the projects of defining and evaluating, but his response also indicates that speculative books with less apparent technology are also valuable. Meanwhile, Hastings agrees with Mendlesohn's concerns about rupture, but regarding her consequences phase, he says:

> it might be argued that the path of children's fiction is a spiral rather than a true circle; the child returns to a stable situation, but one that has been altered (either in external reality or in the child's understanding), so that a permanent change has occurred. If this is the case, there is no necessary barrier between juvenile fiction and "true" science fiction (204–5).

Hastings comes off as very tentative in his passive claim that "might be argued" by someone else "if this is the case." Yet his compromise effectively opens the door for more-subtle consequences, for instance, consequences expressed in the paratextual hidden gems of complex picturebook illustrations, where images may suggest that the speculative or extrapolative question of the book had a subtle impact. I will offer several such examples in the next chapter.

While evaluating the books, I also looked for how intrinsic the sf tropes were to the story, drawing on a complaint written by Hastings that "there is nothing intrinsically speculative in the robot of Dav Pilkey's *Ricky Ricotta's Mighty Robot* (2000); it is simply a large, avenging friend who helps the eponymous mouse deal with bullies (along with a stereotypical mad scientist), filling a role that could as easily be given to the golem of Jewish folklore, a *djinn*, or a benign giant" (207). Mendlesohn also dismisses books that could easily swap out the sf component with something from fantasy or realistic literature without changing the plot. Hastings questions whether books like this that use sf tropes "to give a veneer of the unusual to everyday activities" are really sf at all (207). While he is confusing the projects of defining versus evaluating, his point about that easily replaced robot is important to not only sf standards of quality but also introducing young readers to science-fictional thinking. If the speculative element of sf is missing, the quality suffers.

The above discussions can be condensed into a three-question test to evaluate each book's quality:

1. Is there a speculative "what if" question or extrapolative "if this, then what?" question to the story?
2. Does the ending imply that something has changed in the world or that new possibilities have opened due to the events of the story, however small?
3. Would the story's plot, themes, or lesson be different if you replaced the sf components of the story with something realistic or magical?

Primary sf books do not need to have a very complicated story to include speculation and extrapolation. The detail or plausibility of the science or information is often related, but less important than whether the story asks questions and encourages science-fictional thinking. As per Hasting's spiral compromise, the change at the end need not be dramatic. Just as primary sf should not be held to stricter genre definitions than books for adults, primary sf should not be evaluated on very different terms than sf for adults.

I evaluated 357 primary sf books with these sf quality questions and found that over half passed the test, coming to a total of 243 (68%). I will discuss these 357 books in terms of their formatting in the next chapter. First, to demonstrate how primary sf books must contend with adult preconceptions in order to offer speculation and extrapolation, the remainder of this chapter offers a brief study of just one primary sf theme: robots.

THE CASE OF ROBOTS

The robot, as an sf theme and icon, offers an interesting case of how speculation or extrapolation often operates in primary sf in opposition to adult assumptions about children. There are of course many different popular primary sf icons that I could choose, but the robot offers a potent example, since the technology of robotics is far removed from the natural child. Accordingly, primary sf books with robots demonstrate how adult ideas of childhood manifest in technophobic stories. In addition, Hastings chose a robot as his example of how primary sf fails to employ speculation, and indeed many primary sf books fail to speculate or extrapolate about their robots. However, primary sf robot books also demonstrate how strict adherence to science is not always necessary to achieve valuable speculation and science-fictional thinking.

Primary sf robot books can generally be sorted into two categories: those in which the robot is a friend/pet or those in which the robot is a tool. In the former category, the robot functions as a direct metaphor for humans and animals. For instance, Andrea Baruffi's *If I Had a Robot Dog* (2005) explores the quirks of owning a robotic dog. In *Zoe and Robot: Let's Pretend!* (2011), by Rian Sias, a girl teaches her robot companion how to play pretend. In Dan Yaccarino's *Doug Unplugged* (2013), young robot Doug just wants to go outside and explore instead of downloading information all day. These stories all treat robots as animal-like or humanlike subjects with full AI. This can be a positive source for speculation, as long as the book goes beyond simple metaphor. In the worst of these stories, the author's choice of a robot is pointless, since the book is just a direct metaphor for friendship or pet ownership. The qualities of Baruffi's robot dog can be swapped one-for-one with living dogs, and Yaccarino's Doug is a straightforward representation of children who are bored with sedentary classrooms.

However, *Zoe and Robot* is an example of a book that successfully speculates about how a robot might be a unique companion, and what robots might gain in companionship. Zoe attempts to teach the robot, simply named Robot, how to pretend, despite its protests that this is not possible for robots. The resulting story encourages speculation about both human and robot thinking patterns. The book begins when Zoe tries to play pretend with Robot, who explains, "ROBOTS DO NOT KNOW HOW TO PRETEND," and later, upon failing, concludes, "ROBOT CAN NOT PRETEND" (Sias). The conflict circles around Zoe wanting the robot to learn how to pretend, while the robot insists that robots do not or cannot pretend. For children, the speculation here concerns what robots are capable of doing and how much they can be like us. For an older or particularly self-aware reader, the speculation may also turn to what a child's creative engineering and openness to serendipity could do for the development of AI.

At first glance, Robot could be replaced by a child who is resistant or feels insecure about playing pretend. However, what is key to this book is that Robot makes it an issue of his programming and status as robot when he states, "ROBOTS DO NOT KNOW HOW TO PRETEND" (np). Using the plural "ROBOTS" subtly shifts the story from a narrative about one robot's abilities to the inherent abilities of an entire line of robots. After all, if this robot can learn to pretend, then the implication is that all similar robots by extension can do the same. The speculation generated here asks what else they might learn to do. The story hinges on Robot's ability to learn a human trait that had separated it from Zoe at the start. At the very end, Robot initiates the next round of pretend, potentially implying that it may be good at pretend or excel more quickly than Zoe. This echoes a common theme in sf stories about what happens when robots learn a skill that was previously exclusive to humanity—and then surpass humans at it.

Another category of primary sf books about robots features robots as unreliable tools. Some of these books are so similar that they follow a nearly identical plotline. Take, for instance, *Robot-Bot-Bot* (1979) by Fernando Krahn, *The Trouble with Dad* (1985) by Babette Cole, and *Robot Man* (2010) by Paul Orshoski and Jeffrey Ebbeler. In all three stories, a father buys or builds a robot that will do household chores, but the robot ends up making a funny mess of things instead. In *Robot Man*, the malfunctioning robot even presents a Freudian threat when it ultimately tries to take over the father's job of kissing the mother. In the end, the stories emphasize that the robots are not as good as humans and are better off used for recreation or thrown out altogether. This type of book declares that human work is more valuable and should not be replaced. These robot books present antiscience messages to young children. They seem to suggest that technology is invented for the lazy and is dangerous because it can go wrong at any moment, especially if it is made to replace human labor. Even worse, some of these books imply that children and robots do not mix well. In *The Trouble with Dad*, the robots accidentally take over a town because a baby got hold of the remote control, while in *Robot-Bot-Bot* the little girl opens the robot's head and ties its wires into a knot. Fortunately, these two books are also the oldest in this set of examples, while the newer books seemed less likely to show children as inherently poor custodians of technology.

Books that offer oversimplified or technophobic robot stories for children may result from a general lack of faith in young children as robotics engineers. Even while robots are becoming an increasingly large part of everyday life, adults are concerned about whether children can recognize robots as nonliving entities. Researchers seem to obsesses over when and how children are able to distinguish between robots and humans. Many studies over the years have been dedicated to showing that the average child learns to identify humanoid robots as nonliving entities between the ages of three and four.[9] The sheer quantity of these studies reveals more about adult anxieties than about children's science understanding.[10] It is clear that the goal is for children to "correctly" perceive robots as objects and machines. It is also clear that there is a generational divide about this. Even in 1999 Sherry Turkle wrote, "People who grew up in the world of the mechanical are more comfortable with a definition of what is alive that excludes all but the biological and resist shifting definitions of aliveness. . . . Children who have grown up with computational objects don't experience that dichotomy. They turn the dichotomy into a menu and cycle through its choices" (552). The more steeped in technology each generation becomes, the more this may be the case.

Children in these research studies seem to resist the idea of strictly separating human and robot processes. In a 2008 study by Sharona T. Levy and David Mioduser, kindergarten children were asked to program a robot to do simple tasks. The children treated it as a technology problem until asked to program complex tasks, at which point they combined technological and psychological logic about the robot. In other words, they considered not just what the robot could do but also what it "wanted" to do (345). The researchers emphasized in their report that they do not think the children believed the robot was alive, but that thinking about complex tasks in terms of this hybrid logic was simply easier (351). This is a sort of science-fictional thinking.

Science-fictional thought about robots may be useful. Karen Spektor-Precel and David Mioduser used data from a test group of children to develop a model akin to theory of mind, the psychology term for the ability to understand that other people have beliefs and desires different from one's own. Spektor-Precel and Mioduser call their model the theory of artificial mind, or the understanding that robots require direct operation or programming, behave according to environmental conditions and make decisions accordingly, and the combination of those two. They concluded that theory of mind and theory of artificial mind were not directly connected, but rather that children in their study progressed along a continuum from attributing a theory of mind model to robots to a fully technological theory of artificial mind model:

We found that ToAM is comprised of the following: [. . .] A model of the artificial mind with the following continuum: (a) a ToM-like model completely based on children's model of the human mind; (b) a ToM-based ToAM-technological model referring to the artificial mind but using elements borrowed from their model of the human mind; (c) a partial ToAM-technological model referring to the existence of the artificial mind (i.e. , reference to the input and output of the robot), but not to the content or processing of the artificial mind; (d) a fully technological ToAM model. (340–41)

Should we ever achieve true AI, the fully technological model would not be as helpful for scientists working with robots that have advanced malleable intelligence. Instead, scientists would be working closer to the middle of the continuum, combining technological models with human mind models, much like the kindergartners did in Levy and Mioduser's previous study. Yet this is not something that the researchers thought about, and I do not really expect it to be part of a programming lesson. This is the lesson of science-fictional thinking.

Exposure to sf helps develop this type of thinking. Even just exposure to pop culture robots helps develop it. The study "Children's Knowledge and Imaginary about Robots" by Leopoldina Fortunati, Anna Esposito, Mauro Sarrica, and Giovanni Ferrin found that the more sf pop culture robots a child could name, the more that child associated robots with humanlike characteristics such as "It looks into my eyes" alongside mechanical char-acteristics like "It has gears" (693). The children did not exchange mechani-cal for human traits but described robots as having both. Of course, these researchers also made sure that the children could differentiate robots from humans, revealing that persistent adult concern. The children in the study could indeed distinguish among robots, humans, and toys—the study's third comparison category—but a higher exposure to popular culture robot stories increased the nuance with which the children approached robots, treating them as something not-human but more human than toys.

Books like *Zoe and Robot* encourage this kind of fluid, science-fictional thinking. Speculative primary sf books completely defy the fully techno-logical theory of artificial mind, because when the robots are personified and given full AI, children must apply a more psychological approach to understand the story. These robots do not seem to be running on a simple program, but rather they can grow and change their programming. Children must read these books with a mixture of theory of mind and theory of artificial mind to combine human and robot brain processes. Notably, the more strictly accurate primary sf books do not encourage this science-fictional thinking about robots. After all, the technophobic robot books depict plausible technology: robots do what they are told, and if they do it wrong, it is due to faulty programming, input error, or malfunction. Yet these books also focus on robots as dangerous and a poor replacement for human work. Applebaum fears that technologically savvy children may be put off from books altogether if they see only technophobic stories. The primary sf books that take greater freedoms with plausibility seem to reap a higher reward when they succeed in offering speculation/extrapolation.

In the end, robots are an interesting example of how primary sf can include valuable speculation and extrapolation, but only when adults do not infuse it with their own beliefs about how children understand science and technology.

CHAPTER 2

COMPREHENDING GENRE

As discussed in the previous chapter, the very existence of primary sf runs up against long-held beliefs about the nature of childhood and children's capacity for thinking about science. However, I argue in this chapter that even the youngest child is suited for sf. Following Gubar's kinship model, young audiences require similar but slightly different approaches to sf books than adults. Younger children are likely to have relatively less exposure to the sf intertext and less developed literacy skills in general. Without becoming too different from YA and adult sf, high-quality primary sf books must account for children's varying grasps on literacy. The most effective examples take advantage of children's developing literacy and the children's book formats that are already structured to support literacy development.

This chapter begins by exploring the processes and protocols of reading sf, and how those processes may differ for young readers. I then examine how the features of different children's literature formats—board books, popup books, picturebooks, early readers, comic books, graphic novels, and hybrid novels— support young readers as they develop and hone their sf reading skills.

HOW READERS READ SCIENCE FICTION

According to the reader response theory of reading, first described by Louise Rosenblatt, meaning is created through the interaction between the words and the reader. In opposition to the older idea that objective meaning is waiting to be discovered within the text, reader response theory acknowledges that different readers will find different meaning in the same text, due to bringing different interests and backgrounds to what Rosenblatt refers to as the reading transaction. Research on reading comprehension since then has been exploring how readers tap their background knowledge, or schemata (singular: schema), to make meaning from the text. While skills like being able to sound out words are also important basic parts of the reading process, without a schema the reader has no framework for comprehending what those words and sentences mean. For instance, when a layperson reads a dense passage of jargon, they may be able to read the words, but they will likely have no idea what the passage is attempting to communicate.

A reader's schema is all about the familiar, but the sf genre inherently celebrates the unfamiliar. In his poetics of sf, Darko Suvin emphasizes the importance of cognitive estrangement, that sense of a strange new world, and novums, or the new concepts that distinguish the sf setting. Departure from one's background experiences is at the heart of sf, and this feature makes comprehending it more of a challenge.

Fortunately, knowledge of the genre is also part of a reader's sf schema. Familiarity with other sf stories helps readers to build connections across texts, even if an sf setting or novum is far removed from their day-to-day life otherwise. Accordingly, in Orson Scott Card's *How to Write Science Fiction & Fantasy*, he advises speculative fiction authors to use the intertextual terms that people will already know to capitalize on the existing knowledge base of the genre (38). Milner even says that sf can be recognized by "the deliberate use of intertextuality" (13). Sf authors expect to both build on and build up the reader's genre schema.

The sf intertext includes far more than just books, and this helps immensely for young readers who have seen movies, watched TV shows, and played video games and apps before they could read. David Hartwell emphasizes how important this sf exposure is for children in his essay on the golden age of twelve, writing:

The science fiction drug is available everywhere to kids—in superhero comics, on TV, in the movies, in books and magazines. It is impossible to avoid exposure, to avoid the least hint of excitement at Marvel Comics superheroes and *Star Trek* reruns and *Star Wars*, impossible not to become habituated even before kindergarten to the language, clichés, basic concepts of science fiction. Children's culture in the contemporary U. S. is a supersaturated SF environment. By the time a kid can read comic books and attend a movie unaccompanied by an adult, his mind is a fertile environment for the harder stuff. Even the cardboard monsters on TV reruns feed the excitement. The science fiction habit is established early. (84)

For Hartwell, this early exposure was essential for setting up that golden moment of discovering written sf. Since Hartwell penned these words in the 1980s, sf influences on young children have become exponentially more pervasive due to widely consumed reboots of *Star Trek, Star Wars, Doctor Who,* and the highly successful Marvel cinematic universe—not to mention new sf series, spinoffs, and films. By this measure, contemporary children should be very well prepared to read sf.

This schema can help a child reader understand what might otherwise be incomprehensible. When Jane Yolen's editor expressed a concern that children may not get all Yolen's puns in *Commander Toad in Space* (1996), Yolen wrote back with the retort: "Any kid who has seen Star Wars, Star Trek or Battlestar Gallatica [*sic*] has heard the phrase deep hyper space and will get the pun" (Box 7, Folder 26). Yolen expects children to come to her *Commander Toad* books fully equipped with sf awareness, not from books, but rather from any one of several possible TV shows. This sf schema provides a framework for sf terms and jokes and even for Yolen's plot overall. Children who are familiar with space travel and spaceship crews can approach the story knowing something of what to expect and use it not just to get the jokes but also to help comprehend what they are reading.

Knowledge of the sf intertext is an important part of genre schemata, but there are also specific reading skills necessary for sf. This is what Hartwell is getting at when he writes that "most new readers have to go through a process of SF education and familiarization before they can love it. Just because someone can read does not mean that he necessarily can read SF" (82). Samuel R. Delany suggests that sf can be defined by its reading protocols, and that sf is difficult and off-putting if one does not know these protocols.

In his guide for authors, Card names two major sf reading protocols: abeyance and implication. "Abeyance" refers to actively waiting for more context to understand a term. Card uses as an example the phrase "seed villages," which appears in the first line of Octavia Butler's *Wild Seed* (1980). Card explains:

> Experienced sf readers recognize that they don't know what a seed village is,
> and that the author doesn't expect them to know. [. . .] Instead, this is one of
> the differences, one of the things that is strange in this created world, and the
> author will in due course explain what the term means. But the reader who
> is inexperienced in sf thinks that the author expects him to already know
> what a seed village is. He stops cold, trying to guess what the term means
> from context. But he *can't* guess, because there isn't enough context yet. (91,
> emphasis in original)

This lack of context, in reading comprehension terms, is the lack of appropriate schemata. When the hypothetical reader "stops cold," this reflects an
unwelcome hiccup in what is usually a fluent process.

Card's second sf reading protocol, implication, means that readers must
find hints in the words that they do know in order to get by until they have
more context. Card explains that since readers will know the words "seed" and
"village," they will put these together to theorize what a seed village may be
until they learn otherwise. Card writes that sf authors need to account for the
implications of their words because in the process of this reading protocol,
"the sf reader *will* pick up most or all of these implications" (92, emphasis
in original). Reading teachers will recognize this as the reading strategy of
inferring, or combining evidence from the text with a schema to produce
an educated guess about what the words are not saying directly. Studies like
that by Kate Cain, Jane Oakhill, Marcia Barnes, and Peter E. Bryant (2001)
have shown that proficient readers make more inferences than less proficient
readers. This is not a reading strategy unique to sf, but it is certainly important for reading it. While some sf authors employ the generally disdained
"info dump," or explaining the world in a straightforward but dull "dump" of
information, most well-esteemed sf authors leave many things unexplained,
for the reader to figure out through these reading protocols.

Card's italicized emphasis in the passage above highlights his complete
confidence that sf readers know to read using these protocols, while "mainstream" readers do not. He also notes that the experienced sf reader "expects
the term to be literal, to have a real extension within the world of the story,
while the mainstream audience expects the term to be metaphorical" (93).
This is where the general reading skill of inferring might not be enough—
because the reader must be familiar with the genre in order to adjust their
inferences. Even proficient readers must have the relevant schemata to merge

with evidence from the text. When teaching his students how to read sf, James Gunn explains that "one must identify the genre and then apply the appropriate protocol. If one doesn't know the correct protocol or misidentifies the genre, one is likely to misread something." Card has no interest in how "mainstream" readers learn to make these distinctions and therefore become sf readers, but it must be learned at some point.

A new, inexperienced reader, however, has a few advantages to learning how to read sf. Children are still in the process of learning language. This provides a useful starting point for abeyance and implication, but also a potential pitfall. Farah Mendlesohn writes that children's natural cognitive bootstrapping ability puts them in a better position to figure out sf novums. While most adult beliefs in children's "natural" abilities are largely unfounded, Mendlesohn draws this conclusion from studies on young children learning to figure out language from context (*Intergalactic* 31). Children frequently and skillfully decipher unfamiliar words as part of learning their native tongues. Children are also unlikely to misinterpret phrases metaphorically, since they are not yet very familiar with metaphor.[1] Mendlesohn writes that "these baby talents are the fundamental key to science fiction, that ability to accept new words as both indicative and real, and this is a retention of childlike behavior, rather than a function of maturity" (*Intergalactic* 31). Children may even have an advantage, then, since adults who are inexperienced sf readers must relearn these skills. In addition, young readers receive regular instruction and practice with deliberate reading and comprehension strategies.[2] Students are taught tactics like the "Skip the Word, Then Come Back" strategy, which encourages them to pass over a word that they do not know, but then come back to it at the end of the sentence or passage and think about it with more context—in other words, what Card calls abeyance. They may also receive direct or indirect lessons on how to infer while reading.

However, while these skills and literacy tactics may prevent children from becoming frustrated with unknown words, they will not help children to identify that a term like "seed village" is an indicator of an alternate world. Children may not have the problem of metaphor, but this same tendency to literalize means they may just assume that a seed village is a real thing they simply have not learned about yet. The basis of abeyance and implication is that the reader is holding and investigating these unknown terms as part of figuring out how a new world works. This is why familiarity with the sf intertext and recognition of the genre is a critical starting point. The youngest readers must first realize that they are supposed to be solving a puzzle before they can be expected to treat an unknown term as a puzzle piece. It is easy for experienced readers to take this process for granted, but genres are learned.

SCAFFOLDING PRIMARY SCIENCE FICTION

The belief that children simply cannot understand sf until around age twelve, as discussed in the previous chapter, assumes that children have absolutely no schema or reading skills to use as a starting point. In contrast, Mendlesohn positions children as already independently skilled and beyond the need for any help at all, and therefore the best sf is not "limited by assumptions about what children and teens can understand, all demand more of their readers, all assume that the point is to stretch the reader's understanding" (*Intergalactic* 175). While the former attitude seems to underestimate children's abilities and exposure to media, the latter assumes that children will all have the right skills and experience. This in turn implies that if children struggle, then they must not be trying or interested enough. Both claims would leave many children stranded between a lack of faith and high expectations.

While we can have high expectations for children's abilities, not all children will come to sf from the same place. Some will have less dexterity with applying comprehension skills. Brand-new readers and those who find reading challenging will have to apply conscious attention to comprehending the words and sentences in a way that fluent readers take for granted. They have less free attention for holding terms in abeyance, since they are focused on comprehension at the basic level. In addition, a reader's schema depends upon a lot of variables, such as socioeconomic status. A child who has high exposure to technology or access to sf television and movies will have more applicable schemata than a child who does not.

Thus, children are not all equally equipped for sf reading. Fortunately, high-quality primary sf offers support—or "scaffolding"—for young readers, ensuring that sf is accessible to children of various skill levels and backgrounds. "Scaffolding" refers to supporting a child toward independent competence in a particular skill. This term was coined by Jerome Bruner in the 1970s, inspired by Lev Vygotsky's theory that there are tasks that children can do without help and those that they cannot; in between is what Vygotsky called the zone of proximal development (ZPD), or the range of things children can do with help while actively developing the skills needed to do those things on their own. Scaffolding is the helpful structure that supports children's eventual mastery of a skill. In classrooms, teachers scaffold new skills through guided practice in which they make clear the connections between the new skill and previous skills and lessons. Teachers also connect the new skill to everyday situations in which it can be applied. Using the ZPD like this helps students build on what they know already. Scaffolding also highlights connections across tasks so that students can apply their learned skills to various situations rather than only the specific context of each lesson. In terms of primary sf, the goal is current competence in reading sf as well as preparing for later, advanced readership of sf. The essential idea here is that good primary sf has the same core content and values as sf for older audiences, but with the addition of scaffolding to help readers develop the genre schema necessary to read sf fluently.

Offering support to young readers is not cheating them out of anything. Mendlesohn makes an important point that children are often underestimated in terms of their sf-readiness, and I am sure many children can and do learn sf comprehension skills from advanced books out of sheer interest and determination. It is not that children *cannot* make this leap. My point is that while many children can handle it, there is no need for children to face a gauntlet on their way to developing genre comprehension skills. Gunn writes that his decision to explicitly model how to read sf to his college classes "was based not upon the belief that students had to be taught the SF reading protocols, but that the teaching of all literature is the teaching of reading skills. People can pick them up on their own, and often do, but the principle of teaching (or even fiction writing) is that reinvention is not the quickest or even the best way to approach areas of skill." The same principle applies to children and sf. Luckily, well-executed scaffolding structures offer help for those that need it without hindering those that do not.

Illustrated primary sf offers a particularly helpful kind of scaffolding through the combination of words and pictures. However, while pictures are commonplace and significant in children's literature—which I address further below—they are a marginalized selective tradition in sf aesthetics. Corey K. Creekmur calls his history of sf comics, for instance, an "alternative history" assigned to "the margins of significant SF" (2). Yet, he claims, comics have made a large contribution to sf: "The most prominent function of SF comics has been to actually depict the 'visionary' aspects that are seen as fundamental to the genre" (6). The visual depictions in comic books shaped how sf across formats has imagined classic tropes from robots to space travel. Similarly, Andrew Milner argues that the visual belongs in sf criticism because "the tradition of SF as visual spectacle is as old as that of SF as a literature of ideas" (47). The visual and the conceptual developed side by side. Milner explains that foundational sf theater and movies used "special effects to achieve the visual, as distinct from literary, rendition of a novum" (48). Similarly, J. P. Telotte writes that sf's "potential to 'estrange' how and what we see is also an obvious part of the genre's ties to animation, which has always offered its own strange visions, its own often satiric assaults on given reality" (3). These arguments show that while not often considered central to sf, the visual has a long and valuable history of contributing to the genre.

Yet the illustrations in sf books are not often expected to add much to the written stories. Sf art may even be treated better when it stands alone, without a text, due in part to the history of putting irrelevant, lurid covers on pulp sf magazines to drive sales. *The Encyclopedia of Science Fiction* entry on illustrations says that "there has emerged a robust tradition of sf artworks which are not designed to illustrate texts but rather to stand alone as independent visions of future or alternative worlds. Today, then, one might say that there exist two different ways to create a future world: one may use words (to write narrative prose or poetry), or one may use pictures." The entry explains parenthetically that "there are also genres that combine narrative prose and pictures" and offers links to other entries in the encyclopedia on comics, graphic novels, cinema, television, and videogames. Formats specifically for children like picturebooks are notably left out.

Despite being left out of these accounts, the pictures in primary sf are not simply decorative; they contribute to building genre schema for young readers by constructing an image bank for future reading without pictures. Just as sf comics, theater, film, and animation contributed to the development of common imagination in the sf intertext, the visuals in primary sf offer children an image bank for sf concepts. An image bank is especially helpful since visualization is a reading comprehension skill that is taught to help children engage with text and synthesize what they are reading. In a guide for reading teachers, Tanny McGregor writes:

> Since our students are absolutely accustomed to visual literacies—websites, cartoons, movies, print media, and so on—how smart we would be to regard

this as a teaching and learning advantage! By appreciating our students' affinity for the visual, and by noticing and naming visualization as a thinking strategy, we can bolster motivation and confidence as our kids become stronger readers. (91)

Pictures offer an important piece of scaffolding for primary sf, especially for the preliterate and early-literacy child, since they build on the visual sf inter-text and provide a starting point for further visualizing and comprehending sf text beyond the provided images.

SAMPLING LIMITATIONS

After reading hundreds of books in the service of this project, I collected a list of 357 heavily illustrated sf books to study as a sample of the primary sf that is currently available. This list can be found in appendix A. My choice to include only heavily illustrated books leaves out many classic books and was not a choice that I took lightly. However, it was a useful limitation for several reasons.

First, limiting the selection to heavily illustrated books underscores my argument about the possibility of primary sf by skewing my analysis toward the youngest readers. Previous work in books by Mendlesohn, Noga Apple-baum, and Karen Sands and Marietta Frank has already provided thorough analysis of sf with a focus on text-only or sparsely illustrated novels intended for readers near or beyond the twelve-year-old mark. Yet this focus on older readers could be construed to mean that sf is possible only in those cases because the anticipated readers are closer to the "age of reason" discussed in the last chapter. Much YA and adult sf is also packaged in novels, like books for older children. While books with pictures can certainly be enjoyed by older audiences—there is an especially healthy market for comic books and graphic novels intended for mature readers—the fact remains that illustrated books are associated with and marketed for preliterate children and early-literacy children. Even graphic novels and middle grade novels with many illustrations are usually marketed as easier reads for the notorious "struggling readers" who are working on developing their reading skills. My focus on heavily illustrated sf therefore utilizes extreme sampling to prove a point: if sf can thrive in these formats, then it can thrive in books for any target age.

The second, purely pragmatic reason for limiting the set of books to those with illustrations was that it provided boundaries to my sample, which could have become very unwieldy otherwise. I hope that my work here will be a starting point from which scholarship can launch into further projects that will focus on the many text-heavy books that I had to leave out. There are many avenues left to explore, like the history of the development of primary sf in conjunction with and opposition to juvenile and YA sf. In this book, I am focused on untangling the possibilities and challenges of primary sf and demonstrating that it deserves more attention.

Therefore I am primarily interested in how young children develop and utilize the skills to read sf, despite their relatively smaller schemata and the limiting beliefs of adults. The rest of this chapter is divided by format and looks at how the structure of each children's literature format, especially the use of pictures, can be used to effectively scaffold primary sf. Different children's-literature formats each possess unique relationships between words and pictures that are intended to scaffold different phases of literacy development, and these can simultaneously scaffold genre skill development.

BOARD BOOKS AND CLOTH BOOKS

Children's first encounters with books in general are usually board and cloth books. These formats, intended for infants and toddlers, will not get much attention here. As Perry Nodelman discusses in *Words about Pictures*, these bitable formats are intended to introduce books and allow the youngest children to become familiar with holding them, turning pages, and sometimes tracking text on a page. Babies may also learn the more abstract notion that books have meaning from these formats, according to Nodelman.

Nonetheless, most board books are not sf. They are often realistic fiction or nonfiction concept books like ABCs. I did not find any examples of sf board books that were not reprints of picturebooks, such as the board book version of the Little Golden Book *Robots, Robots Everywhere!* by Sue Fliess (2013). Even the *Star Wars* board books are either concept books, like the *Star Wars ABC* (2010) and *Star Wars OBI-123: A Book of Numbers* (2017), or a nonnarrative string of scenes and jokes for parents, such as the series of board books by Jeffrey Brown starting with *Darth Vader and Son* (2012). These sf-adjacent books develop some marginal sf intertextual awareness, much as board and cloth books in general are intended to develop familiarity with the broader concepts of books as meaningful objects. The board book *Star Wars Block: Over 100 Words Every Fan Should Know* (2018) is explicit in its intention to offer children an image bank that pairs illustrations with the names of various *Star Wars* characters and places. However, it is not itself sf, and the lack of context or explanation potentially undermines the usefulness of this intertextual practice.

PICTUREBOOKS

After children have chewed on board books, but before they can read on their own, children have picturebooks read to them. This is not to say that children never read picturebooks to themselves, but as Joe Sutliff Sanders argues in "Chaperoning Words: Meaning-Making in Comics and Picture Books," picturebooks anticipate an adult, literate reader and a preliterate or early-literacy listener. They are written with the expectation of this shared reading experience, in contrast to other formats, like comic books, that anticipate a solitary reading experience. This expectation of a co-reading experience—regardless of whether or not it is always enacted—means that the books are designed with large, rich pictures for children to interpret while listening to the words.

The pictures in picturebooks are more purposeful than those in general illustrated books. Children's literature theorists have long claimed that picturebooks are defined by the combination of words and complex, complementary, and not merely decorative images. Maria Nikolajeva and Carole Scott classify five different relationships between pictures and words in picturebooks: symmetrical, "two mutually redundant narratives"; complementary, "words and pictures filling each other's gaps"; expanding or enhancing, "visual narrative supports verbal narrative, verbal narrative depends on visual narrative"; counterpointing, "two mutually dependent narratives"; and sylleptic, "two or more narratives independent of each other," which includes wordless books (12). There is a robust field of picturebook theory, all of which generally relies on a core premise: picturebooks can be complex creations worth dissecting, and as such they expect a lot from children.

When listening to a picturebook, the child does not need to focus attention on decoding the printed text but is expected to synthesize the spoken words with the illustrated information. Even the youngest children develop expertise in pictorial interpretation, especially the preliterate and early-literacy audiences of picturebooks. Research like Maureen Walsh's 2003 study confirms that preliterate children from three to six years old receive information from the pictures beyond what is granted them by the reading adult. Evelyn Arizpe and Morag Styles's well-cited *Children Reading Pictures: Interpreting Visual Texts* shows how children are skilled at perceiving details and nuances in picturebook illustrations. Most importantly, picturebooks offer children the chance to use the illustrations to practice inferring, an important sf skill. Lawrence Sipe and Anne Brightman found that second-graders made various types of inferences with minimal guidance when they were asked to explain what happened in between the pictures during the page turn.

Aside from in Mendlesohn's appendix, picturebooks are not often considered a good format for sf. Many of the complaints about sf for children use picturebooks as evidence, like A. Waller Hastings's complaints about *Ricky Ricotta's Mighty Robot*. During an interview with Caldecott Honor–winning picturebook author/illustrator Peter Brown, he told me, "Picturebooks are great for bigger ideas. If you really want to get into science fiction and start thinking seriously about some of these complicated issues, I think you need time and words. You can't cram it into a short picturebook." This statement implies that you need words and length for sf. It also implies that the picturebook format is suited to big ideas but not complicated ideas—at the very least, in Brown's opinion, not the type of speculative and extrapolative ideas found in sf. Notably, a moment later he added, "I'm sure someone will now prove me wrong." Indeed, out of the 164 sf picturebooks in this study, 107 (65%) managed to fit in some speculation or extrapolation.

There may be less text in picturebooks, but there is room for sf to thrive in the format's celebrated use of detailed images, picture-text tension, and iconotextual elements. The scope and detail and artistic techniques of a given image in a picturebook can, for instance, develop the valued sf quality of wonder, or what Istvan Csicsery-Ronay calls the science-fictional sublime. Chris Van Allsburg's black-and-white illustrations in *Zathura* (2002) juxtapose the mundane reality of a living room with the jarring scene of planets and spaceships right outside the windows. Even without the words, these pictures would be quality sf due to making the ordinary feel strange. The illustrations solicit exploration of visual cognitive estrangement and the sf feelings of wonder, awe, and the sublime.

Highly detailed illustrations can also encourage readers to stop and seek out ways that the book world differs from theirs: the novums of the story. Nodelman writes that picturebook layouts call for the reader to pause the plot and peruse the sensations and references of the image. The pictures in Graham Oakley's *Henry's Quest* (1986), for instance, convey a lot of information about the story's setting. Mendlesohn states that the illustrations in *Henry's Quest* contain "informational density that typifies science fiction" (*Intergalactic* 68). The pictures in *Henry's Quest* are so effective because they carry the entire sf context through what Nikolajeva and Scott call "Counterpoint in Genre" (24). The words are familiar fairytale language, narrating the adventures of a peasant bumbling through the countryside, saving the day, and winning a princess. Meanwhile, the pictures focus on a postapocalyptic society. In the illustrations we learn about this new world and how humans recovered after some unknown event that caused a major lapse in technology. The illustrations and words demonstrate different aspects of the basic science of gasoline and flammability. This book requires careful attention to the extremely detailed landscape panels in order to access much of the extrapolative and speculative content.

Wide spreads and landscape images can operate for sf picturebooks like evocative worldbuilding descriptions in novels. Nikolajeva and Scott make a similar point about the illustrations in historical fiction picturebooks, which immerse readers in the details of history "that go far beyond the young reader's experience, and do so in a subtle, nonintrusive way that provides an understanding of unfamiliar manners and morals and the cultural environment in which the action takes place" (63). If picturebooks can introduce children to a historical era that they know very little about, then they can introduce the unfamiliar future or alternative worlds of sf.

The pictures in picturebooks operate alongside the words and other paratextual features, all of which must be interpreted together. Mendlesohn suggests that "the use of intra-iconic (and metatextual) material is particularly useful to sf picture books" (*Intergalactic* 228). This may be an understatement. These paratextual details are not only useful but often the ultimate reason why sf complexity can "fit" into such a short format and do well there despite all expectations to the contrary. There is a lot of interpretive space between these elements for the reader to make inferences to fill in the gaps, exponentially increasing the room for speculation and extrapolation in a given book.

For instance, the paratextual details and word/picture tension in Chris Gall's *There's Nothing to Do on Mars* (2008) challenge Nodelman's concerns that children's fiction patterns are incompatible with sf. Nodelman says that sf for young readers paradoxically sends the message that what is out there to explore in the world is not nearly as good as what you have already. Nodelman offers examples of books that start in an amazing place that the main characters find unsatisfactory, even though that setting is exactly what intrigues the reader. Similarly, the textual narrative in *There's Nothing to Do on Mars* starts by describing a little boy named Davey who is pouting because his family moved to Mars. However, the story starts long before the text. The endpapers, a paratextual element that can be used to maximize the small space of picturebooks, show Davey's "top-secret" journal entries scattered on a Mars-red background. These short entries are primarily complaints, including several about how Davey is bored or how Mars lacks hamburgers. There are also a few pieces of trivia, which are often phrased like complaints: "It takes a year to fly to Mars. I'm glad we didn't go to Jupiter" or "Dad said there is a face on Mars but I haven't seen it." The first full-page illustration shows Davey sitting, scrunched up and cross-armed while the text says that despite his parents' assurances, "Davey knew there was nothing to do on Mars." The next few pages show Davey looking miserable as he tries to entertain himself on Mars. The words contrast action verbs like "zoomed" and "zipped" with the refrain that Davey is bored. In the images Davey also has a perpetually unimpressed expression. However, readers can explore the background and find many intriguing clues that the dry Mars landscape once had water. Readers can also find that face on Mars that was mentioned in the endpapers.

Other pages contradict the boredom in the words with excitement in the images. When Davey's robot dog digs a hole, the text says "all he found was an old bone" while the image shows him biting the tail bone of a gigantic fish skeleton. Similarly, "All Davey found was an old toy" contrasts with an image of a NASA rover. When the words and images are redundant, it is only to emphasize the dry riverbeds and the foreshadowing they offer. As Nodelman sees in the novels he analyzes, the protagonist has found his fascinating, strange world to be wanting, failed to see the interesting things that the reader can see, and is happy only when an older natural order is restored. In this case, Davey accidentally restores water to Mars, and the landscape looks more like Earth. The following page shows him with a surfboard, while the text tells us, "No one was happier than Davey." When Davey's father suggests moving to Saturn next, the text says that "Davey's eyes grew big," but since he is facing away from the reader, we do not know if his eyes are big because he is horrified by another new, boring place or because he is excited. The next page echoes the start of the book, saying "Davey knew there was NOTHING to do on Saturn!" but the image shows him smiling and fancifully jumping above Saturn's rings. The words follow the pattern that Nodelman identifies in longer, text-based books: the protagonist is bored with his futuristic surroundings and goes out to find something more interesting or to revert to a pastoral ideal time. Meanwhile, the images reinforce the reader's position that the setting is awesome, and the pictures and endpapers show that Mars is worthy of interest and examining closely. The final illustration fuels the next phase of discovery rather than contentment. This book pushes back against the idea that sf and children's fiction have conflicting patterns, and the text/picture tension is critical to that message.

In addition to the tension between words and pictures, the gaps between pictures in a sequence help to fit complex plots and speculations into the compact space of picturebooks. In such a short format, a lot happens between the pages and even between the panels on each page. Sipe and Brightman's study demonstrated that children need minimal prompting to make several types of inferences about what happens between the images of a page turn. Similarly, what is called "closure" in comics theory—the space between panels—expects the reader to make inferences. These gaps are immensely useful for fitting a lot of speculation or extrapolation into a short space.

David Wiesner's picturebooks *Flotsam* (2006) and *June 29, 1999* (1992) demonstrate a range of techniques used by just one author/illustrator who is adept at using pictures as well as the space between pictures to tell rich sf stories. These books unite the inferencing skills necessary to interpret closure with the similar process of extrapolating and speculating. Wiesner uses different mixtures of panels and transitions to fit very different speculative storylines into not only the pictures, but the spaces between them. Fewer panels result in bigger closure gaps and more interpretive and speculative/extrapolative effort required, while more panels and smaller closure gaps fit more action but require less mental work.

In the completely wordless book *Flotsam*, Wiesner begins with a series of what Scott McCloud would call action-to-action panels depicting a boy visiting the beach (72). Whenever the boy stops to look at something carefully, like a crab, the panels grow a little larger to encourage the reader to look too. This foreshadows the sf gazing that will happen in this story upon reaching the awe-inspiring novum. When the boy develops some film he found in a camera that washes up on the beach, the panels on the page get increasingly larger and zoomed in until the page is overtaken by the boy's eye staring at the picture in his hand. The next few page turns present a series of bizarre underwater pictures, and Wiesner uses only single- or double-spread aspect-to-aspect transitions between these unearthly photographs (72). The small action-to-action panels at the beginning and end of the book fit all the actual movement of the story into a few pages, while the larger transitions and big spreads encourage readers to join the boy's awestruck perusal of the pictures that he finds. The larger the panel, the more the reader is encouraged to indulge in the lingering gaze described by Nodelman. Readers can pore over the full-page illustrations and piece together the speculation between them but will nonetheless be left with a lot of questions on each page turn. These larger leaps work well for this book, which is essentially pondering the vast unknown of the ocean and how even technology offers us only the most tantalizing little glimpses.

Meanwhile, *June 29th, 1999* contains traditional narrative text and mostly two-page spreads with room for words in the white space around the pictures. These pictures are mostly scene-to-scene transitions (McCloud 71). On each page turn, the setting jumps across miles and between days. These transitions allow the story to cover a wider span of time; the reader checks in with the protagonist only at several key moments. The pictures skip across the landscapes of North America while the words tie these images together as part of a mystery. The pictures are complementary to the text, reflecting the words' matter-of-fact tone by showing the very practical concerns that come up when transporting giant vegetables. For instance, the text is focused on wordplay and alliteration—"Peas from Peoria are shipped down the Mississippi to Mobile in exchange for eggplant"—while the pictures demonstrate that the peas are floated downriver like old-fashioned logging operations while the eggplant travels by train. The keen observer will notice that the train bridge cannot fit the huge eggplant. Other pages feature an expanding text/image relationship, since the pictures alone show people inventing ways to harvest and utilize these giant vegetables. As opposed to Wiesner's other book above, this book expects readers to close the gap between the words and pictures as well as between the pictures.

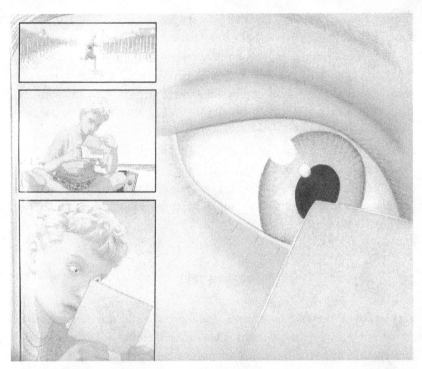

Figure 2. Wiesner's panels grow and zoom in on the boy's eye. *Flotsam* by David Wiesner. Clarion Books, 2006.

Picturebooks have paired well with sf since the format's earliest days. The first modern picturebook, *Little Machinery* (1926) by Mary Liddell, is sf. In the critical facsimile edition, Nathalie op de Beek calls it "a prototypical picture book, a not-quite-missing link between nineteenth- and twentieth-century modes of production" (80). Liddell's book is infused with elements that would later become exactly what scholars love to analyze about picturebooks, especially by calling attention "to the way we interpret words and pictures, the way we scan a composition, and the way the Machinery occupies the frame" (83). Significantly, this prototypical picturebook is also an sf story about a robot.

Little Machinery explored the potential of the format hand in hand with exploration of sf themes for the young reader. Op de Beek says that "Mary Liddell's peculiar text allegorizes the urbanizing 1920s United States via the contemporary form of the picture book. It reflects past children's literature in its depiction of a natural environment and prosaic animals while indulging in speculative fiction about an automaton that springs up in a forest near a railroad track" (94–5). Op de Beek calls it speculative fiction, an umbrella term for both fantasy and sf, but *Little Machinery* is specifically an sf story. As op de Beek points out, this book should be contextualized alongside Fritz Lang's pioneering sf film *Metropolis*, which came out a year after *Little Machinery*. The picturebook explores themes of artificial life and hybridization of machinery and nature. The praise on the back cover includes comments from two engineers, one of whom says, "The joke of it is, the things are rigged up right. They would *work!*" (np, emphasis in original). *Little Machinery* used sf content to develop the parameters and test the strengths of picturebooks. As this early example demonstrates, not only are the sf genre and picturebook format compatible, they can be very well matched and have been since the beginning.

POPUP BOOKS

Very few of the books in my sample of primary sf could also be described as popup books. Popup books are an often-ignored corner of children's literature, possibly due to being an odd format when it comes to their target audience, given that they range from baby's first open-the-flap books to delicate coffee table novelties. Out of the 357 books I gathered, only two were popup books: *Bugs in Space* (1997) by David Carter and *Twinkle* (2007) by Scott M. Fischer. These two books use pictures and the moving parts of those pictures with varying levels of success in speculation and extrapolation.

Bugs in Space demonstrates limited speculation. This title is part of David Carter's *Bugs in a Box* series, making it a space-themed adventure among many other popup bug adventures. Mendlesohn discusses this book in her appendix on picturebooks, noting, "The interaction of this book is explorative, but the exploration is constrained, the popups direct, rather than point outwards and open up the world" (*Intergalactic* 235). She explains that the popup function ruins "the wonder of space adventure," because "each piece of prose is actually an entry, or a directive, demanding a pause for action" (235). Yet this is precisely what a detailed picturebook illustration is praised for doing when Nodelman says that pictures "interrupt the action" and call for detailed perusal (246). In popup books, the reader pauses the action of the story for the action of moving the illustration, while in picturebooks the reader pauses the action of the story for the action of scouring the page for details. Popup art calls for a different kind of viewing: less poring over details and more looking at how it works or how the image changes.

Instead of the inferencing that detailed picturebook illustrations call for, popups and flaps are more like the "special effects" of children's books. Milner spends a good part of his book arguing that the supposedly gimmicky special effects of sf TV and radio are important to the genre's development of visual novums. Telotte even says that the core of the genre in sf film can be located in the development of special effects just as much as in the stories (24). The key in applying this to popup books is determining just how much the "special effects" do or do not create a visual novum and contribute to sf ideas. Just because the popups come with scripted actions for each page does not mean they cannot open the story outward and work for sf themes.

In the case of *Bugs in Space*, the pause on each page to play with the moving pieces parallels and simulates the momentary observation of a new world by the passing captain. The story opens: "A signal from deep in space has been received that tells the world there is life in outer space. And now, Captain Bug Rogers is about to go where no Bug has gone before." The Buck Rogers reference is likely to go over children's heads and make parents or grandparents smile; even in the late nineties when *Bugs in Space* was published, there had been no recent television remakes of Buck Rogers. Children of the right age to appreciate this simple popup tale would be too young to read the more recent comic book adaptations from Dynamite Entertainment (2009–10) and Hermes Press (2012). Children may, however, get the *Star Trek* reference, depending upon their familiarity with the old or remade versions of the series. This second reference is more important to the themes of the book, anyway, since it sets up the book as a journey of observation and discovery rather than change, as per *Star Trek*'s Prime Directive. Each page shows Captain Bug Rogers glimpsing a snapshot of other worlds, and the presence of active life in space is underscored by the movement of the book. Children are called to initiate the movement, but they cannot change it from its intended path without damaging the book. We cannot deny that Captain Bug Rogers has seen and observed and learned new things beyond his planet, though it would have been nice to see how he reports his discoveries when he returns home, and perhaps this would have assuaged Mendlesohn's concerns about opening the discovery outward and providing consequence. The book offers the classic sf voyage extraordinaire in a barebones version. Children who want something complex to think about will not find it here, but the speculation of what kind of alien life may be found in space is a minimal introduction to sf journeys of discovery.

The other popup book, *Twinkle* by Scott M. Fischer, makes more careful and coordinated use of its moving pieces toward the goal of sf. It has only one moving page, but the whole book is set up to draw attention to the book's status as a physical artifact and culminate on that page. This book can be read from either end and concludes in the middle. The front and back covers are nearly the same except for a human on the bottom corner of one cover and a blue-skinned alien on the other. Only the ISBN barcode on the side with the human indicates that it may technically be the back cover—a choice that decenters humanity.

When read from either side, the text of the book is Jane and Ann Taylor's nursery rhyme "The Star"—commonly called "Twinkle, Twinkle Little Star"—while the illustrations reinterpret the words with an emphasis on wonder and exploration. When read from the "front" cover with the alien in the porthole, it tells the story of that alien child mapping a route to a star. The alien gazes off the page, with the star reflecting in their eyes as they look in wonder at their destination. After the ship is smashed by meteors, a human child floats into view through the debris field.

Read from the other end of the book, the poem is the same, but the illustrations follow the human child setting out toward the same star, also crashing, and floating into view of the alien child. The reader must flip the book when changing sides, in order to keep the spine on the left and the text right-side up. This also means that as the reader reaches the middle of the book, the two characters on each end are upside-down relative to each other, evoking the arbitrary orientation of space.

After the two adventurers meet, the centerfold of the book pops out to add another five inches to the top and bottom of the pages. This central page is accompanied by the final stanza "Though I know not what you are, TWINKLE TWINKLE LITTLE STAR!" The picture shows that the two adventurers have connected the remains of their spaceships and are continuing their journey together, with stars in their eyes. The pictures and words demonstrate that for both adventurers, finding this unknown other lifeform in the depths of space expands their personal universes and extends their adventure. This theme is replicated and reinforced by the expansion of the literal dimensions of the book. The creases in the expanding page resemble a starburst, with all crease lines pointing out. The story ends with an outward movement that is reflected both in the plot and in the movement of the page.

However, this book flies in the face of plausibility, given that the human apparently needs no spacesuit and blasts off via a tricycle and a ramp. The alien takes off in what looks like a one-masted galleon with a rocket under the hull. Since both are using dated transportation to achieve space travel, I wonder if it is an intentional play on looking to the stars despite current technological limitations, but that may be a stretch. The text is well known as a lullaby, and the human and alien outfits look suspiciously like pajamas, but this book refuses to frame it as a dream, a common excuse in similar rocketship-in-the-night picturebooks that begin or end in a child's bedroom, like *Harry and Horsie* (2009) by Katie Van Camp and Lincoln Agnew. The reader is left with this ambiguity to decide whether they think the whole thing is a fantasy or just sf with no interest in accurate details.

EARLY READERS

Early reader books—otherwise known as easy readers and beginner books—are the format most clearly oriented toward scaffolding reading. These are intended to be the first books that children read by themselves or with minimal help. In the only critical academic volume about early readers to date, editors Annette Wannamaker and Jennifer Miskec loosely define the format as "those books that children are first able to read entirely on their own" (4). Everything about the format is tailored to that goal. Depending on the publisher, authors of early readers are given limits on their use of vocabulary and sentence complexity. Early readers are often assigned levels to rank the difficulty for new readers.

The pictures in early readers are designed for the purpose of supporting literacy practice rather than for complex meaning-making. Wannamaker and Miskec explain that early readers usually come in a smaller trim size than picturebooks, "because [picturebooks] privilege illustration as an art form," while early readers do not (5). According to Daniel Hade and Laura Anne Hudock, the illustrations in early readers primarily offer clues for readers trying to parse text.[3] They explain that this format's "illustrations usually support a developing reader to independently comprehend the words on the page through letter-picture association or to decorate, extend, and reinforce the story narrative beyond the printed word" (88). The pictures might not go to the extent of the complicated counterpoint or contradiction relationships that Nikolajeva and Scott find in picturebooks; nevertheless, they can extend or reinforce the narrative, offering light picture-word tension that is helpful when words and description may be too complicated, but a picture is efficient and easily understood. In Sarah Albee's *My Best Friend Is Out of This World* (1998), the girl wants to invite her alien friend to dinner, and the text innocuously reads, "This afternoon I called him up." The picture, meanwhile, shows that the girl is not talking on a phone, but rather wearing a helmet headset covered in buttons, switches, and radio receiver/transmitter. This eliminates any need for complicated words about how she contacts her friend; the gap between the word "called" and the picture efficiently extends the meaning.

Only one early reader in my sample used a more complex image/text interaction to add extrapolative content, and it also relied on intertextual knowledge. In *Ant-Man: This Is Ant-Man* (2015), one page features a picture of Scott in a mask and lab coat, spraying gas from a beakerlike jar at the ants, while the text reads: "Soon Scott found a way to talk to ants" (9). His mouth is not open, and he is not talking in any normal sense in the picture, and so it does not match the words exactly. This picture refers to how Ant-Man uses pheromones to communicate with the ants, one of the more extrapolative features of his storyline in the comics and movies. Young readers may or may not gather this from their intertextual knowledge, but that little extrapolation is nonetheless contained in the tension between the picture, words, and intertext for those with the schema to understand it.

Given their relatively simple structure, many sf early readers seem to expect knowledge of the sf intertext. This feature of the sf early reader dovetails neatly with Gretchen Papazian's argument that early readers offer a fascinating challenge to Roland Barthes's concept of *déjà lu* or "already read," which posits that all meaning and understanding of reading derives from previous reading and experience. Papazian explains:

> As a format that generally assumes its reader lacks knowledge of and/or extensive experience with reading, the Early Reader may have revealed a flaw in the theory of *déjà lu*. It might have suggested that there is a beginning to the signifying chain; there is or has to be some sort of denotative meaning upon which to build understanding. Instead, though, the Early Reader's representation of reading practices and processes supports and expands

the theory of *déjà lu* by embedding the "already read" in the text itself via characters and plot sequences; by raising questions about denotative meaning and showing the consequences of such rigid thinking; and by reveling in variety, uncertainty, and possibility. (79)

Papazian points out that by having characters reading books within the book, and other situations that embed reading within the reading, early readers simulate the experience of previous reading. The characters and their fictional reading experience substitute for the real reader's experience. Similarly, sf early readers are not written to be a child's very first encounter with sf, even though it may be their first time reading sf alone. The books simultaneously expect sf schemata and create sf schemata. The early reader format relies heavily on the sf intertext to navigate this balancing act and to offer speculation and extrapolation in very simple stories.

The sf intertext in early readers encourages children to contextualize sf books as part of a genre and as part of a larger category of stories and trends. Much of the intertext in my sample of early readers derives from product tie-ins, series, and the sprawling universes of *Star Wars*, Marvel, and DC that children regularly encounter in other media. All this preexisting material acts like a shortcut, allowing the story to jump past worldbuilding and get right to the action—or speculation. Many of the Marvel and DC early reader series follow the same short, serial pattern of comic books. A good part of the speculation in these books exists solely in the interchange between the book's plot and the broader context of the series. For instance, the extremely short level-one early readers that introduce common superheroes narrate just enough to introduce the hero's name, origin, powers, and allies. There is very little explanation for the powers in *Ant-Man: This Is Ant-Man*, save that they derive from science: "One day, Scott met a scientist named Hank. They talked about science. Hank gave Scott a special suit. Scott tried it on. Scott shrank to the size of an ant!" (7–8). It is hard for the reader to find any extrapolation from current science when the science itself is so vague.

Instead the story speculates about Scott's experiments with ants and how he chooses to use the technology, but primarily between the lines. The super-villains that he punches are not named, and their villainy—like the ethics of Ant-Man's actions—is entirely in the intertext. These books are ultimately tie-ins, and this helps with sf scaffolding. The reader is expected to know the films. In order for the reader to ponder the "what if" about Ant-Man's use/abuse of technology, they would have to know or learn more about the Avengers and these villains. Tie-ins are hardly considered capital-L Literature, but this intertextual linkage makes the book more complex than it would be on its own.

Early readers are also not considered Literature, and while picturebooks have generated a substantial supply of theory and praise, early readers are often ignored entirely in children's literature conversations, due to their perceived mundane content and educational focus. Even in the first and only critical collection seeking to give early readers their due diligence, Papazian seems to excuse this focus on early readers by distinguishing between purely instructional early readers and "literary" early readers that emphasize "theme, character, and story" over things like vowel sounds and sight words (72). Literary early readers, she contends, are eligible for critical readings whereas their purely practical counterparts are less so. Asking early readers to prioritize anything aside from reading practice is antithetical to the format, but clever authors can find their way around these limits in order to provide sf stories that encourage thinking without adding an extra obstacle to reading practice. In my sample, only twenty early readers (53%) passed the speculation/extrapolation test.

COMIC BOOKS AND GRAPHIC NOVELS

Comic books and graphic novels are similar to picturebooks in terms of their image/text interdependency. Mel Gibson asserts that "the picturebook, comic and graphic novel are complex and flexible media linked through their shared uses of image and text" (110). McCloud's comics theory applies well to the picturebooks above, demonstrating the permeable boundaries between picturebooks and comic books. The visual emphasis in comic books and graphic novels offers specific benefits for sf comprehension, but the brevity of comic books and the lower social value of comics formatting in general create unique challenges for sf authors.

Most people have little difficulty with casually differentiating between formats like picturebooks, comic books, and graphic novels until asked to formally theorize the differences. Scholarly attempts have also struggled; the 2012 special issue of *Children's Literature Association Quarterly* was dedicated to wrangling with the theoretical and structural differences and similarities behind picturebooks and comic books. Even this attempt by some of the leading scholars of picturebooks and comics leaves many gaps and contradictions in the theory, due to the frequent crossovers between the formats that make formal distinctions nearly impossible. In response, Sanders argues that the main problem with attempting to differentiate by form alone is that the real differences all lead back to the end users. As mentioned above, he finds

> a reliable and fertile difference emerges between comics and picture books: in general, if the book anticipates a solitary reader who chaperones the words as they go about their work of fixing the meaning of the images, that book is a comic; if the book instead anticipates a reader who chaperones the words as they are communicated to a listening reader, that book is a picture book. (61)

This approach offers a method for distinguishing between the formats and also establishes an anticipated literary timeline: picturebooks are read to children before they graduate to reading comic books and graphic novels independently.[4]

Meanwhile, the very idea of the graphic novel is also contested. Many artists reject the term "graphic novel" altogether and associate it with distasteful marketing contrivances of the publishing industry. Shaun Tan, who was conscripted into the debate when his book *The Arrival*—proposed as a picturebook—was sold and received successfully as a graphic novel, remarks: "I use the terms 'comics' and 'graphic novels' interchangeably, because I don't see much difference between them; these terms both describe an arrangement of words and/or pictures as consecutive panels on a printed page" (2). Some scholars deny that the graphic novel is a format at all. Charles Hatfield's *Keywords for Children's Literature* entry on the graphic novel argues that "the term 'graphic novel' describes neither a discrete literary genre nor a specific publishing format. Rather, it denotes a sensibility: an attitude taken toward comics" (100). Hatfield describes the term as simply a convenient, contemporary publishing niche. He argues that the graphic novel is a workaround for those who want comics to be recognized as a legitimate, respectable format but feel barred from this by the troubled history of comics and children, as epitomized by the Comics Code Authority.

Despite the graphic novel's unstable beginnings, as the term has grown in popular usage other scholars have identified peculiarities that justify the graphic novel as a distinct format and more than an attitude or marketing tactic. The primary argument of this stance positions graphic novels as another medium in the family of comic books and comic strips, distinguished by a greater length and novellike plot complexity. Hatfield describes the comic book as America's previously premier "medium for longform comics narrative," and therefore the "father to the graphic novel" (101). He is following a tradition of treating comic strips and comic books as specific media for packaging a narrative told through a specific grammar of comics, as described by theorists like Thierry Groensteen and McCloud. Even Hatfield, resistant he is to the graphic novel as a distinct format, implies the need for the new medium he describes. Not only does he equate the graphic novel with comic books in the quote above, but he also repeats phrases like "novel-length comic" throughout the entry, a tendency which itself seems to indicate the need for a labeled format that describes novel-length comics. Comic books may be longform in comparison to comic strips, but they are not novel-length unless compiled.

Gibson similarly points to length, stating that graphic novels "share the grammar of comics, as they are longer works in a comic-strip form, containing a single narrative" (101). His emphasis on a single narrative is important, as it distinguishes the graphic novel from European albums and bound collections of episodic comic books. Along the same lines, Michael Joseph differentiates the graphic novel through the length and corresponding binding size, as opposed to the thinner bindings of magazines. He defines them as "a subset of comics generally called alternative comics that, whether by original or subsequent design, find themselves published as books, and which therefore have some definable responsibility to "bookness": that is, to the conventional form, history, or authority of the book" (466). This definition portrays graphic novels as if the result of serendipity—a format that blundered into the space between comics and novels and then made the best of its liminal position.

This serendipitous characterization feels apt, as it encompasses both Hatfield's point that the term gained popularity as an excuse for legitimizing comics, but also acknowledges how the graphic novel's new liminal position has benefited the format and enabled it to become something unique. For instance, the "bookish" binding of graphic novels came with other benefits. Sanders points out that librarians were willing to endorse comics in general only once they became available in "trade album editions, often called 'graphic novels,'" and could therefore sustain the standard library shelving, labeling, and circulation that floppy comic books could not handle (87). The endorsement of librarians is far-reaching, given that these professionals directly impact circulation and awards, lending much credence to the term in popular and publishing circles. Also, since "libraries regularly ghettoize their graphic novel collections in youth departments" (Goldsmith 19), librarians have encouraged the graphic novel's association with children and young adults, for better or worse.

This is all to say that comic books and graphic novels scaffold sf similarly to picturebooks but depend even more heavily on the elements of closure and, for graphic novels particularly, on the story's length. The sheer number of pages and panels in graphic novels, as opposed to picturebooks, provides greater space for speculation and extrapolation from more detailed science. For instance, *A Wrinkle in Time: The Graphic Novel* (2012), adapted by Hope Larson from Madeleine L'Engle's 1962 classic, extrapolates from current understandings of time and space with extra scaffolding from sequential art. Like the original novel, the story unabashedly dives into complex space/ time concepts. In the original, the explanations of tesseract travel and the first, second, third, fourth, and fifth dimensions are accompanied by a handful of small intext illustrations (L'Engle 73–75). Even though L'Engle's ant metaphor for tesseract travel is very concrete to begin with, she and her editors must have expected readers to benefit from the visuals, or they would not have included them in an otherwise purely textual narrative. The graphic novel version, by extension, offers even more guidance for younger readers. The consistently illustrated presentation further grounds these complex concepts by spreading the depiction out onto several pages. Thus, the same explana- tion of tesseract travel and dimensions occurs over five pages composed of twenty-one panels (L'Engle and Larson 138–42). This case of adaptation is particularly interesting because of L'Engle's beliefs, expressed in *Madeleine L'Engle Herself*, that visualization is essential to reading: "To read a book is to listen, to visualize, to see. If the reader, child or adult, cannot create the book along with the writer, the book is stillborn" (164). The graphic novel will provide more of these visuals than the original novel, perhaps opening the door to this story for a reader who might otherwise struggle with visualizing L'Engle's adventure through time and space.

I found only thirty-four sf graphic novels intended for children under twelve,[5] but an impressive 94 percent of them passed the speculation and extrapolation test. Meanwhile, I found 102 sf comic books, of which 68 percent tested well for speculation and extrapolation. Of those comic books that did not make the cut, many were superhero stories with no attempt to explain, extrapolate, or speculate about the superpowers. Of the comic books intended exclusively for young readers—as opposed to those with crossover potential—the comic books that failed most often did so due to two particular problems: prioritizing slapstick and wasting the intertextual potential by using it exclusively to wink at parents. Two such books, both by Art Baltazar and Franco, focus on superhero families or young versions of common superheroes. Baltazar and Franco are by far the most prolific creators of juvenilized comic books.[6] With twelve issues of *Superman Family Adventures* (2013) and over fifty issues in the *Tiny Titans* (2009–12) series, these books are certainly readily available comic books that are intended, in art style and reading level, for the very youngest children. These series both defer to puns and jokes rather than considerations of technology or science, even when the heroes' designs or powers are wide open to such explorations. The creators make the occasional intertextual joke that seems intended for parent-fans of the DC Universe, but even these do not bring in extrapolation or speculation. Other books by Baltazar and different collaborating writers and artists follow a similar pattern, like *Li'l Battlestar Galactica* (2014) and *Li'l Bionic Kids* (2014). These are primarily a host of slapstick situations, with intertextual jokes based on the original television shows *Battlestar Galactica* (1978) and *Six Million Dollar Man* (1973). Given that these shows are not regularly available in reruns and the 2003 remake of *Battlestar Galactica* is very different from the original, these jokes are accessible exclusively by parents. This is particularly odd given the solitary reading experience expected of comic books, unless these jokes are meant to assuage concerned parents who read and approve books before letting their children read them.

The Marvel Universe also has its own line of young hero comic books: *Mini Marvels* (2013) by Chris Giarusso. These stories are similarly juvenile in tone, but, significantly, the jokes about Marvel Universe characters are actually intended for the younger audience. There is even less slapstick in favor of jokes based on the characters' backstories. These books expect that the young reader knows Marvel characters from contemporary movies, television, and other sources and therefore will be in on the jokes. Additionally, what the characters can do with their powers is centerstage, edging the story into speculative territory. For instance, in "Paperboy Blues," when a young Spider-Man shows up at young Xavier's school to collect the school's overdue newspaper fees, the students reveal that they use Xavier's mind manipulation powers to run the place on their own without adults. The characters even dabble in a short debate about the ethics of fooling adult bill collectors in order to sustain their independence. This is all couched in the silly scenario of young Spider-Man's paper delivery job, but there is speculation here about the ethical use of power, unlike anything in *Tiny Titans* or the *Li'l* comics.

More complex comic books in the sample do not infantilize the characters for children—and also demonstrate that not every comic book has to be about superheroes. In the case of *Emily's Intergalactic Lemon Stand* (2004) by Ian and Tyson Smith, the art style's naïveté is similar to that of these other juvenile comic books, but the story does not trade speculation for slapstick. While the plot is silly and humorous, it simultaneously questions what robots are capable of when commanded and created by human greed and competitiveness.

Meanwhile, Marvel also offers less silly comic books for children that are even more inclined toward speculation and extrapolation. The Marvel website has a section for children that includes games, information on the characters, and digital comic book issues. These comic books are produced specifically for Marvel Kids but do not seem to be particularly different from their mainstream comics—save perhaps the lack of especially gritty or gory storylines. They feature well-known and recently cinematized characters like Spider-Man, Ant-Man, and the Guardians of the Galaxy. As in the case of the intertext in *Ant-Man: This Is Ant-Man*, a reader with background knowledge of these characters has a better platform from which to access the stories, but these comic books also stand alone with more successful speculation and extrapolation than the *Mini Marvels* series or the Ant-Man early reader. In *Spider-Man* issue #1 (2010), the hero speculates about the responsibility and consequences of having his Spidey-abilities. In *Ant-Man* #1 (2005), the hero experiments with the biology, communication, and attitudes of different kinds of ants. The team of Guardians deals with being unexpectedly sucked into an interdimensional portal in *Guardians of the Galaxy* #1 (2013). The multimodal format also allows for a direct link to the characters' origins and context. Readers can use the other resources on the website to learn that Spider-Man has powers because of a radioactive spider bite rather than magic. This is an important reminder that the intertext that young readers can draw upon is not only other books, films, and TV shows but also the vast resources of internet reference and fan sites.

In contrast with all these lighthearted comic books, one comic book miniseries, Grant Morrison's *We3* (2004), offered an interesting dilemma for the purposes of this study. I first discovered the title on a list of the "Best 15 Fantasy & Sci-Fi Graphic Novels for Kids (And the Whole Family)" by Perry Rosenbloom on a parental resource website called *Geeks Raising Geeks.* Upon reading the comics, however, I was surprised by their sad tone and the amount of gore and violence toward animals. Blood and guts, in near-photo-realistic detail, spew from the animals and the humans alike. I considered disqualifying it as a story for children under twelve and removing it from my pool of books. Yet the reading level was fine. Furthermore, it was very accessible: the necessary schema for understanding the technology was minimal, and much of the more complicated interpretation was in the pictures. I thought about the usual complaints about "senseless violence" in children's media—but the violence and gore in *We3* are not senseless; the violence is squarely in service of the story's speculation. Instead of glorifying the violence, it becomes a sad, numbing symphony about technology in war and whether humans should drag other animals into our own messes. It is shocking and heartbreaking at times, but a very poignant way to deliver an ultimately antiviolence message that is bound to stick *because* of those very gory images. I ultimately left it on my list, though it does pose a question for future research into other measures of cultural age-appropriateness versus speculative potential.

HYBRID NOVELS

Recent shifts in children's publishing have produced middle-grade novels for ages eight to twelve that rely on frequent, story-significant illustrations. There is not yet a consensus about what to call these books, but the best term to date seems to be "hybrid novels," as defined by Eve Tandoi in the *Edinburgh Companion to Children's Literature.* Tandoi describes this format as a natural evolution in media, and capable of being analyzed with theory previously applied to picturebooks. Despite being of similar length to graphic novels, and occasionally including comic panels, hybrid novels are not defined by the grammar of comics. Instead, they insert illustrations into primarily textual narrative, contributing to the story but not ever taking precedence over the text.

Hybrid novels are the lightest illustrated books in this sample, and accordingly do not rely on the pictures as much as the other formats. Yet these additions help to scaffold a story's speculation and extrapolation in significant ways, and ultimately fifteen (79%) of the books passed the speculation/extrapolation test. In *Cakes in Space* (2014) by Philip Reeve and Sarah McIntyre, the title page is preceded by an illustration. This image shows a brochure about moving to Nova Mundi and a ticket stub that says "family ticket." Like the endpapers in the picturebook *There's Nothing to Do on Mars*, this illustration establishes the setting and the genre early. The brochure is laid against a starry backdrop, and its pictures of life on Nova Mundi include aliens and robots, signaling to the reader to apply sf reading protocols and begin tapping their schema for intertextual connections. The picture also provides information, such as the fact that a family has a ticket to take this trip.

The very first page of *Cakes in Space* uses words and images in tandem to emphasize the science-fictional sublime of space: "The trouble with space is, there's so much of it. An ocean of blackness without any shore. A never-ending nothing. And here, alone in the million billion miles of midnight, is one solitary moving speck. A fragile parcel filled with sleeping people and their dreams. A ship" (1). This poetic opening text is paired with a large black rectangle with some stars on the upper right edges, a lot of empty space in the middle, and a spaceship in the lower right corner. As Tandoi suggests, picturebook codes are helpful for examining this hybrid novel's use of illustration. William Moebius explains that in picturebooks "a character that is on the margin, 'distanced' or reduced in size on the page, and near the bottom will generally be understood to possess fewer advantages" (140). In addition, he explains that something on the right side of the page "is likely to be moving into a situation of risk or adventure" (140). Molly Bang explains that putting a key object in the bottom half of a picture makes it seem threatened or constrained (56), making an object small in the frame makes it seem vulnerable (72), and isolating an object in large amounts of empty space makes it seem alone and vulnerable (84). As these picturebook codes reveal, the intentional layout of the image makes the spaceship seem disadvantaged and insignificant, possibly at risk, and utterly alone in the vastness of space. The design of this opening illustration reinforces the science-fictional sublime of the words.

Other hybrid novels use integrated illustrations to offer information not otherwise contained in the words, such as the comic book panels integrated into *Attack of the Fluffy Bunnies* (2010) by Andrea Beaty and Dan Santat and

The True Meaning of Smekday (2007) by Adam Rex, both of which use comic strips to narrate the backstories of alien invaders. These panels also offer more-detailed depictions of the aliens than words alone, which is especially important in *Attack of the Fluffy Bunnies*, where the wild-eyed aliens look far more menacing in the pictures than in the written description of "bunnies with blackened rumps" (185) and "swirly" eyes (192). The tension between the words and pictures in this text often injects humor into horror and vice versa.

COMPARING FORMATS

The sf quality differs between these formats of children's literature. These differences are difficult to compare in raw numbers, since the total books in each format ranges from 19 to 164. Using statistical tests to account for the very different numbers in each group, most of the formats were not statistically different from one another (see table 1).[7] A logistical regression and Benjamini-Hochberg post hoc comparisons (see appendix A for details) shows that the only statistically significant differences between each format's speculation/extrapolation scores were between graphic novels and comic books ($p =.06$), graphic novels and early readers ($p =.001$), and graphic novels and picturebooks ($p =.04$). Even then, graphic novels and comic books were significantly different only at an $\alpha < 0.1$ level, which means that the probability that the differences in the groups are random was not small enough to dismiss it. This makes sense, given that comic books and graphic novels share roots and qualities, as mentioned above.

When looking at raw percentages, it is tempting to assume that a higher word count offers more room for speculation, confirming Peter Brown's comments. However, while the early reader, picturebook, and comic book categories have the lowest percentages comparatively, over half of the books in each category passed the test despite their short lengths and lower word counts. Additionally, by the logic that texts with more words have more room to speculate, the hybrid novels should have had the highest percentage of success, since they had a higher word count than any of the other categories included in this study. Neither the raw percentages nor the statistical test showed that hybrid novels were demonstrably different from the shorter formats. Only the graphic novel category differed from the shorter formats in the statistical test, and it achieved the highest percentage of speculative/

Table 1. Books That Contain Extrapolation or Speculation

Picturebooks ($n = 164$)	Early Readers ($n = 38$)	Comic Books ($n = 102$)	Graphic Novels ($n = 34$)	Hybrid Novels ($n = 19$)
107 (65%)	20 (53%)	69 (68%)	32 (94%)	15 (79%)

extrapolative books (94%). The graphic novels were not statistically different from the hybrid novels, though. Both formats are defined by their length and complexity, which may help with developing speculative or extrapolative content. The word count, it seems, is not as helpful as the relative length of a story.

Overall, this sample of primary sf books tested well in terms of their speculative and extrapolative content. Of course, this does not mean that all primary sf books make use of this potential; plenty are still only superficially science fictional or too concerned with slapstick to offer speculation. However, the examples of success demonstrate that primary sf is not as much of a paradox as critical comments imply. The varied use of pictures and the sf intertext as scaffolding in different formats for different literacy stages makes primary sf more accessible and comprehensible to a wider audience of children. Some children simply need a little more guidance than others, and those that do not need it can self-advance beyond scaffolded books. The trend cited by Michael Levy and others that children skip to YA or adult sf will probably always be true in part, since many young readers quickly gain the needed sf skills. I do not wish to hold these children hostage in simplified sf, but rather to make sure that the rest of the children who do not jump up merrily into YA and adult titles can make their way to the same place at their own pace. The key is not to condescend to readers of primary sf or write a children's genre unrelated to the adult version, but rather to make sure the doorway to sf is as wide and accommodating as possible.

CHAPTER 3

READING REPRESENTATION

Since reading is a transaction between reader and text, with schema being an essential component of reading comprehension and motivation, then it is also important to consider how readers' identities and cultural backgrounds impact their access to primary sf. Diverse representation—or the lack thereof—signals to the reader who belongs in the genre's readership and the futures that sf often depicts. Emphasizing diversity in primary sf not only enables more readers to participate in the genre but can also introduce children to an important usage of speculation and extrapolation: imagining alternate realities for traditionally oppressed groups. For instance, Lisa Yaszek explains that sf has always been "naturally compatible with the project of Feminism" (1), because many feminist narratives rely on sf's cognitive estrangement and the potential of technological advances to imagine other realities for women. Afrofuturism, Indigenous Futurisms, and Latin@futurism also tap into this potential, as well as many other movements that cannot be encapsulated here.

Generally speaking, sf is diversifying and embracing alternate perspectives. At the same time, conservative groups complain that the increasing prominence of diverse voices is ruining the genre. Even as N. K. Jemesin claimed a well-deserved Hugo Award every year from 2016 through 2018 for her *Broken Earth* trilogy, protest groups launched social media campaigns to try to prevent the books from winning. It is tempting to see these genre battles as irrelevant to the relatively simplified stories of primary sf. However, as foundational texts, these books are in the direst need of attention to diversity.

Children's literature movements such as #weneeddiversebooks operate on the understanding that diverse representation matters, and children's literature needs more of it. The first article on the topic, "The All-White World of Children's Books" by Nancy Larrick, appeared in 1965, but only recently have newer studies and social media campaigns steeply accelerated critical attention to the issue. Representation has been lacking for the last several decades, according to publisher Lee & Low Books, who calculated that only 10 percent of books from 1994 to 2013 included multicultural content, but recent movements have succeeded in raising that number to 28 percent (Ehrlich).

Meanwhile, the numbers are still in need of improvement. The Cooperative Children's Book Center (CCBC) statistics found that out of 4,035 books published in 2019, some 471 (12%) were about Black/African characters, 65 (2%) were about Indigenous characters, 357 (9%) were about Asian characters, 236 (6%) were about Latinx characters, 5 (< 1%) were about Pacific Islander characters, and 35 (1%) were about Arab characters ("Books by and/or About"). When people questioned how books with animal protagonists might be affecting these percentages in 2013, K. T. Horning from the CCBC crunched the numbers coming in for that year to reveal that the problem was still there, even when animal protagonists are taken into account: "Of the 1509 books published in 2013 that we have received so far, 1183 (or 78.3%) are about human beings. [. . .] Of the 1183 books published so far in 2013 about human beings, 124 of those books feature people of color. That's 10.48%" (Horning). While there is nothing wrong with animal protagonists, they cannot replace the need for representation.

Female characters are also underrepresented in children's literature at large. A 2011 study of children's books from 1900 to 2000 found that "on average, 36.5 percent of books each year include a male in the title compared to 17.5 percent that include a female" (McCabe et al. 207). Additionally, they found that "no more than 33 percent of books published in a year contain central characters who are adult women or female characters whereas adult men and male animals appear in up to 100 percent" and "boys appear as central characters in 26.4 percent of books and girls in 19 percent, but male animals are central characters in 23.2 percent of books while female animals are in only 7.5 percent" (McCabe et al. 209). Some attribute this to the commonplace assumption that elementary-age boys will not identify with girl protagonists, though that may be another self-fulfilling prophecy. Never mind nonbinary children, who are not often represented in the books or even considered in these studies.

To compound the problem, the prominence of male characters intersects with the lack of diversity in children's literature. In 2015 eleven-year-old Marley Dias founded #1000BlackGirlBooks, because she was sick of only seeing books "all about white boys or dogs" (Anderson). For her, having an identity at the crux of two underrepresented groups meant an even sharper lack of representation in books. Fortunately, her drive to collect one thousand books received an overwhelming response, and four thousand suggested titles! This girl's success indicates that while diverse books may exist, they are not in common circulation and must be called forth from the edges of children's literature publishing in order to better benefit young readers in a multicultural world.

Primary sf is located at the crux of these fights to keep diversifying sf and children's literature. The sample of books that I gathered indicates that primary sf has the potential to go above and beyond the current shortcomings of inclusivity in both sf and children's literature. High-quality, diverse primary sf books already exist, but they are not getting nearly enough critical attention or support. Some examples of primary sf already include complex intersectional characters and employ culturally rich sf techniques inherited from sf feminism, Afrofuturism, Latin@futurism, and Indigenous Futurisms. These books invite more readers into primary sf, offering more stories that support readers of different backgrounds, while also offering richer speculation and extrapolation about identities and cultures. The following sections will review several sf movements about diversity and explore how the ideas from these movements manifest in primary sf.

FEMINIST SCIENCE FICTION AND PRIMARY SCIENCE FICTION

In *Decoding Gender in Science Fiction*, Brian Attebery explains that while not all sf takes advantage of its historically feminist potential, "gender is not merely a theme in SF," but rather "an integral part of the genre's intellectual and aesthetic structure" (10). In addition, sf feminism is tied to the history of sf illustrations and comics in particular. Corey K. Creekmur explains that the feminist SF of the 1960s and 1970s rose in conjunction with more female comics creators. Sueen Noh argues that sf and comics together explore similar imaginative paths, and that when women entered into the comics and sf industries in the 1960s and 1970s, they used the reality-free arena to tackle patriarchy in different ways. This relationship only grows stronger for children's books. Noh points out that Japanese and Korean comics both make potent use of comics to question and subvert patriarchy and do so mostly in young girls' comics rather than even adult women's comics (209). Today, the largest successful market for young girl's sf is the same as the most successful for young girl's comics: Shōjo, or Japanese girl's manga (Creekmur 4). When these manga are translated, they are the most-consumed sf by girls internationally. Yet in countries that do not have a high respect for sequential art—such as the United States—this market has struggled.

Feminism may be important to sf and sf comics, but Attebery also notes that sf was open to feminist experimentation only once there was a separate YA market to inherit the sex taboo and free up the adult books (6). Due to the associations between children and innocence explored in chapter 1, children's books rarely explore sexual themes. However, primary sf can demonstrate the ideals of sf feminism in terms of gender, starting with simply valuing the presence of girls and femininity in scientific contexts.

Like children's literature at large, primary sf is often aimed at boys. Karen Sands and Marietta Frank write, "Traditionally, children's science fiction has been the realm of boy readers," although they note that sf books for younger readers are better at including women and girls than YA sf books (35). Farah Mendlesohn also says that "the 'children' cited as sf readers are almost always boys," although she mentions no meaningful difference between children's and YA sf women (37). Both studies provide examples of how sf for young readers poorly represents female protagonists and female scientists, often preserving the perception of a boy's genre even when women are included. Mendlesohn explains that the feminist sf writers in the 1970s validated femininity in the context of intellectualism, science, and extrapolative imagination, but "very little of this seems to have permeated through to the fiction written for children and teens: the exceptions stand out" (*Intergalactic* 134). Instead, sf for children and teens often depicts unscientific mother figures and girl protagonists who have no "interests beyond their own emotions" (Mendlesohn 118). In many of the primary sf books in my sample, this held true. From the old 1930s *Flash Gordon* comics to the more recent 2016 hybrid novel *Miles Taylor and the Golden Cape: Attack of the Alien Horde*, female crewmates seem to be along for the ride or appear only as love interests. In other books sisters or moms impede the scientific experimentation or adventuring of their brothers, sons, or husbands. For instance, the little boy in Chris Gall's *Awesome Dawson* (2013) opens the book by speaking to the reader: "Let's go down to my secret workshop. Mom won't find us there." No need to worry about Dad, it seems.

The most effective sf feminism combines integral female characters with speculation and extrapolation. It is the combination of female characters and high-quality sf that sends the message that women belong in the genre at its best. Deborah Underwood and Meg Hunt's *Interstellar Cinderella* (2015) exemplifies the kind of sf book that satisfies feminist ideals but falls short of speculation or extrapolation. In *Interstellar Cinderella*, robots, spaceships, and aliens replace elements of the classic Cinderella story. While the retelling undermines the original Cinderella story to amusing and ultimately feminist effect, it does not make any attempt at speculation or extrapolation. The story structure remains overwhelmingly fairy tale, with an underdog hero, supernatural aid, challenges, and just rewards. This Cinderella proves herself through skill instead of shoe size and refuses marriage in favor of being the royal mechanic. However, the story does not produce any reflection on social or technological science—except perhaps the types of social questions that all fractured fairy tales produce. As a Cinderella tale, this plot has been seen many times in many forms. Technology and science are not important for the story's themes but simply serve as a new setting. This book achieves half of the feminist sf goals: it validates Cinderella as a character with mechanical skill and goals, rather than just emotional concerns, but it falls short of locating women within the consequences of science, or scientific extrapolation. Cinderella and the reader never get to wonder if fixing the prince's spaceship will start a war or birth a new line of dangerously smart spaceships. The mechanical engineering aspect of the story is sidelined in favor of the fractured fairy tale.

Femininity, much like childhood, is often affiliated with the fairy tale and the natural world instead of sf and the scientific, analytic, and technological. Young people absorb these ideas. Carol Haynes and Donald J. Richgels discovered that not a single girl in their study showed any preference for sf at all, despite having equal science abilities in class (17–18). Educational research indicates that girls in elementary and middle school are equally capable in science but are hindered by negative perceptions about women in science careers (Dare iii). In response, educators and educational researchers have developed what is called girl-friendly STEM—integrated science, technology, engineering, and math. Girl-friendly STEM strategies include such recommendations as (1) providing opportunities to be amazed, (2) linking content to prior experiences, (3) providing firsthand experiences, (4) encouraging discussion of and reflections on the social importance of science, (5) showing physics in application-oriented contexts, (6) relating physics to the human body, (7) experiencing physics quantitatively, and (8) engaging in collaborative learning (Dare 29). None of these are inherently "girly" concepts, but all have been found to better engage girls while continuing to support boys. Many of these concepts can be found in high-quality primary sf and may also function, along with female characters, to open up the genre to all genders.

Combining female characters with speculation/extrapolation and girl-friendly strategies offers children more of the benefits of sf feminism. For instance, *Zita the Spacegirl* (2010) by Ben Hatke satisfies several girl-friendly aspects in conjunction with speculation. For one, it offers girl-friendly STEM strategy #1: the opportunity to be amazed, which overlaps with sf's value of a sense of awe or wonder. Sf novums depend upon the unfamiliarity and amazement of exposing the reader or hero to a new world or situation. When Zita lands on another planet, the first six panels of that world serve to emphasize the wondrousness: first a panel of her dazed face asking "where . . . ," and then three panels of various alien closeups of strange faces, strange skin, and even strange socks (Hatke 18). The fourth panel, larger and slightly zoomed out, demonstrates Zita's own awe and shock as well as the tall, intimidating alien menagerie around her (18). Finally, the sixth panel on the next page is even bigger and zooms further out to show huge aliens, robots, and a gargantuan city of strangely shaped buildings. This last panel is unframed and bleeds to the edge of the page, emphasizing the shocking size and extent of the strangeness for both Zita and reader (19). The formatting of the comics panels helps to induce amazement.

Another strategy for girl-friendly science, the social importance of science, can be found in Zita's climactic decision. This girl-friendly strategy from STEM education is the most directly linked to sf speculation, which often questions the social consequences of technology. At the story's climax, Zita must choose whether to use a rare energy source to go home or to save an entire planet that has not been kind to her. She chooses to save them

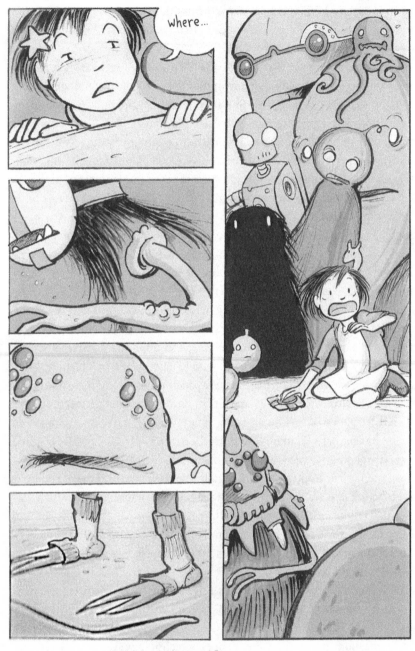

18

Figure 3. The formatting of *Zita the Spacegirl* emphasizes the novum of sf. *Zita the Spacegirl* by Ben Hatke. First Second, 2010.

19

and remains lost in space. This type of choice focuses on speculation about people using technology, rather than hard sf extrapolation. Like many sf plots, the social importance operates on two levels: the literal society of this planet, and the general morals of using science for social good rather than for personal gain.

Another example of these traits operating well can be found in *A Wrinkle in Time: The Graphic Novel*. As explained in the last chapter, this book extrapolates from current understandings of physics to imagine methods of space travel and time manipulation. It does this extrapolative work while including a smart female lead character and incorporating girl-friendly qualities related to physics education. For instance, when Mrs. Which accidentally stops on a two-dimensional planet, the dialogue about how such an alteration to our physical space would feel is supported by a visual depiction (Larson and L'Engle 145). These three panels switch styles to look like depictions of sound waves, and the new text font is reminiscent of a sixteen-bit computer game. These panels allow the reader to glean intertextual details from the visual style to better grasp the concept of 2-D-ness. The visual references rely on familiar concepts and metaphor to express what 2-D might feel like personally, satisfying the girl-friendly STEM strategies of linking to prior experiences and relating physics to the human body.

As graphic novels, the last two examples expect a fully literate reader. There are also exceptional picturebooks and early readers that succeed at girl-friendly, speculative sf for the preliterate and beginner reader. Ryan Sias's *Zoe and Robot: Let's Pretend!* is an easy-reading picturebook that features a girl protagonist and speculation, as described at the end of chapter 1. Zoe's actions in this book also reflect the problem-solving attitude of engineering and follow several girl-friendly strategies. The entire story takes place in a generic middleclass living room, with familiar toys and items all in the service of a common game: pretend. The whole setting satisfies STEM strategy #2: linking STEM to prior experiences. Zoe's solutions are tangible and use familiar tools. When Robot insists "ROBOT DOES NOT SEE A MOUNTAIN," Zoe enacts some creative engineering by painting mountains on the bottom of goggles—at least allowing Robot to compromise between reality and pretend. This book may seem simplistic; it is just that. Sias uses minimal words, effective pictures, sf intertext, and the most straightforward of girl-friendly STEM strategies: linking STEM to prior experiences. This particular STEM strategy is also effective because it relies on the idea of schema.

Picturebooks like Mac Barnett and Dan Santat's *Oh No! Or How My Science Project Destroyed the World* (2010), Judy Sierra and Stephen Gammell's *The Secret Science Project That Almost Ate the School* (2006), and Wiesner's *June 29, 1999* all utilize science class and science fairs as familiar prior experiences along with featuring a female protagonist and simple speculation.

I evaluated each primary sf book in my collection in terms of its gender representation. There were no examples of nonbinary characters in this sample, so I could not explore gender beyond male/female coding. I used the following two questions to test each book:

1. Is there at least one female character in the main cast, as indicated by pronouns in the text or traditional feminine gender markers in the illustrations?
2. Does this character go beyond being an audience, motivation, or antagonist for a male protagonist?

Less than half the books met these standards for the representation of girls, with a total of 135 books (38%) that satisfied both questions. I also looked at how gender was represented in different formats (see table 2), not only due to the formal differences between formats, but because these formats roughly align with literacy stages and therefore ages, as discussed in the previous chapter. Differences in formats may indicate that children receive different messages about gender in sf at different ages.

Splitting the sample by format shows that picturebooks, early readers, and comic books—the three formats defined by brevity—stand out as having fewer strong female characters. A logistic regression and Benjamini-Hochberg post hoc comparisons confirm that comic books, early readers, and picturebooks had significantly fewer female characters than the longer formats (see appendix A for details of the statistical test). The amount of representation of girls in graphic novels was significantly different from the representation in comic books ($p < .001$), early readers ($p = .001$), and picturebooks ($p < .001$). Hybrid novels were also significantly different from comic books ($p = .004$), early readers ($p = .01$), and picturebooks ($p = .002$). However, the short formats were not significantly different from each other, and the two long formats were not significantly different from each other. This disparity between long and short formats is particularly odd, since while speculation or extrapolation could feasibly benefit from more time or space

Table 2. Books That Contain Strong Female Characters, by Format

Format	Female Characters
Picturebooks ($n = 164$)	49 (30%)
Early readers ($n = 38$)	13 (34%)
Comic books ($n = 102$)	33 (32%)
Graphic novels ($n = 34$)	25 (74%)
Hybrid novels ($n = 19$)	15 (79%)
Total ($n = 357$)	135 (38%)

in the narrative, featuring female protagonists does not require longer formats. Around 30 percent of the shorter-format books represented significant female characters—close to the 33 percent of McCabe et al.'s study.

Comparatively, the percentages of the graphic novels and hybrid novels seem dramatically higher. Graphic novels and hybrid novels could be different due to being perceived as for older or more advanced readers, but many of the comic books were not explicitly for young children or new readers either. Even if that were true, there is no good reason to have fewer significant female characters in books for young children. However, another reason that the hybrid novels and graphic novels achieved higher rates of female characters might be the relative newness of these formats. Neither format has any examples in this sample until the late 1970s. Books from prior to the 1970s did very poorly in terms of representing women, with the results consistently less than 50 percent for each decade (see figure 4). Sands and Frank claim, "Female characters in science fiction series for young people have, between 1945 and 1995, increasingly come into prominent positions" (45), and the primary sf in this sample does increase from 1945 to 1995, but the number of books with female representations still does not reach over half during this time span. The only decades in which more than half of the books had significant female characters were the 1930s and the 2010s.

The 1930s stand out since I included only six sf books overall for this decade, all comic books, but nonetheless four of them had significant female characters. Two of these are collected storylines from the *Connie* comics, the less remembered female equivalent of Flash Gordon and Buck Rogers. The character Connie is smart, a leader, and a skilled pilot. While the villains

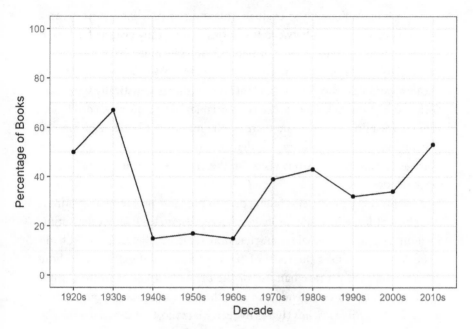

Figure 4. Percentage of books with significant female characters, by decade.

underestimate her because she is pretty, her male companions know better. Connie is also accompanied by Dr. Alden, a rare example of an older female scientist and mother to the dashing-young-man character of the crew. Connie stands in stark contrast to the damsel tradition that pervaded comics for the next decades. In the 1940s and 1950s books in this set, female characters express the desire to overcome gender expectations but nonetheless end up needing rescuing or discover that they should have just stayed at home. "There's adventure among the planets for women too, as well as men! I'm quitting!" declares Tyna to her scientist boss in "Hero of Space" in *Fantastic Worlds* No. 5. Unfortunately, she wants to quit in order to find a more heroic space man and goes on an interplanetary adventure just to learn she loves her original scientist. Perhaps it is not surprising that newer books are more likely to champion women in futuristic narratives, but *Connie* shows that it was possible eighty years ago. Therefore, all the damsels that followed, in the 1940s to 1960s especially, cannot be excused as products of the times. Fortunately, this trend seems to be meandering upward and jumped to over 50 percent in the 2010 books.

Since it is challenging to evaluate this uneven timeline by eye, I ran a Pearson correlation test between the books that met my criteria for female representation and the decade of publication (see appendix A for statistical details). The female characters variable has a weak relationship with the decades variable ($r = 0.17372$), and that relationship is statistically significant ($F(1, 355) = 11.047, p < 0.001$). The two variables have a positive correlation, though, meaning that as years increase the number of books with women gets higher too. It is encouraging that the correlations show a more solid average upward trend than is visible in the graph, even if it is a statistically weak relationship.

It seems that primary sf is falling prey to the same problems as children's literature at large in terms of its gender representation. However, simply including significant female characters only scratches the surface of sf feminism, which also uses the tools of sf to speculate and extrapolate about gender itself. Only a rare handful of the primary sf books in the sample used sf to comment on gender. One of the few examples, an early reader called *Ruthie's Rude Friends* (1984), by Jean Marzollo, Claudio Marzollo, and Susan Meddaugh, shows how a girl's Earth-level strength on a lower-gravity planet saves her male alien friends from a wild animal. After being rescued, her alien friends admire her muscles, and one gives her a demure kiss on the cheek, reversing damsel-in-distress stereotypes. This book's play with gender expectations significantly connects to its scientific and extrapolative themes about gravity and muscle mass. An Earth boy would also be stronger than the aliens and native wildlife, but choosing a girl protagonist evokes the tradition of feminist sf using science to undermine biological determinism that says boys are inherently stronger than girls.

Overall, these examples demonstrate that girl-friendly children's books that satisfy the expectations of sf feminism and speculation/extrapolation are possible, but less common than they could be. Several successful books in this sample set demonstrate how sf matches up with girl-friendly STEM strategies, while also locating women in speculative and extrapolative science situations. While this discussion has been oriented toward male/female divisions, making room for feminine identities in primary sf reduces the association of masculinity with reason/sf, which will hopefully welcome gender-nonconforming and transsexual children in the genre as well. Ideally, these identities would also be clearly depicted in primary sf, but those representations have been slow to reach children's literature in general.

ALTERNATIVE FUTURISMS AND PRIMARY SCIENCE FICTION

Like sf feminism, alternative futurisms use the tools of sf to explore how technology and science might enable alternate realities and futures as relevant to
diverse identities. Isiah Lavender III notes that "feminist sf might be credited
with laying the groundwork for race reading in sf" (188), or the Afrofuturist
selective tradition. De Witt Douglas Kilgore says that Afrofuturist and feminist stories both work against "SF genre's reputation as a repository of boys'
adventure stories descending from colonialist histories of racial exploitation
and exclusion" (Kilgore 11). Kilgore contends that "precisely because of this
history, the tools provided by a Eurocentric culture not only belong to anyone
who has been taught them but also can be used to transform meaning within
the genre" (11). Sf is a flexible enough framework that its own tools can be
used to reframe it, all due to its potent ability to reflect and comment upon
our gendered and racialized reality.

The term "Afrofuturism," popularized in 1994 by Mark Dery in response to
contemporary cultural trends of futurism, was initially defined as "speculative
fiction that treats African-American themes and addresses African-American
concerns in the context of twentieth-century technoculture" (180). Kilgore
writes, "Afrofuturism emerges from and is in conversation with the generic
traditions of science fiction" (6). Afrofuturism thrives in partnership with
sf's rich critical and speculative potential, using the genre's own conventions
to push against the negative cultural concepts that are historically embedded within sf.

Afrofuturism is a relatively well-known movement among sf scholars but
remains a liminal selective tradition: "Sf story collections and histories by
white writers and critics barely mention race as a category of interrogation
or speculation" (Lavender 188). However, the characteristics and goals of the
movement are not new, just newly named. Sheree R. Thomas's first volume
in a line of Afrofuturist anthologies, *Dark Matter: A Century of Speculative
Fiction from the African Diaspora* (2000), includes stories and essays that
date from 1887 to 2000. The titular century of storytelling "showed that the
fantastic is an old and familiar register in African diasporic writing" (Kilgore
3). It has gone unstudied for some time because "sf's frequent assumption of
a colorblind future—whether an unintentional or deliberate privileging of
whiteness—has blinded critics to matters of race" (Lavender 187). Similarly, in
Ebony Elizabeth Thomas's *The Dark Fantastic*, she theorizes that "the silence

and evasion around race in dystopian science fiction" may be intended to imply a pleasant postracial future, but this leads to misreading and situations such as when fans protested that a Black girl was cast as Rue in *The Hunger Games* films (59). By explicitly and clearly imagining inclusive futures, Jabari Asim explains, Afrofuturism has been a constant, healing project that reverses the damage done by historical figures like John C. Calhoun, who "demonstrated an absolute inability to imagine a future that included free Black people thinking and living for themselves" (25).

Afrofuturism, in turn, inspires other alternative futurisms like Indigenous Futurisms and Latin@futurism. Kilgore explains that Afrofuturism offers "a model for how other peoples of color might view the futuristic art they create, allowing them to become conscious of their own imbrication in a technoscientific culture and to resist erasure from the narratives it sponsors" (10). Grace L. Dillon notes that the title of her Indigenous Futurisms anthology "pays homage to Afrofuturisms, an established topic of study for sf scholars" (2). As Dillon's comment indicates, the selective tradition of Indigenous Futurisms is lesser known than Afrofuturism, but is similarly "not so new—just overlooked" (2). Latin@futurism, according to Cathryn Merla-Watson, also "builds upon Afrofuturism" but is not new. She goes on to note that "Latin@futurism dates back to at least the late 1960s, it is just recently that scholars have begun to study it in a focused manner." The earliest story in *Cosmos Latinos: An Anthology of Science Fiction from Latin America and Spain* (2003), edited by Andrea L. Bell and Yolanda Molina-Gavilán, dates from 1913.

Indigenous Futurisms—intentionally plural to reflect the multiplicity of Native tribes and identity—derives from a history of cultural and racial trauma, with a focus on the future. Dillon asserts, "Indigenous Futurisms are not the product of a victimized people's wishful amelioration of their past, but instead a continuation of a spiritual and cultural path that remains unbroken by genocide and war" ("Introduction" 2). This attitude can be traced to one of the movements' foundational authors, Gerald Vizenor, and his concept of "survivance"—the act of not just surviving but going beyond to achieve "an active repudiation of dominance, tragedy, and victimization" (15). David Higgins explains that Vizenor's idea of survivance is particularly poignant in Indigenous Futurisms because "Indigenous sf stories reject victimry" as opposed to "fetishizing the victim role, as mainstream science fictions often do" (53). Dillon explains that Indigenous Futurisms embrace not victimhood but biskaabiiyang, an Anishinaabemowin term for the process of "discovering how personally one is affected by colonization, discarding the emotional and psychological baggage carried from its impact, and recovering ancestral traditions in order to adapt in our post-Native Apocalypse world" ("Symposium" 10). The focus is on reconstructive and productive futures, not compensatory futures.

Indigenous Futurisms challenge the centrality of scientific plausibility in sf aesthetics, as mentioned in chapter 1. Dillon states that this type of literature "sometimes fuses Indigenous sciences with the latest scientific theories available in public discourse, and sometimes undercuts the western limitations of science altogether" ("Introduction" 2) but overall works to demonstrate that "Indigenous science is not just complementary to a perceived western enlightenment but is indeed integral to a refined twenty-first-century sensibility" (3). Dillon notes that this approach to estranging the reader from science itself may grant Indigenous sf "the capacity to envision Native futures, Indigenous hopes, and dreams recovered by rethinking the past in a new framework" (2). However, Miriam Brown Spiers is concerned that Indigenous sf may not be recognized as science at all, but only fiction. She warns that Dillon's choice to reclaim older stories as sf in her anthology risks portraying essential Indigenous worldviews as fiction, and she instead encourages labeling only those stories that pair clearly recognizable sf tropes with Indigenous identities.

Latin@futurism is similarly concerned with locating Latinx people in the future, without erasing the past or present. Merla-Watson defines this alternative tradition: "Latin@futurism excavates and creatively recycles the seeming detritus of the past to imagine and galvanize more desirable presents and futures." She emphasizes that in many core texts of sf like *Star Trek*, "the filmic and more general discursive excision of Latin@s from the future signals a deep-seated and even genocidal desire of white America to disappear Latin@s altogether." Much like "Indigenous Futurisms," "Latin@futurism" is a broad term; it "references a spectrum of speculative aesthetics produced by U. S. Latin@s, including Chican@s, Puerto Ricans, Dominican Americans, Cuban Americans, and other Latin American immigrant populations." This multiplicity of connected and yet different identities, Merla-Watson explains, is important to the overall tradition, which focuses on blurring these abstract borders as well as physical "hybrid and fluid borderlands spaces, including the U.S.-Mexico border."

Alternative futurisms[1] from feminism to Latin@futurism are not isolated; they send ripples through all sf. Stories from these alternative futurism traditions resist the genre's colonialist history and trends and therefore "sometimes intentionally experiment with, sometimes intentionally dislodge, sometimes merely accompany, but invariably *change* the perimeters of sf" (Dillon 3, emphasis in original). The impact goes beyond the stories within these futurisms. Merla-Watson explains that "Latin@futurism and alternative futurisms are revolutionizing how we think about the speculative genre at large." The more we recognize these alternative traditions, the more potential for real change in all sf—including and especially primary sf.

These futurisms contend that the ability to imagine a future for historically oppressed people is an empowering and activist act in and of itself. Rather than perpetuating the convenient erasure in some canon sf, these stories offer validation of people's very existence. With this point of view, the mere inclusion or exclusion of these identities in primary sf becomes a cultural-political statement. Additionally, erased peoples cannot simply be reassigned to metaphorical representation. A key tenet of Afrofuturism, inherited by Indigenous Futurisms and Latin@futurism, is a very literal emphasis on diversity. These stories "eschew SF's more metaphorical approach to the social and political realities of racial difference" (Kilgore 2)—in other words, these traditions reject the idea that a variety of aliens counts as "diversity" in a text and can stand in for real differences. As Sands and Frank point out, sf for children has traditionally "found a way to introduce tolerance by utilizing alien characters, though not trying to represent any particular ethnic group" (93). Teaching tolerance is fine, but in order for a text to be truly diverse, it must contain direct and literal representations of difference.[2]

The Worst Band in the Universe (1999) by Graeme Base is a picturebook full of references to African American culture and musical traditions, but Base conveniently obscures the race of his protagonists by portraying them as green and yellow aliens. The setting is a distant planet where the aliens in power valorize written and traditional songs over new, improvised music, evoking the rebellious history of jazz. A yellow anthropomorphic cat alien named Skat leads the banished musical criminals and serves as a reference to scat singing and the colloquial "cool cat" label popularized by Black musicians like Cab Calloway. The potential diversity of this title is undermined by the use of aliens. Given the history of white musicians coopting African American musical styles and even directly stealing songs, it is not safe to simply assume that these aliens are a representation of African American musicians. The illustrations deny that connection, functioning to extend the technology of oppression rather than using sf to question it. The cultural content does not represent and support readers of color due to the lack of literal depictions.

As I read through the 357 primary sf books, I noted which ones contained real-world diversity. Only 25 percent did. Despite being a low number, my sample fared better than mainstream children's literature representation, especially in recent years. If we compare the 15 years between 2001 and 2016, the CCBC reported that 12 percent of the books they received were about people of color and First Native nations, while my sample shows 31 percent—most of which was racial diversity.[3] This comparison should be taken with a grain of salt, given the much larger sample size of the CCBC data, but it hints at the potential of diversity in primary sf compared to all children's literature.

To examine the extent of the diversity in these books, I coded them into two categories proposed by Lee Galda et al. in *Literature and the Child*: painted faces and culturally rich.[4] The painted faces category refers to a book that offers visual cues of diversity such as characters with various skin tones or disabilities, but no deeper reflection or story content about those qualities. These characters could be changed to different identities without altering the storyline. Painted faces as a category is therefore susceptible to, if not limited to, tokenism. Since my sample focuses on illustrated books, this category usefully highlights the many books that code race only in the pictures. The second category, culturally rich books, refers to titles wherein a nonmainstream culture or identity is integral to the story. Painted faces and culturally rich books were both present in the sample and, to different degrees, succeed at demonstrating diversity in the future or speculative worlds of the books, satisfying the most basic goals of alternative futurisms. In addition, the goals of alternative futurisms often build on speculation and extrapolation. Diverse representation, like gender representation, works best when available in partnership with high-quality sf.

Twenty-four percent of the primary sf in the sample fell into the painted faces category. Several of these books included a character of color in a context that allows the book to be read as an ethnoscape. Lavender explains that in Afrofuturism "reading an ethnoscape" is a specific use of cognitive estrangement that functions by "bringing the language of one world, the fictional world, into collision with the language, experience, and perception of an extratextual reality in which race functions as a technology of oppression" (197). Like sf's more common concept of cognitive estrangement, the ethnoscape is made strange by the racial "ideas and histories that the text uses, defines, discards, renovates, and invents" (189). The most unusual aspect of this approach is that it is not necessarily dependent upon the intentions of the author, but rather how the reader perceives the ethnoscape. One can read an ethnoscape in any type of sf, by looking for "an alternative image that enables us to rethink the intersections of technology and race as well as their political, social, and cultural implications" (189).

In primary sf, reading an ethnoscape can be as simple as representing people of color in scientific contexts in the illustrations, since this choice redefines and refocuses the real history of diversity in scientific fields. In one such example, Brian Pinkney's *Cosmo and the Robot* (2000), the picturebook tells the story of a family of scientists and a dysfunctional robot on Mars. This book was coded as painted faces since the characters are depicted as people of color but the storyline would be the same if they were not. Despite—and perhaps due to—their skin color not affecting the plotline, Pinkney's story normalizes people of color being scientists and encourages more children to see themselves as potential space explorers and settlers. Pinkney's choice imagines a world in which people of color are recognized and valued in astronomy—in direct opposition to the cultural history of erasing their contributions to our space programs. The inclusion of visually diverse characters like this is a political move to normalize nonwhite identities in the future and science.

Just as the presence of girls in sf only scratches the surface of sf feminism, the presence of diversity in sf is important but achieves only one part of the potential in these alternative futurisms. Culturally rich books offer more opportunity for engaging with the ideas of alternative futurisms. However, of the 357 books in this sample, only five (1%) were culturally rich. Two of the books had culturally specific characters and cultural plot points, two included themes about racial stereotyping, and two featured characters with a disability. These books were not, however, automatically better representations of diversity. *The Mighty Odds* by Amy Ignatow included themes about rejecting racial stereotyping of a Middle Eastern character as a terrorist, but it did not clearly condemn the racial fetishization of one character who repeatedly called his African American crush cringeworthy pet names like "my gorgeous Nubian queen" (197).

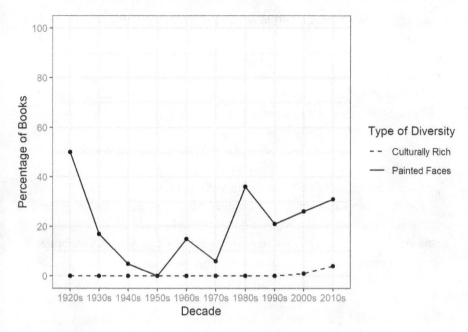

Figure 5. Percentage of books with painted faces and culturally rich diversity, by decade.

As is the case with female characters, representation of diverse characters is slowly increasing over time (see figure 5). Statistically, the books that I marked as diverse have a positive correlation with decades, meaning that as years increase the number of books with diversity gets higher too. The diversity variable's correlation with time (r = 0.21229) is stronger than the correlation between female characters and time mentioned above, and it is also statistically significant ($F(1, 355)$ = 16.755, p < 0.001). Despite this upward trend, no decade in this sample rises above 50 percent. The 1920s sit at the 50 percent line only because I found a total of only two heavily illustrated sf books from that decade, and one of them, a *Buck Rogers* (1929) collection, showed superficial diversity. *Connie* is the only diverse title of the 1930s, with a storyline that discovers Tibetans living on Jupiter. This is a painted faces representation, as the story does not focus on the Tibetans or their culture. Meanwhile, culturally rich primary sf does not even appear in this sample set until 2007.

Fortunately, several books incorporated real cultures in the future in a rich and positive way, such as in Cathy Camper and Raúl the Third's graphic novel

Lowriders in Space (2014). This alternate version of our world is populated by humanoid animals rather than people, but instead of treating this as an excuse to avoid assigning racial traits to the protagonists, this story's animals are clearly Mexican American. Their word balloons are peppered with Spanish words and phrases. The final pages of the book include a glossary of "Mexican-American slang, car, and astronomy terms" (57). This glossary values cultural slang and car jargon equally alongside astronomy, which tends to be given more mainstream value. Likewise, the mere existence of the Spanish language in an sf context locates many Spanish-speaking Latinx people in the future, fulfilling the basic goals of alternative futurisms.

Lowriders in Space is culturally rich, since the cultural context is integral to the story. The author's note explains that building lowrider cars is a Mexican American tradition that began in post–World War II Southern California. This story purposefully brings an uncommonly recognized version of science and engineering into the sf spotlight and makes sure that young readers have that context available in the paratextual material. The author's note explains, "This book was written to celebrate the artistry, inventiveness, mechanical aptitude, resilience, and humor that are all part of lowrider culture" (57). The mention of "inventiveness" and "mechanical aptitude" makes it clear that lowrider modifications are scientific, engineering endeavors. Today, these modifications are often associated with low-income hobbyists, not engineering, but this book emphasizes how cars are complex machines and their modifications can be extrapolated into the future just like any other engineering endeavor.

Lowriders in Space demonstrates *rasquachismo*, a concept important to Latin@futurism criticism. According to Tomás Ybarra-Frausto, *rasquachismo* refers to a sensibility rather than a style. He explains that it is a culturally and community-acquired sensibility about "making do with what you have." Creating lowriders from bits and pieces, he notes, is a prime example of *rasquache* art. At the climactic car show, the bystanders' speech bubbles emphasize how the car is both old and new, while the caption reads: "Every part of it was fixed and painted, shiny, recovered, and rediscovered." Even the art itself reflects this theme, drawn on what looks to be reclaimed, stained paper in black, red, and blue ballpoint pen—pens that the illustrator's note says he often finds on sidewalks.

Furthermore, the plot of *Lowriders in Space* is not concerned with hard scientific explanations of the car's components, demonstrating the fluidity of Latin@futurism. Many of the book's explanations are richly wondrous and poetic rather than scientifically accurate—such as catching the entire Pleiades star cluster and using it for a steering wheel—but this too is culturally grounded. Merla-Watson explains that "Latin@futurist texts often blend speculative genres, such as sci-fi, fantasy, horror, whereby they create new, hybrid forms reflective of cultural mestizaje." Several modifications to the car look like the magic of fantasy rather than the science of sf, because this entire distinction is rejected by Latin@futurism. In fact, the mixture of realistic and unrealistic modifications in *Lowriders in Space* creates *rasquachismo* in microcosm: a cosmic lowrider crafted from both engineering and magic. The story sits comfortably on the border of fantasy and sf, recalling Merla-Watson's point that Latin@futurism revolves around representation of borders. *Lowriders in Space* belongs in this discussion of sf not despite these fantastic elements but because of them and their cultural significance.

   Lowriders in Space is all the more valuable because it is only one of three books in the sample to feature Latinx characters, accounting for less than 1 percent of the sample. Additionally, *Lowriders in Space* is one of only two books in the sample to include the Spanish language. The other book, Judy Schachner's *Skippyjon Jones: Lost in Spice* (2009), does not have any Latinx characters and features Spanish-like singsong nonsense words and blatant, harmful stereotypes.

INTERSECTIONS

Of course, gender and diversity overlap, and those intersections are also opportunities to speculate and extrapolate. Therefore, I ran a Pearson correlation test to show whether gender, diversity, and the sf quality of these books—as measured by the presence of speculation/extrapolation in the story—are statistically correlated (see details in appendix A). The results show that quality is slightly correlated with female characters and not reliably correlated with diversity. In statistical terms, the sf quality variable has a very weak bivariate relationship with the female characters variable ($r = 0.13764$), but it is statistically significant from zero ($F(1, 355) = 6.856, p = 0.00922$). Sf quality has an extremely weak relationship with diversity ($r = 0.0475$) that is not statistically significant ($F(1, 355) = 0.803, p = 0.37087$). The lack of a strong relationship between sf quality and the female characters

Figure 6. *Lowriders in Space* demonstrates *rasquachismo* in content and art style. *Lowriders in Space* by Cathy Camper and Raúl the Third. Chronicle Books, 2014.

and diversity criteria is problematic, as it is important to align these under-represented groups with high-quality primary sf. We do not want to offer fuel to those conservative groups who whine that sf loses something when it includes women and diversity.

Female characters and diversity have the strongest—if still relatively weak—relationship with each other (r = 0.2583), and strong statistical significance ($F(1, 355)$ = 25.378, p < 0.001). Since this is a positive correlation coefficient, it means that books with significant women characters are likely to also have diversity, and vice versa. This result indicates that female and diverse characters are likely to appear together or overlap in books, perhaps due to situations wherein the author/illustrator conscientiously makes a choice toward inclusiveness.

Fortunately, the books that included all three variables—quality and women and diversity—were usually stellar and great models for future fiction. When considering the sf quality, girl-friendliness, and diversity on the level of individual books, forty-three (12%) of the books met all three goals, while sixty-eight (19%) did not meet any. Three quarters of the books fell somewhere in the middle. Nearly half of the books met one goal (154 books, 43%), while another quarter met two (92 books, 26%). See table 3 for a breakdown by format.

Graphic novels stand out as having the highest percentage of individual books meeting all three criteria (41%), and zero books that had absolutely none. Considering this alongside how graphic novels consistently had among the highest percentages of positive scores for each individual criterion, the graphic novels excelled in this sample. This success recommends future partnerships between sf and graphic novels for children. There were only nineteen hybrid novels overall, but five of those (26%) met all three criteria. This new format did well across the board, with the most culturally rich books and the highest percentage of books with female characters. These books deserve more attention as a developing format with good potential for hosting primary sf. Both graphic novels and hybrid novels are new formats and may therefore be more likely to reflect modern sensibilities, but most picturebooks and early readers in this sample were also published in the last thirty years, and their results were not nearly as impressive.

Less than 10 percent of picturebooks, early readers, and comic books met all three criteria. Most of these three formats met only one. As the shortest formats, these categories' results seem to reflect the concern that sf needs

Table 3. Individual Books by Category and How Many of the Three Criteria They Met

Format	None	1 out of 3	2 out of 3	All Three
Picturebooks (n = 164)	36 (22%)	76 (46%)	37 (23%)	15 (9%)
Early readers (n = 38)	10 (26%)	15 (39%)	11 (29%)	2 (5%)
Comic books (n = 102)	21 (21%)	51 (50%)	23 (23%)	7 (7%)
Graphic novels (n = 34)	0	9 (26%)	11 (32%)	14 (41%)
Hybrid novels (n = 19)	1 (5%)	3 (16%)	10 (53%)	5 (26%)
Total (n = 357)	68 (19%)	154 (43%)	92 (26%)	43 (12%)

space, though this is a poor excuse, since including female protagonists and painted faces diversity takes up no narrative space. Another likely reason may be the target reader's age. Picturebooks and early readers are for the very youngest children and may be hampered by adult conceptions that children at that age do not need to know or think about gender, race, or other identities. Meanwhile, there were more comics in the sample from earlier decades, and these, unsurprisingly, did not fare as well on diversity and gender representation.

The 12 percent of books in the data set that did fulfill all three criteria demonstrate the value of these overlapping goals. These books include rich portrayals of intersectional identities for children and how representation can work together with alternative futures and science-fictional thinking. One such example, Marvel Comics' *Moon Girl and Devil Dinosaur: BFF* (2016), exemplifies the value of having all three criteria in the same story. With a nine-year-old protagonist, this series invites young readers to revel in a young hero's inventions and love for science alongside the usual adventures and fun of the Marvel Universe. The best part, however, is depicted quietly in the illustrations, without comment in the words: Lunella (code name Moon Girl) is a young African American girl. Lunella's depicted race may not affect the plot, but it is very exciting in context. Marvel announced at the July 2016 San Diego Comic-Con that Moon Girl is now the smartest hero in their entire Marvel Universe, beating out the likes of Reed Richards, Tony Stark, Bruce Banner, Hank McCoy, and the other mostly white, male, adult geniuses that have vied for the title.

This comic book also offers speculation on the intersections between race, age, and gender in a world of superheroes. Lunella functions as a mirror for African Americans, girls, and young people interested in science, and offers them a place in the future and science-fictional superhero adventure stories. Her identities also spark some of her conflicts. During the events of volume 4, Lunella comes head-to-head with the Hulk and calls out his battle with Devil Dinosaur as a "macho slugfest. It's certainly not very smart . . . or safe . . . or even efficient . . . but definitely, definitely not smart." That Lunella calls out the fight as "macho" strongly indicates a gendered commentary—both the Hulk and Devil Dinosaur are gendered male. Lunella's commentary undermines their supposed combination of smarts and strength, questioning whether these qualities can function together. While the story elsewhere offers extrapolation on biowarfare and other technologies, in this moment it focuses on speculation about the use of intelligence for violence. Marvel often depicts its smart men getting into fights and then using their intelligence to bolster their strength through mutations or inventions. The Hulk is a potent example, as his genius experiments result in his greater strength and size, but his transformation is triggered by anger, a decidedly "macho" emotion.

Yet this ability to use intelligence for strength is depicted as off-limits to Lunella because she is a girl. In this scene, Lunella shouts and tries to stop the fight, drawing comparisons with the usual background female in superhero fights who weeps and wails helplessly while her hero and the villain duke it out. When Lunella decides to enter the fray, she wields a homemade electric gun and a cartoonish boxing glove device. Despite her gadget's direct punch to Hulk's face, the fight stops only because Devil Dinosaur uses his tail to protect and block her while the Hulk laughs it off. Like the usual smart Marvel hero, Lunella tried to enter the fight with strength from her intelligent inventions but was denied access by both her ally and her enemy. In this moment, Lunella's age intersects unhelpfully with her gender. The Hulk's laughter echoes cultural expectations that she is young and female, and therefore only able to land comically weak blows. Devil Dinosaur's protective reaction sends the same message that she is unsuitable for fighting. Being perceived as innocent is a historical triumph for black-skinned children, who, as demonstrated in Robin Bernstein's *Racial Innocence: Performing American Childhood from Slavery to Civil Rights,* have not always received the benefit of childhood innocence. At the same time, this innocence is a defeat. The

Hulk and Devil Dinosaur both telegraph that fighting is not an acceptable action because she is a child, and a female child at that.

Lunella's attempt to intervene backfires when it allows the Hulk to deliver a final punch and stand triumphant and cocky over the dinosaur. Yet the authors have already developed empathy for Lunella at this point, and the Hulk—despite being a longtime hero in the Marvel universe—is not to be cheered here. The narrative sets him up to look like a jerk. He lectures Lunella about being too young and not smart enough. When he mentions being the eighth-smartest person in the world, readers who know that Moon Girl will soon outrank him enjoy a special laugh at the Hulk's expense. Gender and age are working against Lunella, but the writers ask the reader to be frustrated along with her in the face of these pressures. It is significant that this obstacle for Lunella is presented by a known and loved hero, and not by a villain. Children who encounter laughter or incredulity about their interest in sciences, for instance, can expect it to come from trusted and loved ones. It is good to see a model that even heroes are sometimes limited in their perspective, and resilience is worthwhile.

Overall, Moon Girl's intersecting identities provide a chance for representation and for more young readers to see themselves in the expansive Marvel Universe. At the same time, her intersecting identities are not passive tokens of diversity, as they offer a productive way to speculate about how identities operate in the fictional world, as well as in our own.

Another example of intersecting identities, Adam Rex's hybrid novel *The True Meaning of Smekday* relies on the common allegories associated with alien invasion sf, but couples them with real racial diversity and cultural richness. Sf narratives often speculate about our alien encounters through allusions to colonial conquest, and *The True Meaning of Smekday* follows suit. The behavior of the first alien race to invade, the Boov, runs clearly parallel with the United States' history of behavior toward Native Americans. In their first broadcast, the Boov announce that "A. The Boov had discovered this planet, so it was of course rightly theirs," and "B. It was their Grand Destiny to colonize new worlds, they *needed* to, so there really wasn't anything they could do about that" (Rex 60, emphasis in original). The parallels do not stop with this nod to Columbus's "discovery" and the concept of Manifest Destiny. The leading Boov captain, Smek, calls humans "the Noble Savages of Earth" and declares: "I generously grant you Human Preserves—gifts of land that will be for humans forever, never to be taken away again, now"

(63). Each region has its own preserve, and all Americans are crowded into Florida. Of course, the Boovs later decide they like oranges, take back Florida, and re-relocate the Americans to Arizona. The allegory is unmistakable and intended to replicate and reinforce the American Indian cultural experience of diaspora through a familiar emotion for young readers: "it's not fair!" In many sf novels—even for adults—this sort of allegorical sympathy for the colonized is often the extent of the diversity.

Rex also includes real diversity and multiculturalism. The protagonist, Gratuity Tucci (Tip), just so happens to be biracial. This is not played up as important, but rather depicted as matter-of-factly normal. Since Tip is the narrator as well, she does not bother to describe herself. In fact, her race is not mentioned directly for quite some time—though readers may notice her slightly shaded skin in Rex's frequent black-and-white Polaroid picture illustrations. Eventually, though, Tip's gender and race begin to leave a small trail of microaggressions throughout the plot. For instance, the small refugee population of boys hiding under Happy Mouse Kingdom reject her outright just for being a girl, despite the life-or-death scenario. Similarly, when Tip tries to find her mother through the Bureau of Missing Persons, the worker's assumption that her mother is also dark-skinned completely undermines the search and needlessly extends their separation. Tip's identities are not always center stage, but they influence her path through this postapocalyptic landscape.

Rex makes another, potentially more significant, move toward cultural richness by not stopping at allegorical references to Native American diaspora. In all 357 books in this study, *The True Meaning of Smekday* features the only Native American character, which is less than 1 percent of this sample. The one Indigenous character is called Chief Shouting Bear, but we later learn his real name is Frank. His parodic fake name, like much of his depiction, turns out to be part of the novel's prejudice theme. Tip's initial description of him reads: "He otherwise wore the same clothes as anybody else—no buckskin or beads or anything. I'm probably an idiot for even mentioning that" (Rex 252). This moment shows Tip becoming aware of her own prejudices and rejecting them mid-narration, setting a model for young readers of all backgrounds to deal with internalized stereotypes.

Frank undermines the archaic stereotypes that often freeze Natives in old colonial depictions. Tip finds him running a junkyard in Roswell, hiding alien livestock and an alien spaceship under the guise of an obviously fake spaceship. He actively uses the community's social assumptions to hide these artifacts, explaining that he "played the crazy Indian bit to the hilt" (Rex 326). Frank forces the prejudices leveled against him to work for his benefit and in doing so makes a place for himself in the future. He is the only adult with competence in futuristic alien technology and has taken good care of the ship's most delicate working parts and even got the ship flying once. Once the invasion hits, he continues to investigate alien technology and captures the one alien tool essential to the story's resolution. His competence is not because he is particularly capable of understanding alien things—which would court the "magical native" trope—but simply because he has worked for his understanding. It also helps that he is not panicking. The other adults depicted in the story are busy struggling to accept their new reality, bordering on mania as they try to force things to continue resembling "normal." Meanwhile Frank accepts the invasion due to both his long knowledge of aliens and his Diné identity. The parallels to Native American history are not lost on him. He perceives the aliens' treatment of humans through generations of cultural mistreatment, as opposed to a new experience. For him, it is more of the same. Frank's depiction does not necessarily qualify the book as Indigenous Futurism, but it productively locates a Native person in the future and allows reading an ethnoscape of Native American identity in the larger story. Rex accomplishes only the first step of the Indigenous Futurisms concept of *biskaabiiyang*, since the storyline does not move beyond "discovering how personally one is affected by colonization" (Symposium 10). Rex also weakens the potential representative power of this novel when he has the only Indigenous character die at the end.

While Rex's depiction of Indigenous identity in the future stands alone in this sample set of books, it is far from perfect. As Debbie Reese notes in her review of the book, Rex misses several important opportunities to undermine stereotypes with this character. For instance, Tip keeps calling him "the Chief" even after she learns his real name. Reese sums up her thoughts at the end:

> Rex dropped Papago in the story early on and came back to it later, correcting its use. I wish he'd done that here, dropping "the Chief" from Tip's way of thinking about him. Nowhere do I see backstory or story itself that says Frank Jose was a leader of the Dine (Navajo) people; hence, calling him "the Chief" is incorrect. As I read this book, there were times when I thought that Rex seems to know so much! He critiques so much, and yet, leaves this and other things intact. Why? His character knows better, doesn't she? (np)

Rex's attempt to undermine stereotypes goes above and beyond the rest of this sample, but it is only one step toward better, representative primary sf. Perry Nodelman responded to Reese's commentary:

> I like how the Chief slyly manipulates stereotypes of angrily politicized Native Americans in order to keep people from interfering in his life. He creates a safe space for himself by pretending to be something that confirms other people's negative stereotypes and makes those other people want to avoid him. But while the distance between the stereotype and the real, clever, kind man who hides behind it seems to imply the falsity of the stereotype, it also in an odd way also confirms the stereotype: the novel never suggests that there aren't a lot of angry Native Americans who shout too loudly about their land and their rights, etc. Nor does it suggest that the anger is justified and even necessary, or that is anything but just silly and laughable. Indeed, the novel seems to be sending up the supposed silliness of politicized Native people who want to make others aware of their rights at the same time as it seems to be expressing concern about how powerful outsiders oppress people and deprive them if their rights. The novel is just too interested in making jokes and being funny to be consistent enough to be effective as satire. As a result, it undermines its own satire.

Nodelman sets up the problem as a conflict between diverse sf and children's literature conventions about humor.

Overall, the story offers the reader the chance to compare the story's speculative interspecies prejudices to a variety of real-world prejudices. Prejudice is depicted as coming from people—or aliens—in power, but also exchanged between victims. For example, Frank's hospital roommate Mr. Hinkel "thinks Indians like me ought to live somewhere else," but Mr. Hinkel is in the hospital because he "got beat up pretty good by someone who thinks gay people like *him* ought to live somewhere else" (321–22, emphasis in original). It is worth noting that this moment "doesn't sit well" with Reese but draws on the idea that oppressed groups often become oppressors of others, as described by Paulo Freire in *Pedagogy of the Oppressed*. This tendency, Freire explains, prevents effective struggles for liberation and needs to be called out.

Without Tip's identity, *The True Meaning of Smekday* would have sent yet another message that white or male characters are the most suitable protagonists for sf. Without Frank's identity, it would have told a Native American theme while erasing the real people. Rex weaves the female character, culturally rich diversity, and speculative content together. He manages to tackle real problems through sf for a young audience, indicating that others can do it too—and future authors can also fix the problems that Rex propagates despite his better intentions. Rex himself has embraced Reese's criticisms and says he will do better.

CONCLUSION

Overall, primary sf already boasts wonderfully diverse and high-quality books, but they are not getting the critical attention and support that would encourage the important work that they perform. The examples covered above prove the potential and possibility of diverse primary sf, and how it can manifest the types of culturally relevant speculation and extrapolation going on in larger sf traditions like Afrofuturism. Painted faces representation can be as easy as altering the illustrations to include nonmainstream identities, but even this simple act can make a world of difference for the message it sends about diversity in the context of sf and the future. Culturally rich diversity requires more work on the part of the author but is clearly possible to do well in primary sf. The representation of specific groups in primary sf says a lot about who is included in scientific dialogue of the future, and whose science counts.

Children's literature is only just gaining steam for diverse representation and gender equality, and primary sf still suffers from the same issues of representation as children's literature overall. Indigenous Futurisms and Latin@ futurism were represented by very few books in my sample, and many other gender, race, nationality, and religious identities were absent entirely. I hope that future research on primary sf will be able to look at more identities than I have been able to here as representation improves and expands into more varied identities like disability and LGBTQIA identities. There is more work to be done. Primary sf could easily be the leading children's literature genre in terms of representation; the framework is already there in sf's history. If accomplished in tandem with fully extrapolative and speculative sf, then children will be encouraged to imagine a wider variety of people as important agents in our collective future.

CHAPTER 4

THE CASE STUDY

I will now turn to the voices of real children, along with the professionals who work with children and their books. This chapter offers interdisciplinary, grounded evidence of children reading primary sf and how adults mediate children's encounters with sf. Children's literature theories are often untested with actual young readers, due to the conceptual concerns noted in chapter 1 but also due to disciplinary boundaries. As Lawrence Sipe comments, "Given the considerable amount of theoretical work [. . .] that has been done on picturebooks, [. . .] I am struck by the avoidance of actual, 21st-century children" (4). There are only a few well-referenced studies that have tested theoretical, literary picturebook codes with actual children, such as that by Evelyn Arizpe and Morag Styles. Adjacent fields like comics theory are also rarely studied with reading children, with a few exhaustively referenced examples such as Angela Yannicopoulou's study of preschoolers reading speech and thought bubbles. In response to this lack, Marah Gubar calls for "more particular discussions of how young people have responded to individual texts" through methods usually reserved for educational and psychological research ("On Not Defining," 215). These fields, Gubar notes, all complement one another but rarely communicate. In Victoria Ford Smith's words, "childhood studies' interdisciplinary approach is one of the most promising means for scholars to pursue a criticism that not only deals with figures of childhood but also continually seeks out ways to ethically and usefully account for the lived experiences of real young people" (260).

Through this chapter I offer a glimpse of real children reading sf and share the thoughts of the adults in the field alongside those children. The mixed methods case study that I designed and conducted for this book includes three sources of data: 1) a data set of school library lending during the 2016–17 school year from across the United States; 2) a survey of teachers and librarians concerning their beliefs and habits regarding sf and children; and 3) recorded read-aloud sessions with primary school students. In the sections below, I describe the theoretical framework of the whole case study before moving on to sections containing the methodological details and results from each of the three data sources.

CASE STUDY DESIGN AND THEORETICAL FRAMEWORK

The three data sources described in this chapter are intended to work together as a case study in order to answer the question: *How do readers under age twelve interact with illustrated children's science fiction?* One method for effective case study research is to use multiple lenses to explore the research question. Accordingly, this case study of primary sf consists of three methods that function as three different lenses: statistical data modeling, an online survey, and recorded reading sessions. The interdisciplinary nature of these data sources is especially helpful for complementary description. I employ methods and theories from across fields for a stronger analysis that utilizes the strengths of these methods.

Combining methods and disciplines is justified by a pragmatic paradigm of research. Deborah Dillon, David O'Brien, and Elizabeth Heilman explain that in pragmatism, "conducting inquiry to useful ends takes precedence over finding ways to defend one's epistemology" (1118). Under pragmatism the usefulness of methods and frameworks is more important than defining a paradigm and defending methods as coming from a similar basis of assumptions about research and knowledge. In this way, I can combine broad statistical analysis with personal student read-aloud quotes. I am not concerned with scholarly debates over whether quantitative research is too broad or qualitative research too narrow, because in this situation they helpfully complement each other. This study benefits from the inherent variations in epistemology between methods and disciplines included, as the case only becomes a richer and more reliable portrayal with a broader set of perspectives.

Nevertheless, my results are inherently limited by the problematic nature of interpreting children's motivations and books through an adult lens. Ever since Jacqueline Rose's *The Case of Peter Pan, Or the Impossibility of Children's Fiction*, children's literature scholars constantly grapple with the assumption that children's books are at all representative of children or their interests. As mentioned in chapter 1, Rose proposes that children's books are nostalgic products created by and secretly for adults; this relationship potentially skews all interpretations of children's literature. Without going into the myriad theoretical responses and debates inspired by Rose's claims, this problem is an excellent reason for mixing interdisciplinary methods. The read-aloud study helps address this concern by giving the children a chance to explain themselves. I feature direct quotes from these read-alouds to include children's voices and help ensure that the survey data as well as my own interpretations are not too influenced by the unfounded assumptions that adults often carry about children and their books. With these data sources side by side, I also have a clearer picture of how adults mediate primary sf access and readership. In addition, the library circulation records show what children are choosing to check out. There is no feasible way to entirely remove adults from primary sf or this study, but these methods should check and balance one another for a fairer portrayal of the case than any one alone would accomplish.

Since I want to describe how contemporary children interact with sf in everyday life, I chose methods that try to measure children's encounters with sf as they exist in ordinary reading situations. The library lending study is the least intrusive and most objective, since it measures the lending of school libraries retrospectively. The survey measures what adults with a strong role in children's literacy practices say about science fiction, but they might not answer honestly, wholly, or objectively. The recorded read-alouds with children allow me to measure children's engagement through a familiar way of reading books at school and are therefore a better choice than literacy methods that put children in unfamiliar reading situations, like think-aloud reading sessions.

SCHOOL LIBRARY CIRCULATION STUDY

Participants

The school libraries were chosen through stratified random sampling. I used a random number generator to select schools that serve PK–5 from the National Center for Education Statistics database of public schools. I stratified this sample geographically by selecting one random school from each of the fifty states of the United States. Since the PK–5 limitation reflects this study's focus on children under twelve, libraries that served multiple schools with other grade ranges were excluded. If the selected school had no library or librarian contact information, I had the generator produce a new random number. This stratified random selection method makes this study the most generalizable of the three. Since the schools were chosen at random, the sample can be interpreted as representative of United States public school library lending. As the US is a large place with regional differences, the stratification by state ensures that the sampling does not favor any one geographical area.

Once schools were randomly selected, I reached out to each librarian by email and requested their 2016–17 library lending records, as well as a report of their library holdings overall. Ultimately ten librarians chose to participate. Notably, the relatively small sample size of ten schools means that the generalizability of this data is a little less dependable than I would have liked.

To preserve confidentiality, each library is described here only by region and an assigned letter (e.g. , Southeast A). One school requested that it be identified only by region, and not state, and so all schools are identified that way to match. Other demographic information about the school is limited to its locale and generalized size, as reported to the National Center for Education Statistics.

The demographics of each school can be found in table 4, along with the total number of books in its library. The participating libraries came from a good spread of regions and locales. Unfortunately, no school libraries from the Midwest states chose to participate. The participating schools vary significantly in racial diversity and free or reduced lunch–eligible students—a common stand-in measure for students in low socioeconomic homes. All schools reported an even split of male/female students, so that is not reported here. The sizes of the schools fell mostly between 401 and 799 students.

Table 4. School Demographics and Library Totals

Library	School Locale	School Size*	Grade Range	% White	% Free/Reduced Lunch Eligible
Southeast A	Rural	Small	KG–5	80%	68%
Southeast B	Rural	Medium	KG–5	65%	73%
West A	City	Medium	KG–5	6%	74%
West B	Suburban	Medium	KG–5	80%	47%
West C	Suburban	Medium	KG–5	78%	36%
Southwest A	City	Medium	KG–5	32%	57%
Southwest B	Suburban	Large	PK–5	3%	85%
Northeast A	Suburban	Medium	KG–5	65%	46%
Northeast B	Rural	Medium	KG–5	86%	14%
Northeast C	City	Small	KG–5	78%	12%

*Small < 400 students in 2016–17, Medium = 401799, Large > 800

Statistical Measure

There have been many collections and syntheses of school library circulation records concerning students' motivations or linking higher academic achievement and reading proficiency with library use (see Clark 2010, and Clark and Hawkins 2011), but very few analyses of genre-specific lending. One such study by Gemma Moss and John McDonald made use of one elementary school's library circulation data to explore children's reading preferences in relation to the three different classrooms studied and their respective classroom reading cultures but looked only at the differences between the broad genre categories of fiction, nonfiction, and poetry (405). This study revealed the significant impact that the books available and their teacher's approach to these books had on children's recreational text choices, alongside the impacts of peer pressure. Unfortunately, the current study cannot emulate all aspects of Moss and McDonald's qualitative examination since many school library systems do not store information about the students who have checked out the materials.

The quantitative analysis of this library data is useful for the overall case study as a contextual glimpse of larger trends. The checkouts in this study are meant to represent how much sf is being read, based on the reasonable assumption that the children who check out books also read them. There may be cases in which a book is checked out and not read, but I will treat this as an uncommon event and, given the large size of the library circulation data sets, unlikely to skew the results. These data also cannot account for books that were read within the library, without being checked out at all.

Since library records systems do not categorize books by genre, I manually coded each title as "Science Fiction," "Fantasy," "Historical Fiction," "Realistic Fiction," or "Nonfiction" to provide the variable of primary interest, sf lending, and to enable a comparison with other major genres. These genres are generally considered the broadest categories, as represented in children's literature textbooks like that of Galda et al. While coding, I collapsed any books with multiple copies into one data point with the sum of the different copies' circulations, since genre would be the same between copies. I also removed entries for technology lending like DVDs from the data, as this study is focused on books, and the DVDs were mostly instructional videos for classroom use.

The coding process itself was bound by the complexity of distinguishing genres that are not clearly separated from one another. I approached this coding task under the guidance of Brian Attebery's concept that genres are best seen as fuzzy sets, as described in chapter 1. While Attebery's suggestion is meant to curb the harsh distinctions between genres and allow "for partial membership in genre categories" (33), the needs of quantitative analysis require distinct categories for variables. I focused on Attebery's "core example" to code each book based on its relative similarity to a genre's core examples. I determined this similarity through my own experience as a reader, and in consultation with professional online reviews and publisher categorizations. In the case of books that straddled the differences between genres, I coded based on whichever genre bore the greatest emphasis on the structure of the book and its plot devices—in other words, whichever fuzzy set it resembled most.

Fantasy and sf include a wide array of subgenres and sister genres. However, it was not practical or necessary for this analysis for me to code each subgenre. Therefore, each code was inherently applied to a wide array of titles belonging to many subgenres, but I applied the fuzzy-set approach in these instances as well. I coded genres that are sometimes considered speculative fiction but not specifically sf or fantasy by their strongest affiliation. For instance, horror fiction, a subset of speculative fiction that is often distinguished from fantasy and sf, was coded as fantasy if it made use of magic or supernatural elements, and sf if it relied on technology to fuel the plot.

Nonfiction coding provided its own set of challenges, since this category can be very broad and not necessarily devoid of fiction, despite the name. I determined nonfiction books through Galda et al.'s idea of "emphasis": if the book puts the greatest emphasis on conveying information, as opposed to telling a story, then it is nonfiction—even if there is also some sort of narrative aiding in the information delivery (280). If the book happens to convey information but is primarily a story, then it belongs in another genre. This approach is very similar to Attebery's fuzzy sets. Based on this measure, I included concept books within the nonfiction group, as well as biography and creative nonfiction.

I then conducted a statistical analysis to evaluate whether the genres had different circulation rates and whether the demographic information impacted genre circulation. Since the data are nested in schools, it was necessary to control for differences between schools, especially since previous studies on library circulation cited above show a lot of influence from peers and librarians that varied between locations. Therefore, a hierarchical model was appropriate, as it allows for estimating variance attributable to both school context and individual books. The percentage white and free or reduced lunch variables, being characteristics of the school as a whole, must be placed on the second level—the school level—while genre, being a characteristic of the books whose checkouts I am counting, must be placed on the first level—the book level. Since the library circulation numbers are count data, which tend to skew toward low numbers, a Poisson curve was the best choice. After running several iterations of the model, I found that a conditional means model provided the best fit to the data, since conditional means models allow the intercept for each school to vary but assume that the impacts of each variable are relatively constant across schools. The final model is reflected in the equation:

$$\text{Circulations} = \beta_{oj} + \beta_{1j}(\text{Genre}) + \varepsilon_{ij}$$
$$\beta_{oj} = \gamma_{oo} + \gamma_{o1}(\text{Percentage White}) + \gamma_{o2}(\text{Percentage Free/Reduced Lunch}) + \eta_{o}$$

For those unfamiliar with these terms, generalized linear mixed models are statistical equations intended to predict circulation patterns based on the observed data and determine what can be attributed to random chance and what is a reliable pattern.

Table 5. Total, Averages, and Median Books by Library

Library	Total Number of Books	Total Number of Checkouts	Average Checks/Book	Median Checks/Book
Southeast A	6,037	6,863	1.14	0
Southeast B	10,356	19,731	1.91	0
West A	10,921	22,521	2.06	1
West B	9,193	22,035	2.40	0
West C	7,057	11,442	1.62	0
Southwest A	12,752	6,670	0.52	0
Southwest B	23,728	18,945	0.80	0
Northeast A	12,457	29,759	2.39	0
Northeast B	12,066	26,286	2.18	0
Northeast C	15,971	22,956	1.44	0

Results

The data show sf readership that both agrees with and challenges the critical conception of sf for young children. Overall, these data reveal that while there are not as many sf titles in circulation as other genres, children are checking out those sf books with more regularity than the other genres.

While the sizes of the participating schools are mostly between 401 and 799 students, their library holdings vary significantly in size, from 6,037 to 23,728 books. Therefore, average checkouts per book are helpful, since they allow comparison between libraries of different sizes (see table 5). Most schools had over one checkout per book on average, with four schools averaging over two checkouts per book. This average was pulled down, since many books in any given library are not checked out over the course of a year. Accordingly, the median checkouts were zero for all but one library.

Figure 7 shows what percentage of each collection fell into the five broad genre categories used in this study. The distributions were extremely similar, with the libraries overall averaging 49 percent nonfiction, 25 percent fantasy, 19 percent realistic fiction, 5 percent historical fiction, and 3 percent sf. It is fascinating that this trend remained consistent between different schools, regions, and library sizes. The nonfiction totals ranged the most, with a maximum difference of sixteen percentage points between West A (56%) and West

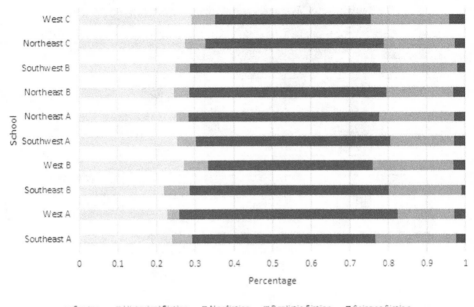

Figure 7. Percentage of library collections by genre.

C (40%). Fantasy had a maximum range of only seven percentage points, realistic fiction had six, historical fiction had four, and sf had three. It is not surprising that nonfiction is so well stocked, since many different books are needed to cover a wide range of reference topics. Yet the distribution of fiction genres also shows a curiously consistent pattern across schools.

These results show that while genre supply is similar among schools, genre circulation differs much more among schools. Nonfiction checkouts show a wide range of twenty-four percentage points between the different libraries. Fantasy and realistic fiction have a similar range of fourteen and thirteen percentage points, respectively. Historical fiction and sf stayed consistent between most schools, with both ranging by only five percentage points. These results imply that each library has internal influences on what gets checked out. Other library studies show that the social dynamics of peers and teachers dramatically influence library lending patterns. The present results confirm that each library has differences in circulation but follow a larger trend.

It would be reasonable to assume that libraries are stocked based on what is in demand by readers, but when we look at how often these books were checked out, the results do not support that idea. Figure 8 shows percentages

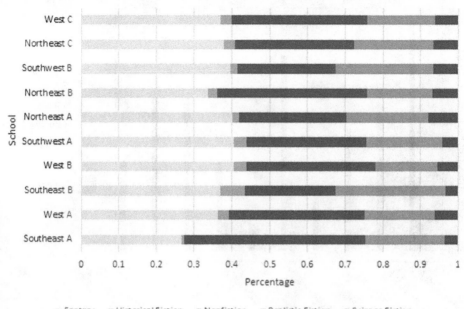

Figure 8. Percentage of library checkouts by genre.

of the overall checkouts for the year in each library. The average checkouts were 37 percent fantasy, 34 percent nonfiction, 21 percent realistic fiction, 6 percent sf, and 3 percent historical fiction. If the distribution of genre in library collections was based on readership, then I would expect the available titles in each genre to approximately parallel the checkout percentages. In these data, that is not the case.

All ten libraries show a relatively small number of sf titles and circulations compared to other genres. Given the similarities between sf and fantasy, the vast difference between their circulation is glaring. Fantasy is clearly a favorite above and beyond all the others. Historical fiction and sf have the lowest number of titles, but sf has far more circulations than historical fiction.

These data support critical commentary that there is not much sf available for children under twelve. However, these stacked graphs do not do justice to the dramatic, exponential difference between the number of sf titles and the number of sf circulations, as compared to the difference in other genres. To look at each genre more closely, I calculated the average circulations per book for each category. This number examines how much usage each genre is getting, compared to how many books are available. Figure 9 depicts the

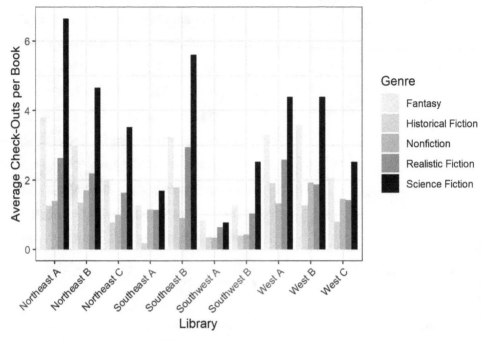

Figure 9. Average checkouts per book by genre.

average number of checkouts per book, by genre and within each school. The sf category had the highest average checkouts per book in every library except Southwest A, where it was 0.1 below fantasy. This pattern shows that sf is often available in lower quantities than other major genres, but children compensate by checking out those books more often per book than other genres. Fantasy took second place for the most checkouts per book in all cases but Southwest A, where it topped sf. The other genres varied in average checkouts, with realistic fiction taking third place in seven out of ten libraries. Nonfiction most often came in fourth, while historical fiction had the lowest average checkouts per book in seven out of ten libraries.

It is worth noting that sf and historical fiction were consistently the genres with the lowest/second-lowest number of books in each library, but sf's usage was concentrated enough to achieve the highest average checkouts per book, while historical fiction mostly had the lowest averages. This indicates something beyond availability at work.

I also checked to make sure that sf's higher averages are not due to extreme cases skewing the average. The median of circulations by genre, across the

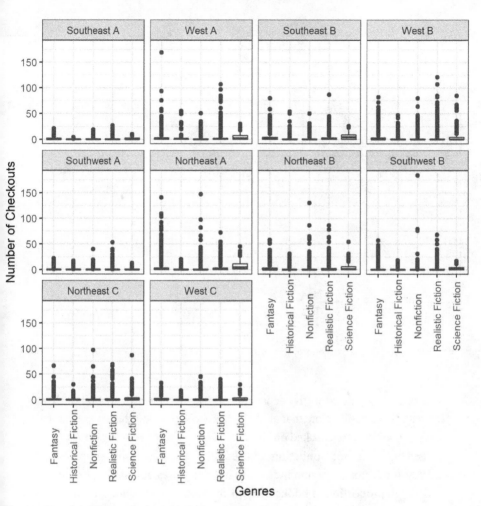

Figure 10. Box plot of library checkouts by genre.

schools, is zero for all genres except sf, which is one. However, sf did not ever have the highest extreme case in any of the schools, as can be seen in the boxplots that plot the outliers in each genre (see figure 10). In five libraries, nonfiction books were the highest extreme cases: two *Minecraft* handbooks, two Raina Telgemeier memoirs, and one dictionary. In four libraries the highest extreme cases were realistic fiction from *The Diary of a Wimpy Kid* series. Only one library's highest extreme case was fantasy: a book of ghost stories.

Rather than being due to high extreme cases, sf achieved the highest average per book by consistently having a good distribution of checkouts across titles.

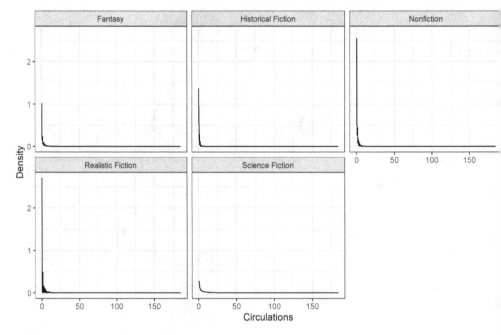

Figure 11. Density map of library checkouts by genre.

This can be visualized in the density plot in figure 11, which combines data from all the libraries. Note that all the data are clustered on the left side, since so many books were checked out never or once over the course of the year.

The big spikes for nonfiction and realistic fiction and smaller spikes on fantasy and historical fiction indicate that these genres, across all the schools, had a high proportion of books with no checkouts or one checkout over the course of the year. Meanwhile, sf's low, rounded spike shows that the books in this category, across all the libraries, were frequently checked out two or more times during the year.

While this is all to say that there is no statistical basis for concern over sf's extreme cases, my personal observations while coding led me to have some concern about the impact of *Star Wars* books. Statistical tests like those represented in figures 10 and 11 indicate that no single book is overly skewing the data, but there is no direct way to test for the influence of an entire series of media tie-ins. Additionally, *Star Wars* was also a consistent theme in the read-alouds and survey data. Timewise, *Star Wars* poses an interesting threat to the validity of the data due to the release of *The Force Awakens*

Table 6. *Star Wars* and Non–*Star Wars* Sf Titles and Checkouts

Genre	Titles	Checkouts	Mean Checkouts per Book
All sf together	3,176	11,429	4
Non–*Star Wars* sf	2,772	8,606	3
Star Wars sf	404	2,823	7

a year before the library circulation window. Due to these reasons, I began coding *Star Wars* books in the data set to ensure that these media tie-ins are not the force—pun intended—behind the entire sf category's results.

Star Wars books accounted for 404 (13%) of the 3,176 sf books across schools, and 2,823 (25%) of the 11,429 sf checkouts. *Star Wars* books do not make up the majority of titles, or even the majority of the circulations for the genre. The most intriguing result is the mean checkouts per book. Without *Star Wars*, sf circulation per book drops only from four times per book to three times per book (see table 6). However, the *Star Wars* books by themselves have an impressive seven circulations per title.

To see if the *Star Wars* books would change the relationship between sf and the other genres, I ran a Poisson general linear model with non–*Star Wars* sf as the intercept. All the genre coefficients were still negative and statistically significant, showing that even when *Star Wars* books are taken out, regular sf is checked out more per book than any other genre. Therefore, I did not use the specific *Star Wars* variable in the final hierarchical linear model; the *Star Wars* books are included under the sf category.

The final hierarchical linear model compares the genre lending and demographic influences while accounting for differences between schools. With sf functioning as the reference category in each model, each genre variable's coefficient indicates the difference between the log of sf's mean and the log of the mean for that category of book (see table 7). Meanwhile, the white and reduced lunch variable coefficients indicate the difference to the log of mean book circulations at schools with higher percentages of white students and higher percentages of free or reduced lunch–eligible students, respectively. Gender was not included, since there was no difference in gender balance between the schools.

The negative results of the other genres show that on average, for every increase in 1 log unit of sf lending, each other genre was checked out less than once. Fantasy was checked out 0.420 times less, nonfiction 1.224 times

Table 7. Poisson Hierarchical Linear Regression Coefficients and Means

	Parameter	Standard Error	p
Fixed effects			
(intercept)	0.821	0.146	< 0.001
Fantasy	-0.420	0.010	< 0.001
Nonfiction	-1.224	0.010	< 0.001
Historical fiction	-1.299	0.016	< 0.001
Realistic fiction	-1.224	0.010	< 0.001
Percentage white	0.007	0.003	0.026
Percentage free/reduced lunch	> 0.001	0.004	0.987
School level variance	0.190		
Goodness-of-fit			
Deviance	654479.6		
AIC	654495.6		
BIC	654573.2		

less, historical fiction 1.299 times less, and realistic fiction 1.224 times less. All these relationships show $p < .001$, meaning that these trends are not due to random chance but are reliable observations.

The demographic coefficients were both positive, although the percentage free or reduced lunch coefficient was very small. The percentage white coefficient indicates that overall lending increases by 1 log units for every 1 percent increase in white students. This was also $p < .001$ and therefore not due to random chance. However, the free or reduced lunch–eligible variable was not significant and therefore shows no significant relationship with library lending.

The demographic data are being modeled by overall lending, and not specifically the sf lending. To see how the demographics relate to sf lending in specific, I created a subset of only sf books and conducted a generalized linear model for just sf books. These results showed no statistically significant relationship between the percentage white students and percentage free/reduced lunch–eligible students and sf checkouts.

Discussion

The library circulation results indicate that book production or library stocking practices do not match up with the usage by children in these schools.

The statistically higher lending rates of sf indicate that we need a better understanding of children's interest in sf texts and that this needs to be translated into change in the production and distribution of genre. The higher lending rates for *Star Wars* sf also indicate that this popular culture sf text has an influence on the reading of sf. Quantitative data like these are useful for pointing out trends, but other sources must investigate the why and how behind the trend and initiate the required changes. I shared the preliminary results of this study with the participating librarians, along with resources to help them acquire more high-quality sf for their library collections, in the hope of instigating some small change.

The library circulation results also indicate that racial diversity and economic status of students affect their likelihood of checking out books in general but have no relationship with the checking out of sf books. Schools with student bodies that were poorer and had more white students had more books checked out in general, but there is no demonstrable difference in sf checkouts for either demographic variable. This result counteracts the relative whiteness of sf, as demonstrated in chapter 3, and perhaps reflects how sf is doing marginally better in overall diversity than children's literature broadly speaking. There is not much previous work on sf, socioeconomic status, and children to compare with, but socioeconomic status does not seem to impact sf lending in this sample. This study also revealed that historical fiction is slightly better stocked than sf, but particularly unpopular in comparison. Some genre scholars like to casually say that sf and historical fiction are two sides of the same coin: one speculating into the future while the other speculates into the past. I am reminded of this relationship by the genres' similarly low availability, but it is interesting that historical fiction shows very different circulation patterns than sf. This may indicate a worthwhile avenue for future research into the popularity and lending of historical fiction for young children.

LIBRARIAN AND TEACHER SURVEY

Participants

Participants were recruited through online snowball sampling. I sent the survey link to listservs, message boards, and social media groups for teachers and/or librarians and requested that they forward and pass along the survey.

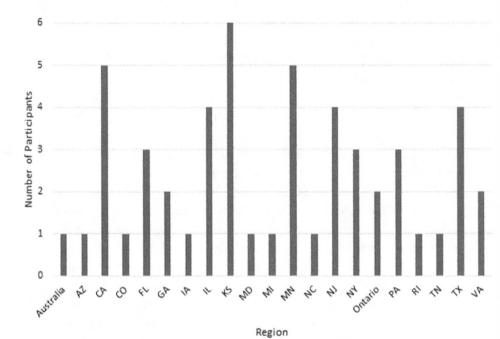

Figure 12. Survey respondents by location, based on where they logged on.

Overall, fifty-nine professionals who work with children responded to the survey. However, several did not finish or opted to not answer certain questions. Therefore, each question has between fifty-two to fifty-nine respondents. Since I am not examining the responses as cases across questions, but rather question by question, I did not throw out incomplete survey responses.

Of the fifty-nine respondents, fifty-two allowed the survey software to perform geolocation (see figure 12). These respondents logged on from nineteen different states in the United States as well as from Canada and Australia.

Of the respondents who answered demographic questions (see table 8), the large majority, forty-five respondents (86.54%), identify as female. The majority are also librarians (39, or 75.00%). Two individuals selected the "other" category for profession, but only one wrote in "Library Director." Similarly, thirty-eight respondents (73.08%) claim to be fans of sf. The write-ins for the "other" category include one "casual fan" with a preference for fantasy, one nonfan whose favorite book is *Ender's Game*, and one person who says they are a fan depending upon the topic. A total of 73.08% is an unexpectedly high turnout of fans, leading me to wonder what the respondents' definitions of "fan" may be or if the survey attracted more fans of sf than may be represented generally in the population.

Table 8. Survey Participant Demographics

Gender	Female	Male	Other
	45 (86.54%)	7 (13.46%)	0 (0.00%)
Profession*	Librarian	Teacher	Other
	39 (75.00%)	17 (32.69%)	2 (3.85%)
Fan of sf	Yes	No	Other
	38 (73.08%)	11 (21.15%)	3 (5.77%)

* Participants could select more than one profession.

Survey Measure

The survey offers a broad picture of primary sf across many practitioners and locations. I designed the digital survey instrument for this study using Qualtrics. The survey contains multiple-choice questions, such as which formats of sf they have in their library; yes/no questions, such as whether they recommend sf to children; and short-answer questions, such as what tactics they use to recommend sf to children. This survey was distributed and passed along through online social media. It was not as necessary to get a statistically representative sample, since I do not use this descriptive data to make any claims of generalizability. These teachers and librarians cannot be assumed to represent their entire professions.

After data collection, I performed simple descriptive analysis on the distributions and comparisons between multiple choice and yes/no question answers. For the open-ended questions, I used open coding over several readthroughs to identify trends. I ultimately identified between ten and fifteen different codes for each question.

Results

The responses to this survey offer a glimpse into how sf is being actively used and supported in classrooms and libraries. The resounding tone of the survey responses falls along the lines of "Science fiction is important, just like everything else!" In stark contrast to scholars who dismiss or single out primary sf as problematic, these professionals insisted that sf is equal to, if perhaps less commonplace than, other genres. This is not to say that the survey results show no specific benefits of or problems with sf, just that the respondents repeatedly described sf as a peer to other genres—even as they later go on to describe how the genre is odd and potentially off-putting.

Many of the professionals claimed that they use and treat sf like any other genre of literature. For instance, when asked what, if any, differences exist between primary sf and YA or adult versions of sf, they described differences that would be the same between children's and YA/adult books, regardless of genre. Out of fifty-nine respondents, twelve (20.34%) mentioned relying upon the protagonist's age to estimate an age range for readers. Others found the biggest differences to be in reading level (3, or 5.08%) and vocabulary (5, or 8.47%). The most common response, with twenty-nine (49.15%) respondents, described a difference in terms of child-appropriate content: no sex or violence and low levels of horror and gore.

Similarly, the respondents reported using procedures that are not genre-specific to work with sf. In response to the question of how they identify potential sf readers, thirty out of fifty respondents (60.00%) indicated that they simply ask or observe what children like. This is not a surprising result, as reference interviews and reader's advisory services are significant to libraries. Among teachers, making book recommendations to students is of particular importance to followers of Donalyn Miller's guide *The Book Whisperer*. Both practices are built around observing or asking each child individually about their interests and favorite books in order to recommend further similar reading or to find ways to bridge to new areas of potential interest across genres.

When asked how they recommend sf, most respondents also evoked common practices. Many indicated that they market sf books to children through book talks, another core service of libraries and especially school librarians. Four (8.00%) specifically mentioned book talks by name, while others mentioned the items traditionally included in book talks: plot descriptions (15, or 30.00%), character (8, or 16.00%), theme (2, or 4.00%), and setting (3, or 6.00%). One of the most popular methods, it seems, is simply to act excited about the book with the expectation that the enthusiasm will catch on. Thirteen respondents (26.00%) mentioned excitement, and their explanations made it clear that this strategy is not specific to sf books.

Others did not pay much attention to the sf genre label, with five (8.93%) stating that they choose books for other reasons, like humor, and that these books just happen sometimes to be sf. Also, five (8.93%) said that they use sf in their classes and activities as part of exposing children to all genres as part of general literacy, without any specific emphasis on sf. Three respondents (5.36%) wrote that they had not thought about using sf in lessons or activities before but might, now that the survey brought it to mind. In response to the question "Why do you choose to use or not use science fiction books in lessons or activities?" one respondent wrote, "Interesting, I never realized that deficiency before!" The survey itself, for this respondent, was the inspiration for her to describe sf in her classroom/library as a "deficiency." Instead of answering the question directly, this respondent wrote about her own surprise.

In response to the question about why sf is or is not important to introduce children to, nearly half of the respondents included it as an important part of a varied reading diet. Out of fifty responses, twenty-one (42.00%) firmly stated that it is important for elementary school age children to read sf because they feel it equally important to expose children to all genres. Thirteen respondents (26.00%) specified that anything that gets children interested in reading is worthwhile, while another two (4.00%) mentioned vocabulary benefits of wide reading. Another four (8.00%) explained that all fiction genres are important for developing empathy, including sf.

The determination to hold sf as an equal genre among many can be seen best when respondents were asked to compare the importance of reading sf to each other major genre (see figure 13). For most genres, over 80 percent of respondents chose the "same" option. Only for informational texts/nonfiction did less than 80 percent select "same," but the number was still over 50 percent (32, or 61.54%). Informational texts/nonfiction received the highest number of votes as more important than sf, with eighteen respondents (34.62%). Historical fiction and contemporary realistic fiction were considered more important by six (11.54%) and nine (17.31%), respectively. Fantasy was very close to sf across the board, with only three people (5.88%) ranking it as more important than sf, and none ranking it as less important. In total, no genre was ranked as less important than sf by any more than 5 percent of respondents. This small skew indicates that even while claiming that sf is an equally important genre, these professionals felt that it is not quite as significant as other genres.

Of those who chose to explain why sf is not as important for children to read, two (4.00%) cited the fact that the genre is not on standard tests, and another two complained that it is too sparse to use effectively. Three respondents (5.36%) said that they do not use sf in their activities because they are unfamiliar with it themselves. Meanwhile, one individual (2.00%) explained that she values realistic fiction more, because "I see more immediate need for students to see themselves mirrored in texts and to learn about others who

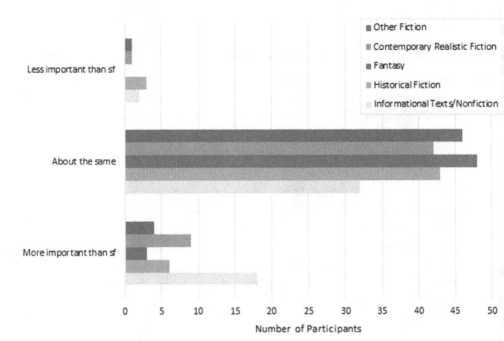

Figure 13. Survey answers to question: Compared to the genres listed below, how important is it to expose children to science fiction?

are different from themselves." This response implies that children cannot see themselves and others as clearly in fantastic stories and may explain why the realistic stories were chosen as more important than sf while fantasy did not receive as much differentiation.

Despite the emphasis on sf as equivalent to other genres, the survey results also include several enlightening comments about the unique benefits and drawbacks of this genre for children. More than half of the respondents (63.80%) reported that they recommend sf to their readers most of the time or often. When answering how they identify potentially interested readers, six (12.00%) used STEM interests as a reason for recommending sf. Another seven respondents (14.00%) explained that they often use children's affinity for common sf tropes like robots and spaceships to determine who may like sf, while four (8.00%) made connections to sf based on a reader's enjoyment of other core texts across media, with *Star Wars* being a commonly cited example. When trying to convince potential readers to take the books, eighteen respondents (36.00%), said that they draw the child's attention to a book's similarity to that child's previous favorites, with five of these respondents (10.00%) drawing comparisons to the child's previous enjoyment of sf tropes, and three (6.00%) making connections to other core genre texts—often, again, *Star Wars*.

Three (6.00%) of the respondents said that they identify readers who may like sf through their interest in speculation; they look for children who like "scientific subjects but are looking for something more than just information on these types of subjects." The phrase "more than just information" is a great way to describe speculation and the exploration and broadening it implies. When trying to convince potential readers to take the books, four respondents (8.00%) reported talking up the technological and speculative innovations of the books.

One popular trend among the ways that the respondents recommend the books is the word "adventure," with eleven respondents (22.00%) reporting this as a successful tactic for making an sf book sound appealing. This calls to mind Hastings's concern that "the trappings of the science fiction novel are used to frame a rather conventional story of adventure and active imagination" (207). Scholars of postcolonial sf, including Afrofuturism and Indigenous Futurisms, have also exhibited concern that adventure or action-oriented sf is often the most prone to colonial and subjugating narratives of encountering and removing the threat of the Other. In the context of these critical concerns, this trend in the survey was disturbing.

Gender concerns were less apparent. One survey respondent mentioned that when recommending sf to children, "if the book has female characters, I point that out to girl readers." Beginning with "if" indicates this librarian's awareness that much sf does not include a female character. Given the benefits of feminist sf discussed in chapter 3, having more than one response of this type would have been helpful.

The most popular (15, or 30.00%) reason for singling out sf as an important genre for children to read is the idea that it could expand a child's mind. Four responses (8.00%) specified that sf books encourage critical thinking, both in terms of what is realistic in fiction and in terms of real-world applications. Ten (20.00%) of the respondents mentioned that sf is particularly valuable as a source and inspiration for speculation and extrapolation about the future. One respondent wrote:

> . . . it exposes them to other possibilities and makes them think about the
> future of their world. It might make them question the current or historical

> practices or actions of our society or race, and where those actions might lead us in the future. It will make them wonder about technology—the possibilities and the pitfalls. It's a fantastic way to express a feeling about something that is currently happening or happened in the past, since sci-fi plots sometimes parallel real events and consequences. They can make kids think about their own values, whether they would be able to survive, make the right decisions, be brave, etc., if put in a similar situation.

This response reiterates the value of speculation, with phrases like "think about the future" and "wonder about technology." Fourteen percent of the respondents similarly wrote in the short-answer box that they use sf in activities because of the genre's ability to inspire critical thinking skills. Their replies talk about encouraging children to think through possibilities and engage their imaginations to analyze real science and society. One respondent wrote, "I think it is an excellent way to explore human nature in an engaging and interesting way."

Many of the librarians and teachers who responded to my survey made connections with science lessons and careers as a means of validating the genre. Twenty percent of the respondents mentioned that sf is particularly valuable, since it can lead to later scientific achievement, citing the cases in which sf has predicted scientific innovations: "Many ideas that were once considered science fiction generations passed [sic] are now realities of today. Before something can be created it must first be imagined!" Sixteen percent of the respondents indicated that sf may encourage an interest in STEM classes and careers, with one person specifically mentioning the potential for girl-friendly sf to inspire girls in STEM. Other responses aligned sf with the STEM practices of creating a hypothesis and problem-solving: "I often find sci-fi books to be very rich mentor texts that can inspire students to wonder, make predictions, ask questions, and learn more. When a child reads about an idea that is just beyond what is known, it pushes them to think bigger." Eleven percent of the responses mentioned science lessons specifically, and one person even mentioned history lessons. One survey respondent worried that reading sf might work against STEM education, expressing concern that "some concepts lead students to believe misperceptions."[1]

In an interesting contrast, three respondents (6.00%) claimed that the genre is helpful for offering escapism—a concept that is often negative and accused of helping readers avoid reality to an unhealthy degree. However, these teachers and librarians invoked a positive use: "Science fiction can be a great escape for children. [. . .] Also, children can relate to the main characters in science fiction and then come out comforted that if the book character could face the uncertain technological future, then so can they." This response portrays escapism in J. R. R. Tolkien's sense of "Recovery, Escape, Consolation": fantastic stories may offer escape, but only in the name of returning to the real world refreshed and better equipped for reality (145).

Similarly, some respondents described a lighthearted, humorous, and hopeful tone in primary sf, especially in comparison to sf for older audiences. Four respondents (6.78%) described primary sf as more hopeful than YA sf. Five respondents (8.47%) said that YA sf tends toward a darker tone than primary sf, and five (8.47%) explained that YA and adult sf is more often dystopian than primary sf. Three (5.08%) also claimed that humor is more important and common to primary sf than to YA or adult sf.

On the whole, the responses show a paradoxical portrayal of sf as both simple and complex. Eighteen respondents (30.51%) found that children's and YA sf differ in terms of complexity, with primary sf offering simpler themes, plot, characters, and ethical dilemmas. Five respondents (8.47%) noted that YA and adult sf have more-complex science concepts. This concern reflects directly on the critical comments by Hastings mentioned in chapter 1. One of these respondents believed that older readers have greater science schemata to use while reading, and so sf for children does not include science explanations:

> In children's books, the "science" in science fiction is often portrayed without explanation, or just in a simple way. By way of example: the focus isn't on how exactly the rocket works, unless the rocket happens to break; the focus is on the adventure of flying in the rocket. Not that detailed explanations are often given in YA/adult science fiction, either, but literate adults can "fill in the gaps" in a way that allows them to move forward in the story without being bothered by details, and they can discern between what details are truly significant, as opposed to complementary.

This respondent suggested that children would be overwhelmed by too much detail and find it hard to find centrally important plot points amidst a flurry of information. This explanation also implies that adults would be "bothered by" too many details, perhaps because with more detail they are more likely to find a flaw or lack of logic. This response raises the challenges inherent to including complex science in any narrative for any age.

Despite their generally positive portrayal of sf, few respondents reported using sf in lessons and activities, with less than half (34.49%) of the respondents professing to use the genre most of the time or often in their activities or lessons. Of those that do, eight respondents (14.29%) said that they use sf in activities because of the genre's ability to inspire critical thinking skills. A total of six responses (10.71%) mentioned that sf is useful for science lessons, and one (1.79%) even mentioned history lessons. One respondent admitted frankly that the genre is not on achievement tests and therefore not prioritized in the classroom.

Many respondents portrayed primary sf as hard to work with in organized, group activities, due to the complexity of the narratives. More than half (65.55%) of the respondents never or rarely used sf in their activities or lessons, while a similar percentage (63.80%) did recommend sf most of the time or often (see table 9). This comparison shows a tendency to encourage children to read sf on their own, but not in guided or group situations. Pearson's chi-square test shows that the distribution of these two questions is not random: $\chi^2(3, N = 58) = 14.28, p = .003$. This indicates that the results show a definitive pattern within this sample toward recommending sf but not using it in groups.

When asked why they did or did not use sf in lessons or activities, many respondents claimed that there are too few primary sf books. Of fifty-six respondents, eighteen (32.14%) reported having few books to choose from, especially at lower grade levels. Another ten responses (17.86%) explained that using sf books in classroom read-alouds or library story time is problematic because the chapter book options are too narratively complex to be suitable for reading aloud over several sessions. Two (3.57%) respondents said that sf books are too long, and three (5.36%) said they are too complex: "I have to appeal to broad ability levels in chapter book read-aloud selections. These books typically have to be shorter, with more simple plots." Others reflected that the books are simply better suited to older children and independent reading: "I will use sci fi pictures [sic] books on occasion in storytime but have always considered the kind of suppositions sci fi is based on to be difficult for younger children to grasp. We do read some sci fi in our middle grade book club." This response is one of the few to acknowledge the possibility of sf picturebooks but simultaneously defers to middle grade books, which range closer to age twelve, as a more appropriate match of content to

Table 9. Survey Questions and Answers concerning Using and Recommending Sf

Question	Never	Rarely	Most of the Time	Often	Total
How often do you use science fiction books with children in lessons or activities?	7 12.1%	31 53.45%	9 15.52%	11 18.97%	58
How often do you recommend science fiction books to children?	1 1.72%	20 34.48%	9 15.52%	28 48.28%	58

age. Overall, these results imply that for most of the respondents, sf seems too scarce and too demanding to be useful for a large group activity.

Several write-in answers characterized sf as odd, even in comparison to similar fantastic texts like horror and fantasy. Throughout the responses, respondents related sf to other genres and subgenres under the speculative fiction umbrella. One person (2.00%) said that sf is a good alternative to horror for children, as it can bring up similar questions without being as scary. Fantasy was mentioned specifically by four (8.00%) respondents as a good way to tell who may also enjoy sf, implying a connected readership between the two genres. When describing the differences between primary sf and YA/adult sf, three respondents (5.08%) placed sf on a sliding scale with fantasy, explaining that "children's science fiction tends to skew more towards fantasy ('soft' science fiction), whereas YA and adult can skew either way—towards fantasy or towards science/technical fiction ('hard' science fiction)." These responses echo Bud Foote's argument, discussed in chapter 1, that fantasy is the genre of childhood, while sf is that of YA.

Sf was also described as weird, unusual, or a last resort, and some respondents even implied that the name of the genre itself was off-putting to children. Respondents said that they could differentiate sf by a specifically weird feel. Three respondents wrote that they recommend sf to readers who like "weird" or "freaky" books. Two respondents reported telling potential readers that sf books are "weird" or "funky" to appeal to them. "Weird" is a historically appropriate word for the genre, given the New Weird movement in 2003 and the magazine *Weird Tales* (original run 1923–54), which is often regarded as foundational in American speculative fiction. This connection with sf history, intentional or not, draws primary sf in line with the overall sf tradition but also characterizes sf as an outsider text.

Respondents seemed to disagree about whether sf is popular or unpopular. Eleven people said that they use the genre in activities because it is popular, and one respondent said that they make sf books sound appealing by telling the potential reader that it is popular among other children. However, another five said that they do not use sf books because the genre is *un*popular. One of these respondents described the paradox: "SF tends to be less popular, seen by them as something you either really love or are not interested in all. For them it's a genre of extremes." This response calls to mind traditional associations of sf with the fervent nerd/geek. These professionals described sf as a genre that elicits polarized responses: either obsession or avoidance. Two respondents reported that they actively avoid the term "science fiction" when recommending the genre. Similarly, four other respondents said that they find success when recommending sf books through other terms instead, like "steampunk" or "humor." In these cases, there is an assumption that the genre's name itself is unappealing. Their responses also indicated that many students may be reading sf without knowing it if professionals avoid the genre's name.

Other survey responses pointed out that sf is well-suited for reluctant readers. Two of the respondents said that they use the genre in activities to help to engage reluctant readers, in part due to popularity and in part due to the frequent presence of pictures in sf. Similarly, two respondents stated that sf is important to read because many reluctant readers are supported well by sf books. One respondent even described the genre as slightly subversive, reporting that the books can be easily recommended to children by pointing out that the genre is not required reading. Five of the respondents mentioned that they recommend sf specifically to reluctant readers or in cases when "traditional fiction and nonfiction does not interest them." This portrayal of sf as a last resort is interesting, especially given the contrast between sf and "traditional fiction" in this last response. This focus on developing readers and subversive reading reveals the belief that sf is a road to other reading, not an end in itself. This is very similar to previously mentioned beliefs that sf is acceptable as a path to science. However, these responses do point to the power of motivation in reading.

Discussion

The survey results demonstrate that for professionals working with children and literacy, sf is largely important as only one of many important genres and paths to reading proficiency. It contains many unique benefits, from science to speculative potential, but also suffers from a perceived lack of availability, higher complexity than other children's books, difficulty to use in group activities, and a feeling of strangeness.

Even while these professionals insisted that the genre was just as important to introduce, their answers revealed stereotypes and indicated that sf books are too hard and science-based for all but the most unusual readers. These experts, who are in close contact with reading children, seem caught in the middle of the paradigm of the natural child and the evidence of children's complex, worldly skills—simultaneously a champion for children's right to read sf and unsure of whether those children have the ability or desire to do so.

Children are certainly savvy enough to become aware of the cultural associations of sf. The children described by these professionals seem to perceive sf as an identity that must be claimed or rejected, but the professionals themselves do not seem to be counteracting this perception of sf as an unusual or extreme genre. Librarians and teachers do not teach just genre definitions; they also convey social cues about these genres. These professionals may be imparting and reinforcing genre biases. The children who enjoy sf may feel that they have to choose to either broadcast or hide their fandom. If librarians and teachers are trying to avoid the situation by recommending sf without using the genre's name, then those children who like sf may not know to look for more sf.

Even worse, internalizing a bias against sf may actually impede the ability to read it. A study by Chris Gavaler and Dan R. Johnson found that adult readers who thought they were reading an sf story were undermined by their own biases. When participants thought they were reading a story in an sf world, they expected lower literary value and inference requirements, and as a result scored lower on comprehension—even though they were given the same story as the control group. The researchers only changed a few words, like "door" to "airlock." Meanwhile, sf often requires more inference requirements than the passage in the study.

In the end, the respondents gave the impression that any more than a taste of sf is best only for the unusual, reluctant, and/or isolated reader. It is no wonder that children seem to be picking up on biases against sf if it is being portrayed as an odd genre for special cases, even while these well-meaning professionals seek to introduce the genre as equally important.

READ-ALOUD STUDY

Participants

The read-alouds were conducted during the free afterschool program at a private, urban school in Minnesota. The location was chosen purely by convenience sampling, due to the ever-challenging process of finding a willing school. The regular attendees of the afterschool program were all invited to participate, resulting in a total of eight participants ranging from kindergarten to fifth grade (male = 2, female = 6). All names used below are pseudonyms to protect the children's identities. While obtaining parental permission forms, I also asked parents to fill out a one-page questionnaire about their home's literacy environment and family sf fandom. Five participants' parents returned the questionnaire.

Parental Questionnaire Measure

The parental questionnaire, distributed with the permission slips, asked parents to select a range of numbers that best represents the number of books in the house, and then if any of those books are sf. Parents were also asked if they read sf books with their children or do science-fictional activities, or if anyone in the home considers themselves a fan of sf across media. These questions are modeled on home literacy surveys like those developed and distributed by Get Ready to Read!, a service of The National Center for Learning Disabilities. This type of survey is founded on the assumption that early exposure to a variety of reading activities and print materials, the home literacy environment (HLE), has a positive impact on literacy development. I altered the survey to fit a modification to the general assumptions about the impact of HLE: a child with exposure to many sf books, activities, and reading models may be better equipped to excel during my read-alouds. Stephen Robert Burgess explains that research with HLE surveys has demonstrated that they are useful and often representative, but the results should be taken cautiously due to the risks inherent in self-reported data (721). These HLE surveys are not primary data sources, but rather are intended to provide context to the main data source: the read-alouds. It is useful to know whether these children come from a background infused with and respectful of sf, especially when considering sf intertext.

Read-Aloud Measure

I recorded the read-aloud sessions and transcribed them for analysis using Lawrence Sipe's picturebook read-aloud categories from *Storytime: Young Children's Literary Understanding in the Classroom* as an axial coding scheme, allowing me to identify different types of responses and then connect them to science-fictional thinking and sf literacy as developed in chapters 1 and 2.

Sipe's picturebook read-aloud method offers a structure for looking at children's verbal literary meaning-making responses, including their responses to visual aesthetics. He does not name the method, perhaps in part because he does not pretend to have invented it—the methods in his book were distilled from observations of teachers who are experts of this reading practice already. However, his grounded theory model results in concrete recommendations for opening up students' literary responses, and then categorizing and analyzing those responses. He does not intend for it to be exclusively for "literacy researchers, theorists, and graduate students" (9) as a research tool—he also wants teachers to adopt this approach to reading picturebooks aloud in everyday classrooms to encourage and evaluate their student's literary understanding.

Sipe ties this method of classroom picturebook read-alouds to scaffolding children's literary understanding. Since I am looking at the literary understanding of primary sf as a scaffold for advanced sf literature, this is a more representative method than an in-depth or unnatural comprehension test like a think-aloud. Sipe's grounded theory categories reflect real classrooms and common reading situations. The experience is more natural and encourages students to produce the normal range of verbal reactions to the story during reading it aloud. Of course, the measure is still not a literal, direct look at students' understanding of sf, but it reflects an authentic reading and response experience along with some ways of interpreting the results.

Ultimately, Sipe's grounded theory offers a handy, well-tested set of categories for analyzing different responses as types of literary meaning-making. He acknowledges readily that there are pitfalls—such as how often silence could be significant, and that it is impossible to accurately determine a student's motivation for a comment. Regardless, he suggests that a researcher or teacher can categorize the student's group dialogue to see what kinds of responses occur. Sipe's grounded theory produced five types of response:

"analytical" response when the child talks about the text as an object; "intertextual" when the child is thinking and comparing across texts; "personal" when the child is connecting the book with their life; "transparent" response when the child merges with the story-world and responds as though a part of it; and "performative" when the child uses the text as a platform for further creativity or manipulation of the story (182). Analytical responses are further broken down into types: "making narrative meaning," or talking about setting, plot, characters, theme, peritext, structure, or speculation on plot and character thoughts; "book as made object or cultural product" when the topic of discussion is explicitly the author/illustrator's choices; "language of the text" when students read the text aloud, repeat sections of read text, ask about meaning of words, offer alternate wording, or use text to prove a point; "illustrations and visual matter" responses specifically concern the pictures and their media, arrangement, color, point of view, or background; finally responses about "relationships between fiction and reality" are about how the story relates to real life, or applying realistic thinking to a story (Sipe 111). For this project, for instance, finding intertextual responses is important as that category shows an emerging understanding of genre traits (143). Additionally, analytical responses show how the children talk through interpreting the pictures versus the words, while their personal and performative responses may show whether they connect to the alienating elements of science fiction. Each category has something to show about the children's engagement with sf texts.

Given my observation in chapter 2 that David Wiesner creates masterful speculation and extrapolation through illustrations, I chose two of his picturebooks for the read-aloud sessions: *Mr. Wuffles!* and *June 29, 1999*. While *Mr. Wuffles!* offers a read-aloud with very few words, *June 29, 1999* features paragraphs of advanced language, creating a comparison of interest between how the two are interpreted. I also chose to read *Zoe and Robot: Let's Pretend!* since this simple picturebook/early reader hybrid would offer more access to the words as well as the pictures, even across a broad range of reading abilities. Additionally, *Mr. Wuffles!* and *Zoe and Robot* both employ comics panels and speech balloons.

Results

The parental questionnaires reveal that most of these participants come from book-filled homes and homes with sf readership and fandom, indicating that these children are well positioned to comprehend sf for their own age. Of the five parental questionnaires returned, the results were consistent. All but one parent reported having 100+ books in the home. The differing parent reported having between fifty and one hundred books. Additionally, every parent reported that these household books include sf. I have no way of knowing how many are sf—and did not want to ask such a difficult question—but the presence of any sf in their home library indicates that these children are coming from an sf-friendly home environment, at least.

Four parents reported doing sf activities with their children, and the same four claimed to have sf fans in the home. The written-in explanations are listed in table 10. The parents' answers about activities indicate that at least four of the eight participants in the read-aloud sessions can be expected to have some exposure to sf intertext. Similarly, four out of eight participants have sf literacy role models at home. *Star Wars* appears in five of these eight answers, revealing that the parents regularly returned to this core genre text as an example of their home sf environment. It is true that I mention *Star Wars* as an example in the activities question, but the other common examples were not echoed in this way. Only three parents reported reading sf with or to their children, and one of them wrote in that these readings were often *Star Wars* books.

The read-aloud data demonstrates that the participating children are perfectly capable of reading quality sf. In the read-aloud sessions, the children were happy to speak about the books in ways that range through all five of Sipe's categories of read-aloud talk. Overall, their conversational turns revealed valuable literary engagement with sf, from tropes to speculation. The children interacted with the books as literary objects while also engaging with the story's speculation and extrapolation, and their comprehension and analysis were on par with Sipe's general observations.

My distribution of read-aloud codes is close to Sipe's results (see figure 14). Sipe's study found that "approximately 73% of the children's conversational turns" were analytical (85). Meanwhile, 10 percent were intertextual, 10 percent were personal, 2 percent were transparent, and 5 percent were performative (86). In my much smaller sample, the children's conversational turns were 76.81 percent analytical, 2.42 percent intertextual, 7.97 percent personal, 5.31 percent transparent, and 7.48 percent performative.

Sipe's first code, the analytical code, includes conversational turns when the children are working through the plot and meaning of the story and

**Table 10. Parental Questionnaire Questions and Answers
concerning Sf Activities and Fandom**

Question	Answers
Do you (or another adult in the home) participate in any other science fiction–themed activities with your child(ren) such as watching movies like *Star Wars*, playing science fiction video games like *Halo* or *Portal*, dressing up like aliens or robots, etc.? If yes, please briefly list some activities:	watch *Star Wars* watch *Star Wars*, princess Leia for Halloween movies, videogames, action figures, Legos watch *Star Wars*, draw or make robots
Would you describe yourself or anyone in your home as a fan of science fiction books, movies, or other media? If yes, please list who, by relation (father, sister, etc.):	little brother (4) is the biggest fan of *Star Wars* adults and children like *Star Wars* uncle—pseudo father figure because father is deceased mother, father

demonstrating their understanding. This category was the most common code to come up during Sipe's observations. It also came up the most often in my own sessions. In my three read-alouds, I had slightly more analytical conversational turns than Sipe. This is could be due to variance in sample, but it could also reflect extra interpretive effort that the children had to spend interpreting sf elements, since Sipe did not have any sf books in his study. The analytical code is significant for refuting the scholarly concern that children may not understand sf. The read-alouds demonstrated children working with their schemata and prior literacy skills to arrive at comprehension.

While reading *Zoe and Robot: Let's Pretend!* several of the children became involved in a discussion about programming in robots, based on what they knew about robotics and computer science already: in other words, applying their schemata to the text. All I had to do was read the title and show the cover to the children before they started discussing what they knew about robots as programmable technology and how that differs from human brains:

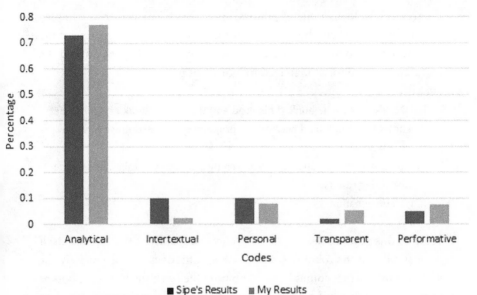

Figure 14. Percentage of codes from all three read-alouds, compared to Sipe's storytime codes.

MARIA: I think Robot has no idea about how to pretend because of the question mark above his head.

JOHN: Yeah, because they only do what's programmed in them. They don't know how to pretend! [. . .] They have no imagination. [. . .] Unless they put a BRAIN inside its head.

In this exerpt, each child's comments fit into Sipe's analytic code. Maria, a pensive girl around fourth grade, analyzed the semiotic significance of a question mark floating above a character's head and synthesized this information with the book's title. John, an enthusiastic *Star Wars* fan of the same age, carried on this thought by applying his schema about robotics and programming to explain why Robot might not be able to pretend. His next comments then speculate that programming does not include imagination, but putting an organic brain inside a robot might allow for imaginative capabilities. This conversation displays sophisticated understanding of the limits of programming and the complexity of organic brain functions.

The children returned to this same idea of programming several times throughout the reading, to explain Robot's actions. At the end of the story, the robot falls down a pile of pillows, upon which Zoe was trying to play pretend mountain-climber. The robot then surprises Zoe by successfully pretending that one pillow is a cloud. After reading this part, I asked the children how the robot managed to figure out pretending:

> JOHN: It's because he bonked his head and things got shook around so he knows how to pretend because the program got messed up so now, now he can . . .
> ME: So if you messed up a program even by accident, you might have some interesting results?
> JOHN: Imagination!

Prior to this reading session, I had not even considered that the fall itself is what allowed the robot to pretend. What John does here is precisely the sort of thinking that comes from combining the scientific view of robots as things to program and science-fictional thinking about robot potential, as discussed at the end of chapter 1.

These examples of the analytic code show how this category captures the moments when these children were working through both the plot and the speculative elements of the book. The only book with narrating words, *June 29, 1999*, had the lowest percentage of analytic conversational turns overall (see table 11). This distribution seems to speak to the books' differences in layout rather than in sf content.

The smaller word count in *Mr. Wuffles!* and *Zoe and Robot* seems to have instigated more spoken explanations of what was going on in the story. The children were happy to fill in for narration, especially when there were no words at all. Their interest in interpreting the pictures was actually directly vocalized during *June 29, 1999* when the first page was wordless:

> ME: So this is like the first page, and there's no words on it. So what do you think? What are we supposed to do with that? Should we just skip it?
> EVERYONE: No!
> RACHEL: No, that is the time to look at the picture.

Rachel, a high-energy girl around second grade, was very matter-of-fact in this moment. She had enough experiences with books to know precisely what

Table 11. Axial Coding of the Read-Alouds, Using Sipe's Codes from *Storytime*

Code	Mr. Wuffles!	June 29, 1999	Zoe and Robot
1: Analytical	131 (77.06%)	108 (71.52%)	79 (84.94%)
1a: "making narrative meaning"	110 (64.71%)	90 (59.60%)	57 (61.29%)
1b: "book as made object or cultural product"	0 (0.00%)	2 (1.32%)	0 (0.00%)
1c: "language of the text"	9 (5.29%)	5 (3.31%)	13 (13.98%)
1d: "illustrations and visual matter"	7 (4.12%)	0 (0.00%)	8 (8.60%)
1e: "relationships between fiction and reality"	5 (2.94%)	11 (7.28%)	1 (1.08%)
2: Intertextual	0 (0.00%)	10 (6.62%)	0 (0.00%)
3: Personal	9 (5.29%)	18 (11.92%)	6 (6.45%)
4: Transparent	5 (2.94%)	13 (8.61%)	4 (4.30%)
5: Performative	25 (14.71%)	2 (1.32%)	4 (4.30%)
Total Conversational Turns	170	151	93

is expected of readers when there are no words. *Mr. Wuffles!* was full of this kind of work, which is captured in Sipe's analytic subcategory 1a: "making narrative meaning." Sipe explains that "the responses in this subcategory comprised over half of the responses in Category 1: literary analysis was clearly of prime importance in the children's developing literary understanding" (91). Likewise, this subcategory comprised the majority of analytical responses in all three of my books.

Making narrative meaning, subcategory 1a, described 65 percent of the conversational turns during the reading of the mostly wordless book *Mr. Wuffles!* Due to different attendance and signups on different days of the afterschool program, there were only two participants present for reading *Mr. Wuffles!*: John and a bubbly kindergartner, Celia. The panels in this story are numerous, with sometimes only seconds or moments passing between panels. I found that John and Celia were quick to zip through small action panels until they found an interesting panel to talk about or I directed their attention to one. Full-page spreads brought on the most conversation, due to having the largest space for closure and the most details. Upon turning to the page where the aliens find the insect's wall drawings under the radiator, we had the following conversation:

> ME: What did they find under there?
> CELIA: Scary stuff and weird stuff.
> ME: Yeah.
> JOHN: They found ancient drawings.
> ME: Ancient scary drawings?
> JOHN: By the ancient cave ants, or ancient cave bugs.
> ME: Oh, it's the bugs that drew all these? How do you think the bugs feel about the cat?
> JOHN: They feel like they want to battle him.

Celia's response reveals her competence in interpreting illustrations, since she reads the tone of the picture. Her two choices of "scary" and "weird" acknowledged that the cave paintings look violent and that these paintings are an unexpected thing to find under furniture. John's analysis applied art and anthropology to recognize the naive art style as an allusion to cave painting. He then noted the insects on the far right of the page and extended his interpretation to conclude that they are the artists and, by extension, also ancient and cave-based. He then noted the tone of the spread—or accepted Celia's interpretation—when he decided that the drawings are hostile and indicate a desire for battle. They extracted valuable information about the characters in this story while talking through this spread.

Celia and John were highly competent at deciphering Wiesner's detailed art and interpreting the panel transitions. However, their analysis misinterpreted the most extrapolative part of the book: the set of discs that appear to be a crucial part of flying the spaceship. I pointed out the alien's broken power-discs when they first appear, and we had the following exchange:

> ME: What's that, you think?
> CELIA: Um, it's something to—
> JOHN: Oh, I know! A broken artifact.

ME: Hm!

JOHN: Or, you know, a broken plate because someone was just pretty angry at dinner.

[CELIA and I laugh]

CELIA: Oh, I know this one! Um, the cat is getting up and all they're thinking, "Oh no, our plates are broken!"

ME: That would be a funny thing to focus on, if you were being attacked by a cat.

Plates! Over here they're looking at the plates again.

JOHN: They're thinking, "Jeez somebody was pretty angry at dinner."

John's use of the word "artifact" draws on the phrase "alien artifact" as a term found in sf stories or historical mysteries about finding aliens or ancient clues about aliens. He used his schema to interpret this story, making this an analytical response rather than an intertextual one. He then offered another, sillier interpretation about dinner plates. Celia's response took up John's humor while also recognizing that it would be absurd to be mourning broken plates while a giant predator looms nearby.

I did not correct them or push them to understand my own interpretation of the discs. After all, my undergraduate children's literature students usually develop a solid hypothesis about the discs only on their second or third readthrough! More importantly, Celia and John did not focus for long on the mystery of what these objects were or why the aliens cared about them. Their lack of deep understanding was quickly glossed over with humor, and they continued reading without consequence. They missed out on the plot point that the broken discs prevented the aliens from flying away immediately, and the potential extrapolation about future technology when the aliens slice replacement discs. Yet this absence did not seem to faze either child or impede their enjoyment of the story. As sf reading protocols require, they moved on and waited to see if it would be clearer later. Most importantly, this confusion did nothing to hinder their access to the speculative question about alien encounters. In the end, both John and Celia responded to the final image by speculating on how the alien visit made an impact. Celia said, "They changed it, they did." She was likely referring to the insects' new cave drawing, which depicts the recent battle and the aliens. John reiterated her statement with one profound alteration: "They changed." John's simple sentence encapsulates a lot of alien encounter speculation and indicates that he has noticed that this book has the type of broad, altered ending that Mendlesohn hopes for in sf.

While Sipe's narrative meaning code was common, his code 1b, "book as made object or cultural product," came up in only one book, *June 29, 1999.* Rachel noted that it looked like "an old-school book," and Maria wanted to know why Wiesner did not add a timeline to the same book. These responses display familiarity with books in general and with the informative illustrations found in nonfiction books.

The children's analytic work during the *Zoe and Robot* read-aloud was more heavily directed at reading and interpreting the speech bubbles, as captured by the much higher percentage of code 1c, "language of the text." This code captures instances of children reading the words aloud, asking language-specific questions, and debating the meaning of words. In *Zoe and Robot,* there are speech balloons in nearly every panel, and these contain early-reader-level words. Several of the 1c conversational turns were focused on how to read robot dialogue. When I turned to the first page of *Zoe and Robot,* Maria spontaneously read the robot's speech balloon aloud in a robotic monotone:

MARIA: [robotic voice] "No, Zoe. Robots cannot climb mountains."
ME: Oh, robot voice. Why do you know to do a robot voice?
MARIA: I don't know.

Maria could have been picking up on the all-caps way that Robot's dialogue is written, but it is more common for all-caps to be interpreted as shouting. Her impromptu vocalization adeptly interprets language and signification, drawing on the intertext for experiences with pop culture robots and the semiotics of written language. Even though real robots like automatic vacuums are becoming household items, these rarely have monotone robotic voices like the robots of cartoons and movies. Her exposure to pop culture robots is broad enough that she could not even name what source she is relying on for her robot voice. Throughout the story, several other students also tried their hand at reading the text with their own robot voice.

Sipe's subcategory 1d, "illustrations and visual matter," came up infrequently. This code does not refer to reading the pictures for meaning—that is part of 1a—but rather it refers to talk about the style, layout, and art choices. We discussed the backgrounds in *Zoe and Robot* and the way that the artist drew multiple cat tails to demonstrate movement in *Mr. Wuffles!*, but *June 29, 1999* did not elicit this type of conversation at all, perhaps due to its more conventional illustration choices and layout.

In contrast, Sipe's subcategory 1e, "relationships between fiction and reality," came up most often during the reading of *June 29, 1999*. This book is speculative and outlandish from the beginning, but there are no overtly sf tropes until the end. Until then, it could just as easily have been fantasy. This genre uncertainty provoked mild interpretive tension between some of the children. John was convinced that aliens were involved from the start, but Mackenzie, a reserved older girl, constantly refuted his predictions and attempted to shut down anyone who repeated it, on the grounds that aliens do not exist. There are also no giant vegetables falling from the sky in our reality, but this plot point did not receive her criticism. The other books that we read had obvious sf tropes from early in the plot, but the aliens of *June 29, 1999* are withheld as a surprise on the last two pages. This late reveal seems to have exposed Mackenzie's resistance to sf tropes but not to fantastic premises. For Mackenzie, aliens were a less desirable explanation than just about anything else, and she missed clues that other students noticed because she was so resistant to an sf explanation. While no one else but John explicitly said they were sf fans, the other younger students did not show this resistance to sf. Mackenzie was the oldest participant in the read-alouds and may have had more exposure to bias against sf.

My percentage of intertextual codes was much lower than Sipe's. Sipe explains that this category helps readers develop an awareness of text sets and genres, similar to my discussion of sf intertextual tropes and schemata in chapter 2. Some of the difference between my results and Sipe's can be attributed to sample size, but I also noticed that the children were displaying their intertextual understanding in ways other than the explicit comparisons that would be coded as intertextual in Sipe's system. When the children read Robot's dialogue in robot voices, for instance, their analysis of the language depended on their intertextual knowledge of robots, but since they did not talk directly about other robot stories, these conversational turns were not coded as intertextual.

Sipe's intertextual code came up twice in the read-alouds, both times during the read-aloud for *June 29, 1999*. First, after I read the title on the cover, Mackenzie commented, "It sounds like a horror movie," though she did not offer any explanation. Later, the other children took up this idea again when we reached the inside title page:

JOHN: This sounds like, this sounds like one of those movies that's like "there's an Armageddon happening," because it's like June 29, 1999. That sounds, that sounds . . .

ME: Does that really specific date make it sound menacing like we were saying before?

RACHEL: That sounds like a horror movie!

JOHN: That sounds like a horror movie like *Friday the 13th*.

In this excerpt John compares Wiesner's book to an entire set of apocalyptic stories as well as to a specific horror film, *Friday the 13th* (1980). This movie is not sf, but the horror genre is often grouped with fantasy and sf under the speculative fiction umbrella. The connection is worthwhile for John's analysis, as it allowed him to reflect on how a specific date seems to point to a large event. Large, world-shifting events often cause the novums of sf. Later in *June 29, 1999*, when the illustrations show giant vegetables falling from the sky, Maria compared the story to a popular fantasy story: "It's like *Cloudy with a Chance of Meatballs!*" Whether she meant the book or the movie, she was performing the same work of comparing across the fantastic. In this way a knowledge of other speculative fiction genres might factor into children's interpretations as they work to comprehend sf books.

The only specifically sf intertextual connection was also a conversation about scientific language. When Wiesner threw the phrase "extraterrestrial conditions" at us, not only did we have a silly tongue-twister moment, but the children wove together sf intertext with scientific language and speculation:

ME: What are extrater—extraterre—I can't even say it! Extraterrestrial conditions.

JOHN: I'm pretty sure it's something to do with aliens.

ME: Alien conditions?

JOHN: Because I'm pretty sure E.T., he stands for extraterrestrial.

ME: Oh, yeah, so thinking of the E. T. movie, if E. T. means extraterrestrial, then that associates it with aliens, yeah.

MACKENZIE: I feel like extraterrestr— . . .

JOHN: terrestr—

MACKENZIE: terre—"extraterrestrial" might be a word for growing things or like earth forming?

RACHEL: Now—

ME: Oh, yeah, that word "Terra" is in there, and that means Earth.

RACHEL: Now that we got more into the story, I think they're sending food to aliens.

ME: They're sending food to aliens?

RACHEL: I think so.

MACKENZIE: There's no aliens . . .

Here, again, John was happy to jump into sf concepts with aliens, through a clever intertextual interpretation. *E. T. the Extra-Terrestrial* (1982) draws clear associations between the term "extraterrestrial" and aliens, and so John wielded this popular culture connection to help him define a large, scientific term. Mackenzie took a more strictly scientific route, making connections to the root word "terra," which I can only assume she had heard in other agricultural and scientific contexts. As the oldest student present, Mackenzie would have had the highest accumulation of science classes and more exposure to scientific terms. Meanwhile, Rachel ignored Mackenzie's definition. Her response returned to the analytic mode to combine John's alien connection with the plot thus far in an attempt to predict the ending, an example of the most popular analytic subcode 1a: making narrative meaning. Mackenzie is not willing to abandon known science and realism, however. Her response, as noted above, falls into the analytic subcategory 1e: the relationship between fiction and reality.

While my participants were not explicitly talking about intertextual comparisons, even this talk following John's connection reveals an underlying understanding of tropes like aliens. Mackenzie and Rachel both knew, without hesitation, what an alien was. Mackenzie was aware that they are not a scientifically proven idea, and Rachel's response reveals that she knows that aliens are associated with space—since the food was being sent up in balloons. While Sipe's coding scheme does not acknowledge that their knowledge here is inherently intertextual, they are relying on their schemata in order to produce their analysis.

Next, the personal category of response reveals personal connections to the story. Sipe explains, "If children draw the story to themselves in these easy and down-to-earth ways, and are not discouraged by their teachers, they may develop the ability to make much more important and meaningful connections as they become more astute and sensitive readers" (153). Sipe warns not to treat this category as insignificant, since it teaches the ability to apply stories to life situations. Comprehension education specialists like McGregor refer to this type of response as "text-to-self connections" and consider it to be a valuable comprehension strategy for applying schema to a story (36). This category can seem trivial, but it captures children's reflections about the way that the sf world is similar yet dissimilar to their own world, encouraging them to reflect on the novums and cognitive estrangement of sf. This code was most popular in the reading of *June 29, 1999*. The children were excited that they knew the vegetables, and several shouted out when the pictures revealed a vegetable that they personally enjoy:

> RACHEL: [gasp] I love lima beans!
> JOHN: I like cucumbers. I'd probably just go home and eat it.
> ME: Oh, you'd just eat it?
> RACHEL: Mmmm, lima beans.
> ME: Would you want a gigantic lima bean?
> RACHEL: YEAH, I would just eat it! [munching sounds]

While this category of response does not reveal much in terms of how children are understanding the science or speculation of the story, it shows that they became invested in the story enough to imagine themselves in the story-world. This personalizing speculation reflects some of Mendlesohn's and Nodelman's concern that children's literature is inward focused, because at this moment the children were not concerned with the larger consequences of a world covered in giant vegetables. They were expressing their individual likes and dislikes. Yet these children were taking up the speculation, merely on a small scale. They wondered what they would do were the strange events to happen to them, and they concluded that giant vegetables were unusual but still, in the end, vegetables. After all, many advanced sf books function well because they challenge the reader to step into alternate points of view. The children's focus may have been on only one tiny piece of the speculative content, but it became a scaffolded version of a more advanced sf thought experiment.

The last two codes, the transparent and performative categories, are similar. Sipe explains that "they represent two different, contrasting enactments of what I call the aesthetic impulse" (169). In my read-alouds, both types of aesthetic response reflect children engaging with the awe and wonder of sf. Transparent responses are the "receptive aspect," and performative responses are the "expressive aspect" of the aesthetic impulse (180).

The transparent category includes moments wherein the children are fully "immersed in the storyworld" (Sipe 173), experiencing and reacting to Istvan Csicsery-Ronay's science-fictional sublime and Joan Gordon's statement that quality sf includes "that nebulous attribute, a sense of wonder" (2). Transparent conversational turns can demonstrate only the audible evidence of a child's absorption, "providing only tantalizing glimpses of what was probably happening inside the children's minds" (Sipe 86). This also makes it the most subjective to code. I had to evaluate whether I thought the child was reacting reflexively due to being absorbed in the story, or if they were performing for peers.

In the read-alouds, transparent talk most often manifested as exclamations upon the page turn, revealing the power of this paratextual element. On the first few page turns of *June 29, 1999* there was a chorus of shouts and screams and Rachel frequently exclaimed "OH MY GOODNESS" at each new giant vegetable. Even our group's resident skeptic, Mackenzie, murmured "really big . . . " when the first batch of enormous vegetables was revealed. Similarly, during the reading of *Mr. Wuffles!*, both John and Celia held out a long "ooohhh" on the page turn that revealed the insects' cave painting. These transparent responses are testaments to Wiesner's mastery of the page turn as a means of capturing the awe and wonder of sf. In contrast, Sias's illustrations evoked character-driven joy. When Robot finally succeeded at pretending, Rachel and Maria both exclaimed, "Yay!" This response is equally transparent, but less to do with sf awe. Sias's book is meant to be domestic and familiar, however, so this is not a surprising or even unintentional lack. Overall, my sessions produced more transparent responses than Sipe's, perhaps due to the valued quality of wonder of sf.

Finally, the performative category, Sipe explains, is the least likely to be encouraged or tolerated in literary settings. On the surface, the performative category seems to contain irrelevant or analytically useless responses from the students. These "responses were often mildly (or wickedly) subversive and transgressive; in some quarters, they would probably be considered totally off-task. They threatened to deconstruct the story into a totally free (and in some cases anarchic) play of signifiers" (Sipe 174). Yet understanding and active interpretation are preconditions for these performances. Sipe claims, "If, as I have argued, the findings of these studies indicate that the children were astute literary critics and displayed various types of literary understanding, the children's performative responses display their abilities as specifically *deconstructive* literary critics" (180, emphasis in original). This code is particularly interesting, as it shows that adult biases are not exclusive to sf but apply to children's literary engagement more broadly. Sipe noted that children were doing very clever things in their performative talk, but the teachers in his study had to be willing to allow it and then to see past the apparent raucousness to appreciate the children's interpretive work. Similarly, adults may have to look beyond the obvious to see evidence of children understanding sf.

The picturebook with the most performative responses by far was *Mr. Wuffles!* After the first alien speech balloons appeared, John said:

JOHN: "Waaa!" That's what I think that says

ME: You think that says "Waaa!" Why do you think that?

JOHN: I don't knoooow.

ME: Could you read this?

CELIA: [silly nonsense noises]

ME: Hm! It could say that. I definitely can't read it. What do you think they're doing?

CELIA: Um. They're making something, like a trap for the cat. Or the cat wouldn't like it. I can read those, I think. [pointing to the next alien speech bubbles]

John's interpretation of the first speech bubble sounded like a cry of surprise and had a solid basis in the illustrations: the aliens' hands are thrown up in the air, with wide eyes and open mouths. His drawn-out "I don't knoooow," accompanied by a bashful smile, indicated that he knew he had done something silly and was waiting to see how I would respond to his performance.

When I encouraged the performance by asking whether they could read the symbols, Celia ran with it. Even when I tried to steer us back to the next panel by asking what the aliens were doing, she answered quickly and then went back to the speech bubbles and how she could read them. Her phrasing "I can read those, I think" is almost an exact reversal of my prior statement "I definitely can't read it." Sipe says that several aspects of Mikhail Bakhtin's carnival apply to the performative code, including "the common people assume roles of power usually held by their masters" (180). Celia's performances reveal delight in being able to do what I—the adult and supposed expert reader—could not do. From that point on, Celia was determined to vocalize dialogue for every single balloon in the book. Her alien speech consisted of a series of squeals, pops, shrieks, beeps, and some monkeylike noises. John's occasional contributions indicated that he accepted without question that Celia's performances were valid and sought to support them, even though she was significantly younger:

> CELIA: I can read these ones, I think! And this one says, and that one says
> . . . [silly noises]
> ME: Why do you think that's that one? [pointing to last panel, which got a
> screamlike reading]
> JOHN: Because because they look scared!

John had noticed that Celia's alien language was informed by the expressions of the aliens in the panel. She interpreted their facial cues and expressed her analysis through the tone of her noises. At times John also offered recommendations for her performances based on his more advanced knowledge of written language as an older student, such as when he noted, "I don't think that one would be [exclamatory nonsense sound]. I think that would be [questioning nonsense sound], because there's a question mark." At one point, he experimented with transposing Wiesner's set of geometric shapes into phonemes based on association: "That one looks like it says [carefully enunciated nonsense word], because that one looks like an eight, that one looks like a D, that one looks like an O." The intentional, evidence-based nature of Celia's and John's sounds became even clearer when we reached the insects' speech balloons:

> ME: What do you think—this looks different. How do you think the ants talk?
> JOHN and CELIA, together: [skittering noises]
> ME: Oh, yeah! Like little bug skittering noises? [laughs as they both continue
> making noises] It's kind of scary sounding! What's happening over here?
> CELIA: Oh, it's saying [alien noises].
> ME: And what's the bug saying?
> CELIA and JOHN, together: [skittering sounds]
> ME: Do you think they can talk to each other? Do they understand each other?
> JOHN: Probably.
> CELIA: I think they kind of do.

Their performance of insect language sounded completely different from the aliens, reflecting the different shape and content of Wiesner's speech bubbles. It incorporated a knowledge of insects, and their conclusions about the alien-to-insect communication derived from the series of conversations depicted across the panels on that page. It even led to some surprising speculation when John wondered if the bugs were aliens too.

John's and Celia's performances were informed by the context of the image and revealed analysis and expression all at once. They were not talking to me in measured, academic language about their interpretation. They did not translate the alien and insect speech bubbles into English. Yet their subversive "reading" performance revealed inferences and critical reading, even as they took joy in flooding our read-aloud with silly sounds.

Sipe's transparent and performative codes describe aesthetic responses, and in total the children's conversational turns were 5.31% transparent and 7.48% performative. These results are two to three percentage points higher than Sipe's overall observations, indicating that the children in this study were more aesthetically engaged in these sf books than might be expected from an average read-aloud.

Discussion

The read-aloud data show that these children were capable and willing to delve into analyzing and enjoying sf. They engaged in a variety of valuable literary conversations about sf picturebooks. Their talk ranged from insightful to enthralled, indicating that sf can be understood and enjoyed by these children. Considering the participants' home sf environment, as indicated by the questionnaires, they are probably representative of well-prepared children who have a decent sf schema. Others with less-literary home environments, less exposure to the sf intertext, and fewer sf role models may not produce the same quality of read-aloud talk. These read-alouds offer a detailed glimpse into the comprehension and engagement of several children on the higher end of sf preparedness—a picture of what is possible for primary sf, given good conditions.

CONCLUSION

Overall, this case study suggests that sf is accessible and desirable to children but limited by the adult perceptions that reinforce stereotypes and potentially

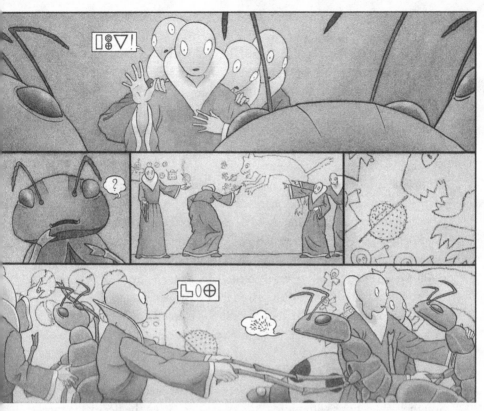

Figure 15. The speech bubbles in *Mr. Wuffles!* are open to interpretation. *Mr. Wuffles!* by David Wiesner. Clarion Books, 2013.

keep availability low. The children in the read-alouds aptly applied both their general literary skills and their intertextual awareness of sf to the stories to interpret them. They displayed great interpretation skills and compensated for the challenges of sf. The examples of the analytical code in the read-alouds, in particular, demonstrate that the children could parse the words, illustrations, and general plot in these examples of primary sf, while also accessing the science-fictional thought. The read-alouds were conducted with picturebooks, but the surveyed professionals who said that sf is too complex and challenging for use in group activities were talking about chapter books and novels. Practicing sf skills on picturebooks can be carried forward into these longer and more text-heavy sf books, but teachers and librarians must first provide this opportunity to develop sf reading skills through choosing sf picturebooks for storytime, even with older children.

Meanwhile, the library lending results indicate that American elementary children appear to be reading sf, but the production does not meet the demand. The children could make discriminating choices from the variety of titles in the other genres, but they had to compensate for the low availability of primary sf by concentrating their readership on fewer titles. Since adults control production, this is not surprising. If the prevailing discourse is that children do not or cannot read sf, then there is no motivation to create or acquire more of it. If the demand is invisible, then even the low availability is not going to change. The low availability seems to be common knowledge among librarians and scholars, but not the demand. In my survey 32 percent of the teachers and librarians reported that they did not use or recommend sf in their classrooms and libraries due to having few books to choose from, especially at lower grade levels. Only one individual reported that she never recommends sf, but she blamed this on a lack of available books for her grade level. Meanwhile, the librarians who contributed their checkout records for my circulation study were unsurprised by the low percentage of sf, but they were surprised by the high concentration of readership. While librarians usually take their circulation trends into account when acquiring new books, none of the libraries' databases categorized the books by genre, and so they had no way of knowing how many of their checkouts were sf books. Without this information, these librarians are not using their precious resources to fill out their collections with more primary sf titles. Given the nearly identical percentages of genres across all the libraries in my study, these librarians seem to be following commonplace, tried-and-true patterns of acquisition. Sticking to these patterns also reinforces the low availability of sf. Children's book publishers, who rely heavily on libraries, do not want to produce books for a low demand. A small publisher of children's and YA sf and fantasy told me that the sf titles sell the least, and so they do not regularly acquire books in that genre.

The surveyed professionals clearly recognize the benefits of sf and want to treat it as an equal literacy opportunity, but they may be affected by lingering biases that then become passed on to their students. Yet sf is not as "weird" as it used to be. In the words of Neil Gaiman, "Nowadays, people own their nerd-dom" (qtd. in Westcott). Professionals may need to adjust subtle aspects of their classroom and library practice to avoid stigmatizing the genre. If librarians and teachers do not use it in activities, then this lack of academic endorsement and usage makes sf less visible and less modeled to children as valuable literature. Even if home environments include sf representation, the disparity between home and "official" literacy arenas may depict sf as only for pleasure reading. This disparity risks perpetuating old ideas of sf as exclusionary or frivolous reading material, which might dissuade young readers and other professionals from taking the genre seriously. This, in turn, only supports the assumption that the genre is divisive, or only for personal reading, as seen in the survey results. Young readers will likely keep reading it anyway, but with the impression that it is not worth thinking about—effectively undermining the benefits of science-fictional thinking and leading to situations like Gavaler and Johnson's study of poor adult sf reading comprehension. In addition, the attitudes about sf held by librarians and teachers can reinforce the negative concept of sf held by scholars and editors. This entire system of assumptions among editors, publishers, librarians, teachers, and scholars runs the risk of being a closed loop, without ever once reflecting the actual reading desires of many children.

CONCLUSION

Contemporary children are finding and reading sf regardless of adult concerns, seizing control of their literacy choices within the adult-controlled framework of available books. Poorly rendered primary sf may sate some children, but quality primary sf is important for developing science-fictional thinking and practicing the sf reading protocols needed for more advanced literature. As the previous chapters have shown, adults must be willing to challenge several dearly held beliefs—not just Romantic notions of childhood but also the related exclusionary definitions of sf that impose unnecessary restrictions on primary sf—for primary sf to expand beyond its current status.

One potent example of genre ostracism became unexpectedly significant as this project developed: the case of *Star Wars*. This example demonstrates how adult beliefs about the boundaries of genre and the limits and interests of childhood can undermine potentially beneficial primary sf. While working on this book, I have received many passionate—and occasionally condescending—lectures about how *Star Wars* is really fantasy and not sf at all. As discussed in chapter 1, this reaction is an example of confusing the projects of defining the genre with evaluating it. At the heart of it, this type of genre denial attempts to validate sf as a serious genre by elevating it above the popular and the fantastic. While there is certainly merit to discussing the fantasy elements of *Star Wars*, denying its obvious sf tropes and its key place in pop culture's understanding of sf is not helpful.

Star Wars became increasingly significant for this project with each new source of data. This extensive story-world came up in each of the three data sources, often without provocation. In the survey results, the teachers and librarians did not mention many specific texts by name, but when they did mention anything, it was usually *Star Wars*. Two respondents mentioned *Star Wars* by name when explaining how they recommend books, four mentioned using *Star Wars* to identify potential sf readers, and one mentioned *Star Wars* while talking about how sf is great for engaging "reluctant readers." In the parental questionnaires for the read-alouds, the parents also mentioned *Star Wars* by name in four out of five responses. One of my read-aloud participants, John, proclaimed himself a *Star Wars* fan and eagerly showed me his newest *Star Wars: Rogue One* informational book after the reading sessions. Even though *Star Wars* was not mentioned during the read-aloud recordings, this context was informative, since John was one of the most active and reflective participants.

While coding the data for the library circulation study, I had noticed many different *Star Wars* books from a variety of series that all seemed to be getting high numbers of checkouts. After noticing how *Star Wars* kept coming up in the other two studies, I returned to these data and coded these books as a separate variable at the last minute. As described in chapter 4, it turns out that the *Star Wars* books accounted for only 13 percent of the sf titles, but 25 percent of the sf checkouts. These books by themselves received over double the average circulations of the other sf books. The *Star Wars* books were not carrying the circulations for the entire genre, but the high average circulations demonstrate that sf readership is more intense around this story-world.

I also noticed *Star Wars* was a significant presence while collecting my sample of 357 heavily illustrated primary sf books. I set a limit of three books from a single series, but I put no limit on books from the same story-world. There are enough different *Star Wars* series that the sample includes four early readers, two picturebooks, and one graphic novel. One of the early readers is a mashup, *Angry Birds Star Wars: Yoda Bird's Heroes* (2013), which demonstrates that *Star Wars* is such a pervasive cultural text that publishers expect level-one new readers to enjoy mashups and puns between the characters from the first *Star Wars* film trilogy (1977, 1980, 1983) and the relatively new *Angry Birds* (2009) characters. Other examples like Jane Yolen's *Commander Toad in Space* (1996) and Elys Dolan's *Nuts in Space* (2014) make references to *Star Wars*, among other core sf texts.

Star Wars was clearly an important reference point for the sf intertext and probably accounts for a large portion of many children's genre schemata. Yet, of the official *Star Wars* brand books in the sample, only the books with original trilogy characters have demonstrable extrapolation/speculation. The books based on the first films, like *Star Wars: The Mystery of the Rebellious Robot* (1979) and *Star Wars: The Maverick Moon* (1979), feature situation-based plots, while *Star Wars: Finn and Poe Team Up!* (2016) and *Star Wars: Rey Meets BB-8* (2015) show characters interacting with one another. Even recent books based on old characters, like *Star Wars: Trapped in the Death Star!* (2016), include speculation and/or extrapolation through a focus on the situation or event. Recent books with brand-new characters outside the movies, like book 1 of *Star Wars: Jedi Academy* (2013), also did not include speculation/extrapolation. The stories with old characters tend to be all about what the characters are doing, not who they are. The writers seem to assume that children will already know the characters of the old films and therefore do not require an introduction. There seems to be more space for speculation in a story about a situation than a story introducing characters. This may reflect on Disney's interest in selling new characters, more than an interest in telling thought-provoking stories.

What the case of *Star Wars* indicates most, in the context of this study, is that this expansive story-world holds a lot of responsibility for children's intertextual familiarity with sf. Primary sf is already a limited pool with con-centrated readership, and the popularity of *Star Wars* further focuses that readership in one area. Its popularity is not necessarily a problem, but the speculative sf content of these books may not encourage sf reading beyond the brand. Given how frequently *Star Wars* came up during my research, these books should be evaluated carefully in terms of whether they develop the reader's science-fictional thinking and skills. Disney is unlikely to change its strategy anytime soon, but teachers, librarians, and parents can choose to buy and recommend those *Star Wars* books that do engage in speculation. After all, the films—despite being space opera and often dismissed by hardline sf definers—offer plenty of speculation about the reach of government power, the ethics of rebellions, the use of advanced technology for weapons, and so forth. If this speculative content in the films does not deter children, then there is no reason to think that children cannot enjoy these ideas in books, too.

PRIMARY SCIENCE FICTION IS THE FUTURE

Clearly primary sf is possible. However, it is scarce. In this respect I com-pletely agree with previous commentary. Nodelman writes of the "shortage of good SF for young readers" ("Out There" 294). Levy comments that for readers under twelve, "there is relatively little" (421). Mendlesohn writes that there is "nowhere near enough" (*Intergalactic* 4). My data also reflect this scarcity. The library circulation data show that sf represents, on average, only 3 percent of the circulated titles, and the survey respondents complained of having few books to choose from. In comparison to other genres—especially sf's sister genre, fantasy—there are simply fewer primary sf books. When the available supply of books is so small, the poor-quality examples are more pronounced. This may feed into the impression that primary sf is poor sf, as described in chapter 1. This bad impression, in turn, only reinforces the cultural narratives that science in sf is too hard or not interesting to children, which surfaces even in the survey responses.

Yet, given the evidence that primary sf can and does include high-quality and inclusive titles for a range of literacy levels, the scarcity of primary sf is a call to action, rather than cause for despair. Adults may not be able to—and probably should not—try to control children's reading of sf, but instead we can work to improve the availability, quality, and diversity of primary sf books. More than anything else, I am calling for adults to use their power as adults to give a boost to primary sf so that it represents the best that the genre can offer.

First, this means rejecting limiting theories of childhood that sow doubt about childhood abilities and interests. Scholars can contribute through more research with real children in order to ground our ideas about the sf genre in real children rather than ideological ones. On the practitioner level, if primary sf is receiving the highly concentrated lending shown in my library circulation results because of the low number of available titles, then librarians and teachers have good reason to expand their sf holdings. They must have faith that children will read these titles, and they must also make sure that their usage and presentation of these books do not communicate negative biases.

Second, adults need to give adequate attention to primary sf books that are high quality and represent various identities. As librarians and teachers expand their collections to include more primary sf, this is also a great opportunity for the demand to be filled not just with any books but with more high-quality, inclusive titles in particular. Books that demonstrate good gender and diversity representation are a small part of my sample, but there were more available, proportionally, than in children's literature at large. These exemplar books are worth seeking out. The act of seeking them out may even increase their production if publishers take note. I hope to have begun that work throughout this book, and appendix B features a list of recommendations.

In the end, it turns out that children read what they want to without any regard for what scholars write about those books. We cannot simply declare that primary sf is impossible and throw our hands up in defeat. With all these young people already out there reading primary sf, everyone involved in children's literature has a responsibility to make sure that the available books are rich with sf value and welcoming to all literary space cadets.

APPENDIX A

This appendix describes and then lists the 357 primary sf books read and analyzed for this study. I gathered this pool of primary sf books from online children's literature blogs, book-rating websites like *Goodreads*, librarian suggestions, books mentioned in appendix D of Mendlesohn's *The Intergalactic Playground*, child_lit listserv suggestions, and ideas from other colleagues. There were three limitations to the books included:

1. Had to be sf, defined as in chapter 1
2. Had to be significantly illustrated
3. No more than three books in the same series

As explained in chapter 2, limiting this list to illustrated books productively skews the sample toward the younger age range. Including no more than three books from a series prevented the overrepresentation of comic books that have run for over fifty years and several other series of over twenty books. While not a formal limitation, all the books included had to be available in English or Spanish due to the practical need for me to be able to read them. I also tried to choose books from the beginning of a series when possible.

I kept looking for and reading examples of primary sf until reaching saturation, or when new books became rare and did not add anything different. This process resulted in 357 books. The books hailed mostly from the United States (303), with others from England (34), Canada (10), Australia (4), France (2), Japan (2), New Zealand (1), and Scotland (1). Most of

Table 12. Primary Sf Book Sample by Decade and Format

Decade	Picturebooks	Early Readers	Comic Books	Graphic Novels	Hybrid Novels	Total
1920S	1	0	1	0	0	2
1930S	0	0	6	0	0	6
1940S	0	0	20	0	0	20
1950S	0	1	23	0	0	24
1960S	0	1	19	0	0	20
1970S	8	0	8	1	1	18
1980S	18	5	4	1	0	28
1990S	22	5	1	0	0	28
2000S	71	8	11	9	4	103
2010S	44	18	9	23	14	108
Total	164	38	102	34	19	357

them were picturebooks (164), along with comic books (102), early readers (38), graphic novels (34), and hybrid novels (19). The sample covers ninety years, from 1926 to 2016. Two-thirds of the initial publication dates were from 2000 and later, and most of the primary sf books in the sample that were published prior to 1970 were comic books (see table 12). Due to the limitations on series and attempting to get books from the beginning of series, many long-running comics were represented in the earlier decades. A longitudinal study of the changes within individual comics over time was outside the scope of this study.

Different formats had different relationships with sf quality, female characters, and diversity, as analyzed in chapter 3. Post hoc comparisons from the logistic regression (see tables 13–15) demonstrate that graphic novels and hybrid novels performed particularly well in this sample.

There was no apparent relationship between the sf quality and the country of origin or publisher, and even the date of publication did not have a large impact on the quality. A Pearson correlation test (see table 16) shows that sf quality does not have a demonstrable relationship with the decade in which the book was originally printed. The correlation is very weak ($r = 0.00181$) and is not statistically significant from zero ($F(1, 355) = 0.001, p = 0.97281$). This means that statistically speaking, the time of publication has no noticeable effect on sf quality. As mentioned in chapter 3, sf quality does have a

Table 13. Post hoc Comparisons from Logistic Regression of Sf Quality with Format, Using Benjamini-Hochberg Adjustment

	Early Readers	Comic Books	Graphic Novels	Hybrid Novels
Picturebooks	0.524	-0.108	-2.142*	-0.692
Early readers		-0.632	2.667**	1.216
Comic books			2.035†	0.584
Graphic novels				-1.451

**indicates the mean difference is significant at the 0.01 level *0.05 level. †0.1 level

Table 14. Post hoc Comparisons from Logistic Regression of Female Characters with Format, Using Benjamini-Hochberg Adjustment

	Early Readers	Comic Books	Graphic Novels	Hybrid Novels
Picturebooks	-0.199	-0.116	-1.875***	-2.175**
Early readers		0.084	1.676**	1.976*
Comic books			1.760***	2.060**
Graphic novels				0.300

*indicates the mean difference is significant at the $p < 0.05$ level **0.01 level. ***0.001 level

Table 15. Post hoc Comparisons from Logistic Regression of Diversity with Format, Using Benjamini-Hochberg Adjustment

	Early Readers	Comic Books	Graphic Novels	Hybrid Novels
Picturebooks	-0.169	0.411	-1.081†	-0.880
Early readers		0.580	0.912	0.711
Comic books			1.492**	1.291
Graphic novels				-0.201

**indicates the mean difference is significant at the $p < 0.05$ level. †indicates 0.1 level

positive, statistically significant relationship with both the female characters ($r = 0.17372$) and diversity variables ($r = 0.21229$).

Given Mendlesohn's focus on the historical shifts to science and sf for children, it is interesting that sf quality did not change enough across the

**Table 16. Pearson Correlation Probability Matrix of
Sf Quality, Female Characters, Diversity, and Decade**

	Female Characters	Diversity	Decade
Sf quality	$r = 0.13764$ $F = 6.856$ $p = 0.00922$	$r = 0.0475$ $F = 0.803$ $p = 0.37087$	$r = 0.00181$ $F = 0.001$ $p = 0.97281$
Female characters		$r = 0.2583$ $F = 25.378$ $p < 0.001$	$r = 0.17372$ $F = 11.047$ $p < 0.001$
Diversity			$r = 0.21229$ $F = 16.755$ $p < 0.001$

$df = (1, 355)$

ninety-year publication timeline to register on a statistical measure. Mendle-sohn explains that publishers changed their approach to sf around 1960, when they also transitioned from the "juvenile" to "young adult" labels. The books in my sample have publication dates ranging from 1926 to 2016, and the percentage of books that include speculation and extrapolation rises between the 1950s and the 1970s (see figure 16). Only in the 1980s does it drop sharply. Mendlesohn's observations about the shift in quality in the 1960s, however, are referring to books for older children and teens. These changing publication attitudes may not have affected primary sf as much. Despite some jumps, each decade shows a total of over 60 percent of the books passing the test for speculation/extrapolation as described in chapter 1, except for the 1940s, when it drops suddenly to 35 percent.

The 1940s group consisted of twenty comic books, of which thirteen did not pass the test. Significantly, they were all similar in theme. Many of them told stories about an upstanding citizen who gains a superpower—often atomic power—and uses this to foil Nazi schemes. The covers, like that of *Startling Comics* No. 27 in 1944, prominently display a superhero punching a Nazi in the face. However, the thirteen stories that failed the test did not include extrapolation about how these atomic powers work or speculation as to why atomic powers are particularly well suited to Nazi-punching. Mean-while, *Atoman* No. 1 in 1946 passes the test because the eponymous hero won-ders if increased nuclear testing and bomb usage will create more radioactive people with his power, and how to ethically use such power. Other Nazi stories without superheroes, like "Poison in the Universe" in *All New Comics* Vol. 1

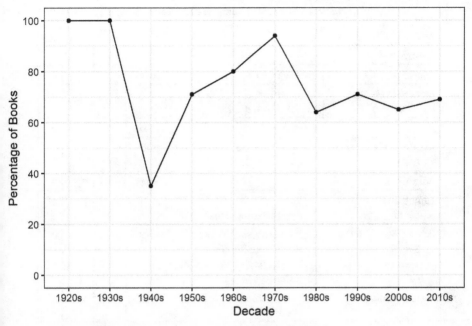

Figure 16. Percentage of books with extrapolation or speculation, by decade.

No. 4 from 1943, speculate whether Hitler's speeches, transferred by radio to a distant planet, could turn a peaceful, technologically advanced society against itself. The superhero-versus-Nazi stories that drag down the average of this decade are more interested in the satisfaction of getting back at the bad guys, without any care for the sf aspects of the superpowers involved.

List of Books

This list of books is divided by formats. Along with the author(s), illustrator, title, and year of publication, I have also included whether I coded the book as a yes (y) or no (n) for speculation/extrapolation (S/E), yes (y) or no (n) for significant female characters (F), and which level of diversity (D): painted faces (pf), culturally rich (cr), or none (n).

Table 17. Primary Sf Sample: Picturebooks

Author(s)/Illustrator	Title	Year	S/E	F	D
Agee, Jon	Dmitri the Astronaut	1996	y	n	pf
Agee, Jon	It's Only Stanley	2014	y	n	n
Alexander, Martha	Marty McGee's Space Lab, No Girls Allowed	1981	y	y	n
Arnold, Tedd	Green Wilma: Frog in Space	2009	y	y	n
Asch, Frank. and Devin Asch	The Daily Comet: Boy Saves Earth from Giant Octopus!	2010	y	n	n
Austin, Mike	Junkyard	2014	y	n	n
Barnett, Mac, and Dan Santat	Oh No! Or How My Science Project Destroyed the World	2010	y	y	pf
Barnett, Mac, and Dan Santat	Oh No! Not Again! (Or How I Built a Time Machine to Save History)(Or at Least My History Grade)	2012	y	y	n
Bartram, Simon	Man on the Moon: A Day in the Life of Bob	2002	y	n	pf
Base, Graeme	The Worst Band in the Universe	1999	y	y	n
Beaty, Andrea, and David Roberts	Rosie Revere, Engineer	2013	y	y	n
Beaty, Andrea, and David Roberts	Iggy Peck, Architect	2007	n	n	pf
Bennett, Jeffrey, and Alan Okamoto	Max Goes to Mars: A Science Adventure with Max the Dog	2006	y	n	pf
Bianchi, John	The Bungalo Boys: Flight of the Space Quester	1993	n	n	n
Bloom, Suzanne	A Mighty Fine Time Machine	2009	n	y	n
Breathed, Berkeley	Edwurd Fudwupper Fibbed Big	2000	y	y	pf
Breathed, Berkeley	Mars Needs Moms!	2007	y	n	n
Breen, Steve	Violet the Pilot	2008	y	y	pf
Brett, Jan	Hedgie Blasts Off!	2006	y	n	n
Brown, Sam	Sometimes I Forget You're a Robot	2013	y	n	n
Brownlow, Mike	Mickey Moonbeam	2006	y	n	n
Bryant, Megan E., and Artful Doodlers	Space Princess Cosma: Sparkle Surprise Party	2005	y	y	n
Butterworth, Nick	Q Pootle 5	2000	n	n	n

Author(s)/Illustrator	Title	Year	S/E	F	D
Cali, Davide, and AnnaLaura Cantone	*Mama Robot*	2008	y	n	n
Camp, Lindsay, and Tony Ross	*Why?*	1999	y	y	n
Canoau, Brittany, Jeffrey Clark, Scott Tilley, and Lori Tyminski	*Hiro and Tadashi*	2014	y	y	pf
Carey, Valery Scho, and Lynne Cherry	*Harriet and William and the Terrible Creature*	1985	y	y	n
Carrick, Carol, and Donald Carrick	*Patrick's Dinosaurs*	1983	n	n	n
Carrick, Carol, and David Milgrim	*Patrick's Dinosaurs on the Internet*	1999	n	n	n
Carrick, Paul	*Watch out for Wolfgang*	2009	n	n	n
Carter, David	*Bugs in Space*	1997	y	n	n
Christelow, Eileen	*Mr. Murphy's Marvelous Invention*	1983	y	n	n
Cole, Babette	*The Trouble with Dad*	1985	n	n	pf
Cole, Babette	*The Trouble with Gran*	1987	n	y	n
Corcoran, Mark	*Star Wars: The Mystery of the Rebellious Robot*	1979	y	n	n
Corey, Shana, and Mark Teague	*First Graders from Mars: The Problem with Pelly*	2002	y	y	n
Corwin, Oliver	*Hare and Tortoise Race to the Moon*	2002	n	n	n
Cox, Judy, and John O'Brien	*The West Texas Chili Monster*	1998	n	y	n
Crew, Gary, and Steven Woolman	*The Watertower*	1994	y	n	n
Cyrus, Kurt, and David Gordon	*Motordog*	2014	y	n	n
Czernecki, Stefan	*Lilliput 5357*	2006	y	n	n
Deacon, Alexis	*Beegu*	2003	y	y	pf
Dewan, Ted	*The Sorcerer's Apprentice*	1997	n	n	n
DiPucchio, Kelly	*Clink*	2011	y	n	pf
Diterlizzi, Tony	*Jimmy Zangwow's Out-of-This-World Moon Pie Adventure*	2000	n	n	n

Author(s)/Illustrator	Title	Year	S/E	F	D
Diterlizzi, Tony, and Angela Diterlizzi	*Adventure of Meno: Big Fun*	2009	n	n	n
Dodds, Dayle Ann, and Kyrsten Brooker	*Henry's Amazing Machine*	2004	n	n	pf
Dolan, Elys	*Nuts in Space*	2014	y	y	n
Dorros, Arthur, and David Catrow	*The Fungus That Ate My School*	2000	y	y	pf
Dyckman, Ame, and Dan Yaccarino	*Boy + Bot*	2012	y	n	n
Elliott, David, and True Kelley	*Hazel Nutt Alien Hunter*	2004	n	y	n
Fischer, Scott M.	*Twinkle*	2007	y	n	n
Fleischman, Paul, and Claire Ewart	*Time Train*	1991	y	y	pf
Fleischman, Paul, and Kevin Hawkes	*Weslandia*	1999	y	n	n
Fliess, Sue	*Robots, Robots Everywhere!*	2013	n	n	n
Foley, Greg E.	*Willoughby and the Moon*	2010	n	n	n
Foreman, Michael	*Dinosaurs and All That Rubbish*	1972	y	n	n
Foreman, Michael	*Nuts in Space*	2003	y	n	n
Freedman, Claire, and Ben Cort	*Aliens Love Dinopants*	2015	y	n	n
Freedman, Claire, and Ben Cort	*Aliens in Underpants Save the World*	2009	n	n	pf
Gackenbach, Dick	*Dog for a Day*	1987	n	n	n
Gall, Chris	*Awesome Dawson*	2013	y	n	n
Gall, Chris	*There's Nothing to Do on Mars*	2008	y	n	n
Ganz-Schmitt, Sue, and Shane Prigmore	*Planet Kindergarten*	2014	n	n	n
Ganz-Schmitt, Sue, and Shane Prigmore	*Planet Kindergarten: 100 Days in Orbit*	2016	n	n	n
Giancola, Donato, and Marc Gave	*Visit My Alien Worlds*	2002	y	y	pf
Glass, Andrew	*My Brother Tries to Make Me Laugh*	1984	n	y	n
Graves, Keith	*Pet Boy*	2001	y	n	n
Grey, Mini	*Space Dog*	2015	y	n	n

Author(s)/Illustrator	Title	Year	S/E	F	D
Grey, Mini	*Toys in Space*	2013	n	y	n
Grey, Mini	*Traction Man Meets Turbo Dog*	2008	n	n	n
Gutierrez, Akemi	*The Pirate and Other Adventures of Sam & Alice*	2007	n	y	n
Hoban, Russell, and Colin McNaughton	*They Came from Aargh!*	1981	n	n	n
Jackson, Alison, and Janet Pedersen	*Thea's Tree*	2008	y	y	n
James, Simon	*Baby Brains and Robomom*	2007	y	n	n
Jeffers, Oliver	*The Way Back Home*	2007	n	n	n
Joyce, William	*A Day with Wilbur Robinson*	1990	y	n	n
Joyce, William	*Sleepy Time Olie*	2001	n	n	n
Joyce, William, and Christina Ellis	*The Numberlys*	2014	n	n	n
Keats, Ezra Jack	*Regards to the Man in the Moon*	1981	n	y	pf
Kirk, Daniel	*Hush, Little Alien*	1999	y	n	n
Kirk, Daniel	*Moondogs*	1999	n	n	n
Knapman, Timothy, and Adam Stower	*Mungo and the Spiders from Space*	2007	y	n	n
Krahn, Fernando	*Robot-bot-bot*	1979	y	n	n
Krull, Kathleen	*How to Trick or Treat in Outer Space*	2004	n	n	n
Lasky, Kathryn, and David Jarvis	*Porkenstein*	2002	y	n	n
Lester, Helen, and Lynn Munsinger	*Wodney Wat's Wobot*	2011	y	y	cr
Liddell, Mary	*Little Machinery*	1926	y	n	n
Loomis, Christine, and Ora Eitan	*Astro Bunnies*	2001	y	n	n
Lucas, David	*The Robot and the Bluebird*	2007	y	n	n
Macaulay, David	*Motel of the Mysteries*	1979	y	y	n
McCall, Bruce	*Marveltown*	2008	y	n	pf
McCanna, Time, and Tad Carpenter	*Bitty Bot*	2016	n	n	n
McClements, George	*Baron von Baddie and the Ice Ray Incident*	2008	n	n	n
McElligott, Matthew	*Even Aliens Need Snacks*	2012	y	n	n

Author(s)/Illustrator	Title	Year	S/E	F	D
McElligott, Matthew	Mad Scientist Academy: The Weather Disaster	2016	y	y	n
McNamara, Margaret, and Mark Fearing	The Three Little Aliens and the Big Bad Robot	2011	n	n	n
McPhail, David	Tinker and Tom and the Star Baby	1998	y	n	n
Moore, Gertrude	Mrs. Moore in Space	1974	y	n	n
Morrissey, Dean	The Crimson Comet	2006	y	y	n
Nolen, Jerdine	Plantzilla Goes to Camp	2006	n	n	n
Novak, Matt	The Everything Machine	2009	y	y	pf
Oakley, Graham	Henry's Quest	1986	y	n	pf
O'Malley, Kevin, and Patrick O'Brien	Captain Raptor and the Space Pirates	2005	y	n	n
Parker, Jake	Little Bot and Sparrow	2016	y	y	n
Peet, Bill	The Wump World	1970	y	n	n
Pinkney, Brian	Cosmo and the Robot	2000	y	n	pf
Pinkwater, Daniel	Guys from Space	1989	n	n	n
Price, Ben Joel	Earth Space Moon Base	2014	y	n	n
Puttock, Simon, and Philip Hopman	Earth to Stella	2005	n	y	n
Reed, Lynn Rowe	Oliver, the Spaceship, and Me	2009	n	n	pf
Regan, Dian Curtis, and Robert Neubecker	Space Boy and the Space Pirate	2016	n	n	n
Rennie, Susan, and Dave Sutton	Kat and Doug on Planet Fankle	2002	n	y	n
Reynolds, Peter H	Charlie and Kiwi	2011	y	n	pf
Reynolds, Peter, and Paul Reynolds	Going Places	2014	y	y	pf
Riddell, Chris	Wendel's Workshop	2007	y	n	n
Rix, Jamie, and Clare Elsom	The Last Chocolate Chip Cookie	2014	n	n	pf
Rosen, Michael, and Neal Layton	Smile If You're Human	1999	y	n	n
Sabuda, Robert	The Adventures of Providence Traveler: Uh-oh, Leonardo!	2003	y	y	n
Sadler, Marilyn, and Roger Bollen	Alistair in Outer Space	1984	n	n	n

Author(s)/Illustrator	Title	Year	S/E	F	D
Samworth, Kate	*Aviary Wonders, Inc*	2014	y	n	n
Sanders, Rob, and Brian Won	*Outer Space Bedtime Race*	2015	n	n	n
Santoro, Scott	*Farm-Fresh Cats*	2006	y	y	n
Schachner, Judy	*Skippyjon Jones . . . Lost in Spice*	2009	n	n	n
Schories, Pat	*Jack and the Night Visitors*	2006	y	n	n
Scieszka, Jon, and David Shannon	*Robot Zot!*	2009	y	n	n
Scieszka, Jon, and Lane Smith	*Baloney (Henry P)*	2001	n	n	n
Seuss, Dr.	*The Butter Battle Book*	1984	y	n	n
Seuss, Dr.	*The Lorax*	1972	y	n	n
Shaw, Nancy, and Margot Apple	*Sheep Blast Off!*	2008	y	n	n
Sias, Ryan	*Zoe and Robot: Let's Pretend!*	2011	y	y	n
Sierra, Judy, and Stephen Gammell	*The Secret Science Project That Almost Ate the School*	2006	y	y	pf
Sims, Lesley, and Annabel Spencely	*Puzzle Journey into Space*	1995	y	y	pf
Smallcomb, Pam, and Joe Berger	*Earth to Clunk*	2011	y	n	n
Smith, Stu, and Michael Garland	*Goldilocks and the Three Martians*	2004	n	y	n
Spires, Ashley	*The Most Magnificent Thing*	2014	n	y	pf
Staub, Leslie, and Jeff Mack	*Time for Earth School, Dewey Dew*	2016	y	n	pf
Talbott, Hudson	*We're Back! A Dinosaur's Story*	1987	y	n	pf
Tauss, Marc	*Superhero*	2005	y	n	pf
Teague, Mark	*Moog-Moog, Space Barber*	1990	n	n	n
Thomas, Frances, and Ross Collins	*Maybe One Day*	2001	y	n	n
Underwood, Deborah	*Interstellar Cinderella*	2015	n	y	pf
Van Allsburg, Chris	*Zathura*	2002	y	n	n
Van Camp, Katie, and Lincoln Agnew	*Harry and Horsie*	2009	n	n	n
Van Dusen, Chris	*If I Built a Car*	2005	y	n	n
Viva, Frank	*A Long Way Away*	2013	y	n	n

Author(s)/Illustrator	Title	Year	S/E	F	D
Wahl, Jan, and Kimberly Schamber	*Rabbits on Mars*	2003	y	y	n
Waldman, Neil	*Al and Teddy*	2013	n	n	pf
Ward, Helen, and Wayne Anderson	*The Dragon Machine*	2003	y	n	n
Watkins, Adam F.	*Raybot*	2016	n	n	n
Whybrow, Ian, and Adrian Reynolds	*Harry and the Robots*	2000	n	n	pf
Wiesner, David	*Flotsam*	2006	y	n	n
Wiesner, David	*June 29, 1999*	1992	y	y	pf
Wiesner, David	*Mr. Wuffles!*	2013	y	n	n
Willis, Jeanne, and Tony Ross	*Dr. Xargle's Book of Earthlets*	1988	y	n	pf
Wilson, Sarah, and Chad Cameron	*George Hogglesberry, Grade School Alien*	2002	y	n	n
Winkowski, Fred	*The Martian Crystal Egg*	1980	y	y	n
Wood, Audrey, and Bruce Robert Wood	*The Christmas Adventure of Space Elf Sam*	1998	y	n	n
Wright, Walter	*Star Wars: The Maverick Moon*	1979	y	y	n
Yaccarino, Dan	*Doug Unplugged*	2013	n	n	n
Yaccarino, Dan	*If I Had a Robot*	1996	y	n	n
Yamada, Kobi, and Mae Besom	*What Do You Do with an Idea?*	2014	n	n	n
Yorinks, Arthur, and Mort Drucker	*Tomatoes from Mars*	1997	y	n	pf
Yorinks, Arthur, and David Small	*Company's Coming*	1988	y	y	n

Table 18. Primary Sf Sample: Early Readers

Author(s)/Illustrator	Title	Year	S/E	F	D
Albee, Sarah, and Nate Evans	My Best Friend Is Out of This World	1998	y	y	n
Amos, Ruth	Angry Birds Star Wars: Yoda Bird's Heroes	2013	n	y	n
Baruffi, Andrea	If I Had a Robot Dog	2005	n	n	n
Bell, Cece	Rabbit & Robot: The Sleepover	2012	y	n	n
Buller, Jon, and Susan Schade	Space Rock	1988	y	n	pf
Buller, Jon, and Susan Schade	Baseball Camp on the Planet of the Eyeballs	1998	y	n	pf
Carbone, Courtney, and Erik Doescher	Supergirl Takes Off!	2016	n	y	n
Catalanotto, Peter	Monkey & Robot	2013	n	n	n
Cowley, Joy	The Jigaree	1983	n	n	n
Dalton, Julie, and Gregg Schiegiel	Llama Drama	2003	y	n	n
Driscoll, Laura	Wall-E: Smash Trash!	2008	n	n	n
Feldman, Eve, and Carl Molno	We Are Friends	1989	n	y	pf
Frantz, Jennifer, and Marcelo Matere	Transformers: Rise of the Decepticons	2009	n	n	n
Hill, Susan, Andie Tong, and Jeremy Roberts	The Amazing Spider-Man: Spider-Man versus Kraven	2009	y	n	n
Macri, Thomas, and Craig Rousseau	Iron Man: This Is Iron Man	2012	y	n	pf
Macri, Thomas, Patrick Olliffe, and Pete Pantazis	X-Men: Days of Future Past	2014	y	y	pf
Macri, Thomas, and Todd Nauck	The Amazing Spider-Man: This Is Spider-Man	2012	n	n	n
Marzollo, Jean, and Claudio and Susan Meddaugh	Ruthie's Rude Friends	1984	y	y	n
Mass, Wendy	Space Taxi: Archie Takes Flight	2014	y	n	n
Milgrim, David	Go, Otto, Go!	2016	y	n	n

Author(s)/Illustrator	Title	Year	S/E	F	D
Millici, Nate, Andrea Parisi, and Grzegorz Krysinski	*Star Wars: Finn and Poe Team Up!*	2016	n	n	pf
Oliver, Mark	*Robot Dog*	2005	y	n	n
Orshoski, Paul, and Jeffrey Ebbeler	*Robot Man*	2010	y	n	n
Phleger, F and M, and Ward Brackett	*You Will Live under the Sea*	1966	y	n	n
Pinkwater, Daniel	*Mush, a Dog from Space*	1995	y	y	n
Santos, Ray	*Power Rangers Samurai: Rangers Unite*	2012	n	y	pf
Schaefer, Elizabeth, and Brian Rood	*Star Wars: Rey Meets BB-8*	2015	n	y	n
Siglain, Michael	*Star Wars: Trapped in the Death Star!*	2016	y	y	n
Siracusa, Catherine	*The Banana Split from Outer Space*	1995	n	n	n
Spiegelman, Nadja, and Trade Loeffler	*Zig and Wikki in Something Ate My Homework*	2010	n	n	n
Stamper, Judith Bauer, and Jerry Zimmerman	*Space Race*	1998	n	n	n
Suen, Anastasia	*The Scary Night: A Robot and Rico Story*	2010	n	n	pf
Todd, Ruthven, and Paul Galdone	*Space Cat*	1952	y	n	n
West, Tracey	*The Powerpuff Girls: No Girls Allowed!*	2001	n	y	pf
Wrecks, Billy, and Erik Doescher	*Batman's Hero Files*	2015	y	y	pf
Wyatt, Chris, Ron Lim, and Rachelle Rosenberg	*Ant-Man: This Is Ant-Man*	2015	y	n	n
Yaccarino, Dan	*Blast Off Boy and Blorp: First Day on a Strange New Planet*	2000	n	n	n
Yolen, Jane	*Commander Toad in Space*	1980	y	y	n

Table 19. Primary Sf Sample: Comic Books

Author(s)/Illustrator	Title	Year	S/E	F	D
Anderson, Murphy	Lars of Mars No. 10	1951	y	n	n
Baltazar, Art, and Franco	Superman Family Adventures No. 1	2013	n	y	n
Baltazar, Art, and Franco	Tiny Titans: Adventures in Awesomeness	2009	n	y	pf
Baltazar, Art, and Franco	Li'l Battlestar Galactica	2014	n	n	pf
Baron, Mike, and Steve Rude	Nexus No.1	1981	y	n	n
Better Publications, Inc.	Startling Comics No. 27	1944	n	n	n
Better Publications, Inc.	Startling Comics No. 28	1944	n	n	n
Binder, O. O., and C. C. Beck	Fatman the Human Flying Saucer	1967	n	n	pf
Butterworth, Mike	The Rise and Fall of the Trigan Empire	1965	y	n	n
Byrne, John, Arthur Adams, and Dick Giordano	Annual Action Comics No. 1	1987	n	n	pf
Charlton Comics Group	Mysteries of Unexplored Worlds Vol. 1 No. 17	1960	y	n	n
Charlton Comics Group	Mysteries of Unexplored Worlds Vol. 1 No. 20	1960	y	n	n
Charlton Comics Group	Mysteries of Unexplored Worlds Vol. 1 No. 42	1964	y	n	n
Charlton Comics Group	Space Adventures Vol. 3, No. 50	1968	y	n	n
Charlton Comics Group	Space Adventures Vol. 3, No. 60	1967	y	n	n
Charlton Comics Group	Space War Vol. 1 No. 9	1961	y	n	n
Charlton Comics Group	Strange Suspense Stories Vol. 1 No. 73	1965	y	n	n
Charlton Comics Group	Unusual Tales Vol. 1 No. 39	1963	y	n	n
Chaykin, Howard	Marvel Premiere No. 32, Featuring Monark Starstalker	1976	n	n	n
Clevinger, Brian, Scott Wegener, and Ronda Pattison	Atomic Robo Vol 1: Fightin' Scientists of Tesladyne	2009	y	y	pf

Author(s)/Illustrator	Title	Year	S/E	F	D
Dell Publishing Co.	Tom Corbett, Space Cadet No. 4	1953	n	n	n
Eliopoulos, Chris, and Ig Guara	Lockjaw and the Pet Avengers	2009	y	n	n
Elwood, Roger (ed.)	Starstream No. 1	1976	y	y	n
Elwood, Roger (ed.)	Starstream No. 3	1976	y	y	n
Elwood, Roger (ed.)	Starstream No. 4	1976	y	n	n
Fables Publishing Co.	Weird Science No. 6	1950	y	n	n
Fables Publishing Co.	Weird Science No. 9	1951	y	n	n
Fox Feature Syndicate	Cosmo Cat	1959	n	n	n
Giarusso, Chris	Mini Marvels	2013	y	y	pf
Godwin, Frank	Connie: Captives of the Space Pirates	1938	y	y	n
Godwin, Frank	Connie: Master of the Jovian Moons	1939	y	y	pf
Guibert, Emmanuel, and Joann Sfar	Sardine in Outer Space	2000	n	y	n
Hamlin, V. T.	Alley Oop	1939	y	y	n
Hoena, Blake, and Steve Harpster	Eek & Ack: Beyond the Black Hole	2009	y	n	n
Itahashi, Shuho	Cyber 7 No. 1	1989	y	y	n
Jerwa, Brandon, and Ian McGinty	Li'l Bionic Kids	2014	n	y	pf
Kane, Bob	Detective Comics No. 93	1944	n	n	n
Kirby, Jack	Captain Victory and His Galactic Rangers No.1	1981	y	n	pf
Kirby, Jack	The Eternals No. 1	1976	y	n	n
Lee, Stan, Gary Griedrich, and Marie Severin	The Incredible Hulk No. 103	1968	n	n	n
Lee, Stan, Jack Kirby, and Chic Stone	The Fantastic Four Annual No. 2	1964	y	y	n
Lee, Stan, Jack Kirby, and Syd Shores	Captain America Vol. 1 No. 102	1968	y	y	n
Libris, John, and Don Ryan	The Adventures of Captain Havoc and the Phantom Knight No. 4	1949	y	n	n
Mather, Arthur	Captain Atom No. 36	1951	n	n	n

Author(s)/Illustrator	Title	Year	S/E	F	D
McLoughlin, Colin, and Denis McLoughlin	Swift Morgan No. 16	1949	y	n	n
Michelinie, David, Don Newton, Bob Layton, and Liz Berube	Star Hunters No. 1	1977	y	y	pf
Montclare, Brandon, Amy Reeder, and Natacha Bustos	Moon Girl and Devil Dinosaur: BFF	2016	y	y	pf
Morrison, Grant, and Frank Quitely	We3: Vol. 1-3	2004	y	y	n
National Comics Publications, Inc.	Mystery in Space No. 39	1957	n	n	n
National Comics Publications, Inc.	Strange Adventures No. 9	1951	y	n	n
National Comics Publications, Inc.	Strange Adventures No. 60	1955	y	n	n
Nickel, Scott	Backyard Bug Battle	2007	y	n	pf
Nowlan, Phil, and Dick Calkins	Buck Rogers in the 25th Century	1929	y	y	pf
Pilgrim, Corona	Ant Man: Larger than Life #1	2015	y	n	n
Pilkey, Dav	Ricky Ricotta's Mighty Robot	2000	n	n	n
Raymond, Alex	Flash Gordon	1934	y	n	n
Ritt, William, and Clarence Gray	Brick Bradford on the Isles beyond the Ice	1935	y	n	n
Sansom, Art, and Russ Winterbotham	Chris Welkin Planeteer	1951	y	n	n
Scott, Mairghread, and Luciano Vecchio	Guardians of the Galaxy Infinite #1	2013	y	y	n
Siegel, Jerry, and Joe Shuster	Action Comics No. 75	1944	n	n	n
Smith, Ian, and Tyson	Emily and the Intergalactic Lemonade Stand	2004	y	y	n
Spires, Ashley	Binkey the Space Cat	2009	y	n	n
Stamm, Russell	Invisible Scarlett O'Neil	1946	n	y	n
Standard Comics	Jetta	1952	n	y	n
Steet & Smith Publications, Inc.	Shadow Comics Vol. 4 No.5	1944	n	n	n
Stuart, Terry, and Stan Lee	Guardians of the Galaxy Annual Vol. 1, No.1	1991	y	y	n

Author(s)/Illustrator	Title	Year	S/E	F	D
Sumerak, Mark	Power Pack: End of the Rainbow	2006	n	y	n
Super Comics Inc.	Strange Planets No. 10	1963	n	n	n
Super Comics Inc.	Strange Planets No. 12	1964	y	n	n
Tezuka, Osama	The Greatest Robot on Earth	1964	y	n	pf
Tezuka, Osama	The Hot Dog Corps	1961	y	n	pf
Titan Publishing Co. Inc.	Forbidden Worlds No. 35	1955	y	y	n
Tobin, Paul	Spider-Man Marvel Adventures Amazing #1	2010	y	y	pf
Various Authors	2000 AD	1977	y	n	n
Various Authors	All New Comics Vol.1, No.4	1943	y	n	n
Various Authors	Amazing Mystery Funnies No. 1	1938	y	y	n
Various Authors	Atom Age Combat Vol. 1, No. 1	1952	n	n	n
Various Authors	Atoman No. 1	1946	y	n	n
Various Authors	Buster Crabbe Vol. 1, No. 1	1953	y	n	n
Various Authors	Captain Midnight No. 100	1950	y	n	n
Various Authors	Captain Science Vol. 1, No. 1	1950	y	n	n
Various Authors	Captain Video Vol. 1, No. 1	1951	y	n	n
Various Authors	Commander Battle and the Atomic Sub No. 1	1954	n	n	n
Various Authors	Crusader from Mars Vol. 1, No. 1	1952	y	n	n
Various Authors	Drift Marlo No. 1	1962	n	n	n
Various Authors	Famous Funnies No. 72 (Speed Spaulding)	1940	n	n	n
Various Authors	Fantastic Worlds No. 5	1952	y	y	n
Various Authors	Mystery Comics No.1	1944	n	y	pf
Various Authors	Out of This World Vol. 1, No. 1	1956	y	n	n
Various Authors	Planet Comics No. 21	1942	n	y	n
Various Authors	Pocket Comics No.1	1941	n	n	n
Various Authors	Police Comics No.1	1941	n	n	n
Various Authors	Race for the Moon No. 1	1958	y	n	n
Various Authors	Rocket Comics No. 1	1940	n	n	n
Various Authors	Rocket Kelly No. 2	1945	y	n	n
Various Authors	Science Comics No. 2	1940	n	n	n

Author(s)/Illustrator	Title	Year	S/E	F	D
Various Authors	*Spaceman No. 2*	1962	y	y	n
Various Authors	*Superworld Comics No. 2*	1940	y	n	n
Various Authors	*Unknown Worlds of Science Fiction No. 1*	1974	y	n	n
Various Authors	*Wonder Comics No. 1*	1944	y	n	n
Worley, Rob M., and Jason T. Kruse	*Scratch 9: The Pet Project & Cat Tails*	2015	y	y	n

Table 20. Primary Sf sample: Graphic Novels

Author(s)/Illustrator	Title	Year	S/E	F	D
Brallier, Max, and Douglas Holgate	The Last Kids on Earth	2015	y	y	pf
Camper, Cathy, and Raúl the Third	Lowriders in Space	2014	y	y	cr
Chaykin, Howard	American Flagg! Southern Comfort	1987	y	y	pf
Davis, Eleanor	The Secret Science Alliance and the Copycat Crook	2009	y	y	pf
Fearing, Mark	Earthling!	2012	y	n	n
Foglio, Phil, and Kaja and Brian Snoddy	Girl Genius Vol. 1	2012	y	y	pf
Fridolfs, Derek, and Dustin Nguyen	Study Hall of Justice	2016	y	y	n
Gagne, Michel	The Saga of Rex	2010	y	n	n
Gallardo, Adam, and Nuria Peris	Gear School	2007	y	y	pf
Hatke, Ben	Little Robot	2015	y	y	pf
Hatke, Ben	Zita the Spacegirl	2011	y	y	n
Hosler, Jay	Last of the Sandwalkers	2015	y	y	n
Kane, Gil, and Ron Goulart	Star Hawks II	1978	y	y	n
L'Engle, Madeleine, and Hope Larson	A Wrinkle in Time: The Graphic Novel	2012	y	y	n
Lieberman, A. J.	The Silver Six	2013	y	y	pf
Maihack, Mike	Cleopatra in Space	2014	y	y	n
Middaugh, Dallas, and Jeanne DuPrau	The City of Ember: The Graphic Novel	2012	y	y	n
Nelson, O. T., and Dan Jolley	The Girl Who Owned a City: The Graphic Novel	2012	y	y	pf
Parker, Jake	Missile Mouse: The Star Crusher	2010	y	n	n
Pittman, Eddie	Red's Planet	2016	y	y	pf
Pullman, Philip, Stéphane Melchior, and Clément Oubrerie	The Golden Compass: The Graphic Novel Vol 1	2015	y	y	n

Author(s)/Illustrator	Title	Year	S/E	F	D
Roman, Dave	Astronaut Academy: Zero Gravity	2011	y	y	pf
Shiga, Jason	Meanwhile	2010	y	n	n
Siddell, Tom	Gunnerkrigg Court vol 1	2009	y	y	pf
Stevenson, Robert L., Martin Powell, and Daniel Perez	The Strange Case of Dr. Jekyll and Mr. Hyde	2009	y	n	n
Thompson, Craig	Space Dumplins	2015	y	y	n
Tobin, Paul, and Ron Chan	Plants vs. Zombies: Timepocalypse	2015	n	y	n
Varon, Sara	Robot Dreams	2007	y	n	n
Verne, Jules, Davis Worth Miller, Katherine MacLean Brevard, and Greg Rebis	Journey to the Center of the Earth	2008	y	n	n
Wells, H. G., Davis Worth Miller, and Katherine McLean Brevard	The War of the Worlds	2009	y	n	n
Wells, H. G., Terry Davis, and José Alfonso Ocampo Ruiz	The Time Machine	2008	y	n	pf
Winicl, Judd, and Guy Major	Hilo: The Boy Who Crashed to Earth	2015	y	y	pf
Yamomoto, Yun Yun	Swans in Space	2009	n	y	pf
Yang, Gene Luen, and Mike Holmes	Secret Coders	2015	y	y	pf

Table 21. Primary Sf Sample: Hybrid Novels

Author(s)/Illustrator	Title	Year	S/E	F	D
Ball, Nate	*Alien in My Pocket 1: Blast Off*	2014	y	y	n
Beaty, Andrea, and Dan Santat	*Attack of the Fluffy Bunnies*	2010	y	y	n
Benton, Jim	*Franny K. Stein: Lunch Walks among Us*	2003	y	y	n
Brallier, Max, Rachel Maguire, and Nichole Kelley	*Galactic Hot Dogs: Cosmo's Wiener Getaway*	2016	y	y	n
Brown, Jeffrey	*Star Wars: Jedi Academy*	2013	n	y	n
Diterlizzi, Tony	*The Search for WondLa*	2010	y	y	n
Giarusso, Chris	*The G-Man Super Journal: Awesome Origins*	2015	y	y	pf
Hampson, Frank, and Angus P. Allan	*Dan Dare: Pilot of the Future!*	1977	y	y	n
Itnatow, Amy	*The Mighty Odds*	2016	n	y	cr
Judge, Malcom	*Jonny Jakes Investigates the Hamburgers of Doom*	2015	y	y	pf
Nelson, Peter, and Rohitash Rao	*Herbert's Wormhole*	2009	y	y	n
O'Ryan, Ray	*Galaxy Zack: Hello, Nebulon!*	2013	n	n	n
Patterson, James, Chris Grabenstein, and Juliana Neufeld	*House of Robots*	2014	y	y	cr
Reeve, Philip, and Sarah McIntyre	*Cakes in Space*	2014	y	y	pf
Rex, Adam	*The True Meaning of Smekday*	2007	y	y	cr
Richards, C. J.	*Robots Rule! The Junkyard Bot*	2016	y	y	n
Scieszka, Jon	*Frank Einstein and the Antimatter Motor*	2014	y	n	n
Stadler, Alexander	*Julian Rodriguez: Trash Crisis on Earth*	2008	n	n	pf
Venditti, Robert, and Dusty Higgins	*Miles Taylor and the Golden Cape: Attack of the Alien Horde*	2015	y	n	pf

APPENDIX B

This appendix offers a list of recommended primary sf books. This list is not exhaustive, and I would not even claim that it necessarily represents the best books in my sample, but it offers a starting point with some variety in themes and sf tropes. These books all feature speculation or extrapolation, and I have included notes about their representation of gender and diversity. The list is organized by format.

Picturebooks and Early Readers

Oh No! Or How My Science Project Destroyed the World by Mac Barnett and Dan Santat

This story follows an unnamed girl as she considers what she should have done differently to prevent her science project from taking over the city, and how she is going to solve the problem.

Girl Power: The protagonist is a girl with awesome science skills. Her narration throughout the story both points out and pokes fun at doing science for the fun of it (without always thinking through the consequences).

Diversity: The illustrations portray an appropriately diverse world, though the protagonist herself is not given any clear markers of difference. Dan Santat is Thai American.

Beegu by Alexis Deacon

Beegu is lost and cannot find her mother. She tries to befriend several Earthlings, and finds young humans to be the most sympathetic.

Girl Power: Beegu is a gender-neutral-looking alien but receives female pronouns rather than the "default" male pronouns.

Diversity: The illustrations show an appropriately diverse world.

Cosmo and the Robot by Brian Pinkney

Cosmo is heartbroken when the robot Rex, his only friend on Mars, breaks down. His parents offer him a Super Solar System Utility Belt as consolation, but perhaps Cosmo can use it to help his robot friend and even save his annoying big sister, Jewel.

Girl Power: Unfortunately, Cosmo's sister is an antagonist and not a great representation of girls in science here. However, it is pleasant to see that Cosmo's mother is a scientist.

Diversity: While unimportant and unmentioned in the plot, Cosmo and his whole family have dark skin and natural hair. As they appear to be the only family on Mars, this indicates that Cosmo's parents are very important scientists. Given the history of NASA's erasure of African American contributions, this is an important case of visual diversity. Brian Pinkney is African American.

Mr. Wuffles! by David Wiesner

What happens when a cat-toy-sized spaceship catches the attention of a bored cat? This mostly wordless picturebook by David Wiesner offers a fun twist on alien visitation, and plenty of opportunities for inventing dialogue and filling in story.

Girl Power: For better or worse, with androgynous aliens and insects at the fore, gender is not a factor in this book.

Diversity: None to speak of. The only human character is never fully shown but appears to be white.

Weslandia by Paul Fleischman

Now that summer vacation has arrived, Wesley needs a project. Why not build a whole new civilization, starting with a staple crop? The details in this book are great fun, begging to be made into your reader's own summer projects. Written by Paul Fleischman and illustrated by Kevin Hawkes.

Girl Power: There are girls in the background sometimes, but that doesn't add anything in the way of girl power.

Diversity: For a book referencing early civilizations, it is awfully white. No nonmainstream background characters.

Zoe and Robot: Let's Pretend by Ryan Sias

Zoe tries to teach Robot how to pretend but finds that ROBOTS DO NOT KNOW HOW TO PRETEND. In this hybrid early reader/picturebook, beginner readers can read the easy speech balloons and practice their best robot voice.

Girl Power: Unlike in many boy-and-robot-pal books, Zoe's role here is active. She utilizes basic engineering and problem-solving to try to overcome Robot's programming and teach him imagination. Also, Zoe's sense of style is pleasantly quirky.

Diversity: Zoe is racially ambiguous, offering no tangible diversity.

My Best Friend Is Out of This World by Sarah Albee and Nate Evans

In this early reader, Maddy invites her friend Victor to her house. When Victor turns out to be an alien, Maddy's parents struggle to act normally. The plot introduces the classic sf metaphor of fearing aliens simply because they are alien.

Girl Power: Maddy is depicted as female, while her alien friend Victor is depicted as male. She comfortably wields advanced gadgets that look possibly homemade, seemingly with no help from her parents. Written by Sarah Albee.

Diversity: Aside from an impressive head of brilliant red hair, Maddy appears to represent a mainstream identity. Victor's blueness doesn't offer any identifiable diversity to speak of, either.

Comic Books and Graphic Novels

Moon Girl and Devil Dinosaur: BFF by Brandon Montclare, Amy Reeder, and Natacha Bustos

This series by Marvel comics features Lunella Lafayette, age nine, discovering the abilities she will use as the superhero Moon Girl. This volume introduces Moon Girl as she meets and partners up with Devil Dinosaur, a short-lived Jack Kirby character who first appeared in 1978.

Girl Power: At the 2016 San Diego Comicon, Marvel announced that Moon Girl was now the smartest character in the entire Marvel Universe. In this volume she faces off with The Hulk and refuses to be dismissed just because she is a little girl. Cowritten by Amy Reeder, with art by Natacha Bustos.

Diversity: Not only is she a supersmart girl, Moon Girl appears dark-skinned with natural hair, as do her parents. This aspect of her identity is not discussed overtly within the context of this volume but is visually apparent. Lead artist, Natacha Bustos, identifies as Chilean and Afro-Brazilian.

Atomic Robo and the Fightin' Scientists of Tesladyne by Brian Clevinger

The first volume of a series of comic books, this time-traveling and adventurous story packs a lot of snarky humor and history. Over the course of the series, Atomic Robo (invented by Nikola Tesla) travels between 1884 to 2015, punching out bad guys and generally forcing the world to question their definitions of humanity, citizenship, etc. Teachers should watch out for some mild swearing and vague sexual references in some issues.

Girl Power: The creators of this comic book have said that they made a specific effort to avoid the comic book industry's sometimes ridiculous standards for how women look and are framed suggestively in comic book art. Women appear in many different roles from scientists to soldiers. Atomic Robo works alongside competent and smart women, such as Ada.

Diversity: With the main character as a robot with no semblance of race, the diversity in the supporting characters and in the background becomes more important. The illustrations reveal an appropriately diverse world. Characters of color work with Atomic Robo as scientists/soldiers in his unit, such as Vik.

Little Robot by Brian Hatke

This mostly wordless tale by Ben Hatke follows an unnamed little girl as she discovers and repairs a hapless robot in a local dump. After they figure out how to be friends, she must help him evade capture.

Girl Power: This little girl is handy with a wrench and carries her own fully equipped tool belt. Not only that, but she knows how to use it.

Diversity: The pictures portray a little girl with dark skin and natural hair. The narrative also offers hints about her social status: she lives in a trailer park, wears the same white nightshirt every day, and appears to feel judged by neighbors who have houses and swing sets. These identity markers are not overtly mentioned but influence her character and choices.

Secret Coders by Gene Luen Yang and Mike Holmes

Join twelve-year-olds Hopper, Eni, and Josh as they solve mysteries and learn to program at Stately Academy in the first volume of this series. The puzzles and clues beg for you to solve them at home, alongside the characters.

Girl Power: Hopper, named for programmer Grace Hopper, is a basketball-loving girl who excels at programming and solving puzzles alongside her male costars. Hopper stands off against stereotypes from her male classmates.

Diversity: This series offers several markers of diversity, all within the context of intelligence and programming skills. Hopper is biracial and struggles with learning Mandarin from her mother, while Eni has dark skin. Author Gene Luen Yang is Chinese and Taiwanese American.

Space Dumplins by Craig Thompson

Violet Marlocke (vaguely preteen-aged) sets out to find her father after he is lost in a galactic environmental energy crisis: a bout of giant space whale diarrhea. Violet forges a band of alien heroes to help her traverse this junkyard-like version of space.

Girl Power: Violet, with appropriately violet hair, is squarely in the forefront of this adventure. In a twist on old dynamics, she is the one setting out to rescue her burly, lumberjack-styled father.

Diversity: Nothing to speak of here. Unfortunately little diversity in a real, mirroring sense—just aliens.

Lowriders in Space by Cathy Camper and Raúl the Third

Lupe Impala, Flapjack Octopus, and Elirio Malaria decide to make the lowest and slowest car in the world for the universal car competition. In this first volume, their mechanical and design innovations blast them right into space.

Girl Power: Lupe is the mechanical genius behind the space-worthy car. She is also the leader of the team. This series is written by Cathy Camper.

Diversity: The story is set in an alternative Southern California populated by humanoid animals. The text is peppered with Spanish words and phrases. The plot foregrounds the cultural tradition of lowrider cars and is influenced by the Latin@futurist tradition of playing with boundaries between science/ engineering and surreal fantasy. Author Cathy Camper is Arab American, and illustrator Raúl the Third is Latino.

Hybrid Novels

House of Robots by James Patterson and Chris Grabenstein

Sammy Hayes-Rodriguez, fifth-grader, lives in a house full of both useful and seemingly useless robots designed by his genius mother. His middle school life becomes exponentially awkward when his mom sends a new robot to follow him around school, for reasons she won't explain. A good sf story for readers who enjoy the *Diary of a Wimpy Kid* series and the funny middle school situations that author James Patterson is known for.

Girl Power: Sammy's mom is a renowned robot inventor, assisted by one male and one female grad student. Sammy's sister Maddy is not antagonistic, like the sister figure in many sf stories, but refreshingly treated as his best friend in a glowing and emotional sibling relationship.

Diversity: Sammy's second-best friend Trip (his sister Maddy is his first-best friend) is a nonstereotypical person of color. In a second and less common representation of diversity, Maddy has severe combined immunodeficiency. The robots are often utilized as tools to help Maddy access experiences and social situations than she cannot otherwise safely enter due to her disability.

The True Meaning of Smekday by Adam Rex

Recently made into a (very different) animated film, this lightly cartoon-illustrated novel follows twelve-year-old Gratuity Tucci as she sets out with an alien named J.Lo to find her mother and maybe even save the whole planet from two invasions at once.

Girl Power: Gratuity is in charge. She holds her own against both silly and intimidating aliens, and comes up with very clever solutions to old and new problems–the heart of engineering. She also faces off against some boys that, despite an apocalyptic setting, have the audacity to set up a boys-only survivor's club.

Diversity: Gratuity's biracial identity comes up several times throughout the book, including some prejudice and assumptions. The book also explicitly brings up how alien invasion stories often parallel colonial invasions, with a Dine (Navajo) character and conversations about Native Americans today, although it falls short of perfect execution (see Reese 2015).

NOTES

Introduction

1. The book even goes so far as to include extra scientific trivia, beyond the story's necessities. Before we even see that illustration of the lightning scene, an earlier page features a full-page diagram that shows how to calculate the distance of lighting using thunder and the speed of the sound waves. It is labeled "*fig 1.1*" and drawn on a graph-paper background. The book features twenty-five of these textbook-like diagrams that are often above and beyond what the story even calls for.

Chapter 1: Definitions and Evaluations

1. This was not always the case. Prior to the 1960s, sf for adolescents was referred to as juvenile sf. As Mendlesohn explains in *The Intergalactic Playground*, this different label also made different assumptions about what those young people were interested in reading.

2. Some schools are even integrating Indigenous ways of knowing into elementary science. This is not only because "the knowledge students have and how they learn is influenced by their culture, context, and their everyday experiences" but also due to a new movement in science at large wherein "many Indigenous ways of understanding about the world have become accepted by scientific experts and are considered as adding value to science" (Mack et al. 52).

3. I use the compound word "picturebook" purposefully. In the "Picture Book" entry in *Keywords for Children's Literature*, William Moebius indicates that while the term has endured many uses and versions, scholars such as himself have been working to assign the one-word term "picturebook" to a specific type of book "in which pictures and words together are treated as semi-autonomous and mutually attractive chains of meaning, rather than as fixed images serving as a supplement to meanings fixed in words" (169). I therefore exclusively use the term "picturebook" rather than the two-word iteration "picture book" to emphasize the significance of the interplay between pictures and text in this format.

4. A small but growing body of research indicates that sf produces positive thinking about science in children. Fleischmann and Templeton's interview study with NASA scientists revealed that they were introduced to science as children through sf, and that the genre was a tool that shaped how they came to think about science (1). The American Society of Mechanical Engineers similarly published short interviews with engineers who pursued their careers because of sf books and movies that they encountered as children (Brown and Logan 3). Educators and educational researchers have experimented with using science fiction in science programs for teens, such as Yann Brouillette's 2019 chemistry resource guide "Comic Book Chemistry: Teaching Science Using Super Heroes," and Camillia Matuk, Talia Hurwich, and Anna Amato's 2019 study "How Science Fiction Worldbuilding Supports Students' Scientific Explanation." Both focus on high school and college students, though Brouillette mentions the possibility of elementary applications. It is less common to find examples like the Sci-Dentity Project by Mega Subramaniam, June Ahn, Amanda Waugh, and Allison Druin in 2012 that focus exclusively on K–12. The presence of sf in classrooms and library collections has not been studied much for the younger set. After all, if most people believe that young children do not read sf, then no one is likely to research it.

5. For instance, Kathleen Mohr found that when presented with an option to select a book to keep, the children in her study overwhelmingly selected informational books— particularly books about animals. Meanwhile, studies like E. Wendy Saul and Donna Dieckman's showed that many teachers, especially those working with children in the early grades, tend to select fiction rather than nonfiction texts for classroom use, because practitioners feel that informational texts are too difficult and boring for young children.

6. Fortunately, this research has led to changes in educational practice. The Common Core State Standards (CCSS) in 2010 in the US led to a dramatic shift in the way that information is treated: the standards advised that 50 percent of elementary students' book exposure at school should be informational texts (a broad term for nonfiction). This new standard led to the rise of nonfiction in elementary school classrooms and "an unprecedented change for all involved in education, especially teacher education" (Young and Goering 1).

7. In the introduction, editors Gary Westfahl and George Slusser specify that they excluded children's and YA scholars because they wanted to focus on how children are represented in speculative fiction for adults (xi). Accordingly, Foote is interested in what the child means to the adult reader, concluding that these speculative fiction genres "appeal to our sense of wonder in different ways, appeal to different parts of us: the child, the young adult, and the adult" (205). This treatment of the child as part of the adult echoes the concerns voiced by children's literature scholars who worry that books for children also have more to say about adults than about children's abilities and interests.

8. For instance, the Amulet series by Kazu Kibuishi, which I would consider fantasy, primarily features fantasy tropes like epic quests, elves, and magic talismans but also includes a few sf tropes, like robots, aliens, and space travel. The robots are invented by a magical amulet-wielding puzzle maker, evoking Arthur C. Clarke's third law about advanced technology being indistinguishable from magic. Analyzing this story only as fantasy obscures the ways that it speculates about the boundaries of science and magic by playing with both fantasy and sf ideas. The same could be said for many primarily sf stories that include fantasy, as explored in future chapters.

9. See Andri Ioannou, Emily Andreou, and Maria Christofi, 2015; Mark C. Somanader, Megan M. Saylor, and Daniel T. Levin, 2011; Megan M. Saylor et al., 2010; Sharona T. Levy and David Mioduser, 2008; Debra Bernstein and Kevin Crowley, 2008; Jennifer L. Jipson and Susan A. Gelman, 2007.

10. There is also a body of research about adults and robots, but these studies tend to ask whether adults feel empathy toward robots. See, for instance, the work of MIT researcher Kate Darling. No one tests whether adults genuinely believe that robots are alive, though, but rather they test whether adults anthropomorphize robots or feel that robots deserve ethical treatment, similar to animals.

Chapter 2: Comprehending Genre

1. Teachers are not expected to introduce metaphors until fourth grade, according to the Common Core State Standards.

2. Note that children will have different experiences with this, depending upon their literacy instruction. Those who have received direct, explicit comprehension strategy instruction in classrooms will have an advantage.

3. This straightforward image/text correlation would be helpful when an sf novum word does not exist in the real world. Seeing this new word/concept in a picture would help the reader practice the sf reading protocol of implication through clues that do not put added strain on reading comprehension. However, I did not encounter any early readers that made use of this potential—likely because invented words are an unnecessary extra hurdle for children at this stage.

4. Early readers are not usually included in this debate, but they could be seen as the transitional middle ground between picturebooks and comic books since they are often the first books children encounter that have this solitary reading potential. Wannamaker and Miskec speculate that "Early Readers may be especially threatening to parents because they often represent a child's first direct experience with a work of literature that is not being filtered by an adult who can alter or interpret written words when reading aloud to a pre-literate child" (8). Hade and Hudock explain that this liminal position allows for early reader books like Mo Willems's *Elephant and Piggy* series (2007–11), which productively "promotes a pedagogy of multiliteracies" (93) by teaching children to read words and comics conventions at the same time. Annette Wannamaker further notes that early reader series like *Babymouse* feature the young protagonist talking back with significant sass to a seemingly adult, even patronizing narrator, which demonstrates and plays metafictionally with the picturebook adult/child relationship that the young reader is transitioning away from when they move on to comic books and graphic novels.

5. In light of the definitions and history of the graphic novel, I analyze comic books and graphic novels together in this section as formats defined by the grammar of comics. However, when counting the books in my pool of primary sf for quantitative purposes, I distinguish them from comic books by their "bookness": a novel-length narrative and bound as a book rather than a magazine.

6. Note that I included a maximum of three books from any comic book series in my data set, in order to avoid inflating the category with long series that generally did not differ in speculative/extrapolative quality from issue to issue.

7. Note that board books, cloth books, and popup books were not given separate consideration. I found no board books or cloth books that were not reprints of picturebooks. Due to the extremely low number of popup books ($n = 2$), I grouped them with the next most reasonable category, which was the picturebook category in both cases.

Chapter 3: Reading Representation

1. There are several other alternative futurism traditions, but I have focused on the ones most relevant to the discussion of primary sf in this chapter.

2. The act of world building in speculative fiction often includes inventing new cultures. However, often these seemingly alien or alternate worlds reflect and comment upon contemporary culture through allegory. This practice can either reinforce cultural stereotypes or undermine them. Several 1940s and 1950s comic books took racial and cultural resentment from World War II into the future, with caricatures of German and Japanese villains conducting evil schemes in space. Other mid-1900s comics harmfully represented Native and First Nations people through depicting hostile native humanoids on other planets that look suspiciously like green-skinned versions of the stereotypical "Indians" from western films.

3. This comparison is limited to 2001–16, since 2001 is the earliest that the CCBC started distinguishing between books by and about POC, and 2016 is the upper limit of my primary sf sample set.

4. While Galda et al. also include a third category called "culture as a concept," or books that explicitly talk about diversity in the world, these books are inherently nonfiction.

Chapter 4: The Case Study

1. In a practitioner article that I cowrote with elementary-science teacher Bonnie Laabs, we address the potential for misconceptions via *The Crimson Comet* (2006), a steampunk picturebook by Dean Morrissey and Stephen Krensky in which a rocket flies to the moon and reveals that it is lit from within by an intricate engine. Laabs says that her students already come to school believing that the moon is self-lit, and this book risks reinforcing that idea. Yet we recommended using the book to directly address these preconceptions, teach how to distinguish between moon facts and moon myths, and discuss the value of imagining different explanations while still knowing them to be false: in other words, the value of fiction—and unrealistic *science* fiction. This approach requires an adult who has faith that children can understand and make distinctions between fact and fiction, between science and sf, and that both belong in the classroom.

WORKS CITED

Primary Sources

Albee, Sarah, and Nate Evans. *My Best Friend Is Out of This World*. Golden Books, 1998.

All New Comics, vol.1, no. 4, Family Comics Inc. , 1943.

Amos, Ruth. *Angry Birds Star Wars: Yoda Bird's Heroes*. DK Children, 2013.

Asimov, Isaac. "Robot Dreams." 1986. *Masterpieces: The Best Science Fiction of the Twentieth Century*, edited by Orson Scott Card, Ace Books, 2001, pp. 91–96.

Baltazar, Art and Franco. *Li'l Battlestar Galactica*. Dynamite Entertainment, 2014.

Baltazar, Art and Franco. *Superman Family Adventures*. No. 1, DC Comics, 2013.

Baltazar, Art and Franco. *Tiny Titans: Adventures in Awesomeness*. DC Comics, 2009.

Barnett, Mac, and Dan Santat. *Oh No! Or How My Science Project Destroyed the World*. Disney-Hyperion, 2010.

Baruffi, Andrea. *If I Had a Robot Dog*. Sterling, 2005.

Base, Graeme. *The Worst Band in the Universe*. Penguin, 1999.

Beaty, Andrea, and Dan Santat. *Attack of the Fluffy Bunnies*. Abrams, 2010.

Bell, Andrea L., and Yolanda Molina-Gavilán, editors. *Cosmos Latinos: An Anthology of Science Fiction from Latin America and Spain*. Wesleyan, 2003.

Brown, Jeffrey. *Star Wars: Jedi Academy*. Scholastic, 2013.

Camper, Cathy, and Raul the Third. *Lowriders in Space*. Chronicle Books, 2014.

Carter, David. *Bugs in Space*. Little Simon, 1997.

Cole, Babette. *The Trouble with Dad*. Heinemann Young Books, 1985.

Corcoran, Mark. *Star Wars: The Mystery of the Rebellious Robot*. Random House, 1979.

Dolan, Elys. *Nuts in Space*. Nosy Crow, 2014.

Fischer, Scott M. *Twinkle*. Simon & Schuster, 2007.

Frankenstein. Directed by James Whale. Universal Pictures, 1931.

Gall, Chris. *Awesome Dawson*. Little, Brown Books for Young Readers, 2013.

Gall, Chris. *There's Nothing to Do on Mars*. Little, Brown Books for Young Readers, 2008.

Giarusso, Chris. *Mini Marvels*. Marvel Comics, 2013.

Godwin, Frank. *Connie: Captives of the Space Pirates*. Ledger Syndicate, 1938.

Godwin, Frank. *Connie: Master of the Jovian Moons*. Ledger Syndicate, 1939.

Hatke, Ben. *Little Robot.* First Second, 2015.

Hatke, Ben. *Zita the Spacegirl.* First Second, 2010.

"Hero of Space." Illustrated by John Celardo. *Fantastic Worlds,* no. 5, Visual Editions, 1952

Ignatow, Amy. *The Mighty Odds.* Amulet, 2016.

Jerwa, Brandon, Ian McGinty, and Art Baltazar. *Li'l Bionic Kids.* Dynamite Entertainment, 2014.

Kibuishi, Kazu. *Amulet: The Stonekeeper.* Scholastic, 2008.

Krahn, Fernando. *Robot-Bot-Bot.* Dutton, 1979.

L'Engle, Madeleine. *A Wrinkle in Time.* 1962. Square Fish, 2007.

L'Engle, Madeleine. *Madeleine L'Engle Herself: Reflections on a Writing Life.* Shaw, 2001.

L'Engle, Madeleine, and Hope Larson. *A Wrinkle in Time: The Graphic Novel.* Margaret Ferguson Books, 2012.

Liddel, Mary. *Little Machinery: A Critical Facsimile Edition.* 1926. Wayne State UP, 2009.

Marzollo, Jean, Claudio Marzollo, and Susan Meddaugh. *Ruthie's Rude Friends.* Dial Books for Young Readers, 1984.

Montclare, Brandon, Amy Reeder, and Natacha Bustos. *Moon Girl and Devil Dinosaur: BFF.* Marvel Comics, 2016.

Morrison, Grant, and Frank Quitely. *We3.* Vol. 1–3, Vertigo, 2004.

Morrissey, Dean. *The Crimson Comet.* HarpersCollins, 2006.

Oakley, Graham. *Henry's Quest.* Atheneum, 1986.

Orshoski, Paul, and Jeffrey Ebbeler. *Robot Man.* We Read Phonics, 2010.

Pinkney, Brian. *Cosmo and the Robot.* HarperCollins, 2000.

Reeve, Philip, and Sarah McIntyre. *Cakes in Space.* Random House Books for Young Readers, 2015.

Rex, Adam. *The True Meaning of Smekday.* Disney-Hyperion, 2007.

Schachner, Judy. *Skippyjon Jones . . . Lost in Spice.* Dutton, 2009.

Schaefer, Elizabeth, and Brian Rood. *Star Wars: Rey Meets BB-8.* Disney-Lucasfilm Press, 2015.

Scieszka, Jon, and Brian Biggs. *Frank Einstein and the Antimatter Motor.* Amulet Books, 2014.

Scott, Mairghread, and Luciano Vecchio. *Guardians of the Galaxy Infinite.* No. 1, Marvel Comics, 2013.

Shelley, Mary. *Frankenstein; or, the Modern Prometheus.* Lackington, Hughes, Harding, Mavor, & Jones, original in 1818.

Sias, Ryan. *Zoe and Robot: Let's Pretend!* Blue Apple Books, 2011.

Sierra, Judy, and Stephen Gammell. *The Secret Science Project That Almost Ate the School.* Simon & Schuster, 2006.

Smith, Ian, and Tyson Smith. *Emily and the Intergalactic Lemonade Stand.* SLG, 2004.

Spencer, Nick, and Mark Brooks. *Ant-Man.* No. 1, Marvel Comics, 2015.

Startling Comics. No. 27, Better Publications, 1944.

Tobin, Paul. *Marvel Adventures Spider-Man.* No. 1, Marvel Comics, 2010.

Underwood, Deborah, and Meg Hunt. *Interstellar Cinderella.* Chronicle Books, 2015.

Van Allsburg, Chris. *Zathura.* Houghton Mifflin, 2002.

Van Camp, Katie, and Lincoln Agnew. *Harrie and Horsey.* HarperCollins, 2009.

Wiesner, David. *Flotsam.* Clarion Books, 2006.

Wiesner, David. *June 29, 1999.* Clarion Books, 1992.

Wiesner, David. *Mr. Wuffles!* Clarion Books, 2013.

Wyatt, Chris, Ron Lim, and Rachelle Rosenberg. *Ant-Man: This Is Ant-Man.* Marvel Comics, 2015.

Yaccarino, Dan. *Doug Unplugged.* Dragonfly Books, 2013.

Secondary Sources

Aldiss, Brian W. *Billion Year Spree: The History of Science Fiction.* Corgi, 1973.

Anderson, Meg. "Where's the Color in Kids' Lit? Ask the Girl with 1,000 Books (and Counting)." *NPR,* 26 February 2016, npr.org/sections/ed/2016/02/26/467969663/wheres-the -color-in-kids-lit-ask-the-girl-with-1-000-books-and-counting. Accessed October 2016.

Applebaum, Noga. *Representations of Technology in Science Fiction for Young People.* Routledge, 2009.

Arizpe, Evelyn, and Morag Styles. *Children Reading Pictures: Interpreting Visual Texts.* RoutledgeFalmer, 2003.

Asim, Jabari. "Afro-Futurism." *The Crisis,* vol. 123, no. 2, 2016, pp. 22–28.

Attebery, Brian. *Decoding Gender in Science Fiction.* Routledge, 2002.

Attebery, Brian. *Stories about Stories: Fantasy and the Remaking of Myth.* Oxford UP, 2014.

Bang, Molly. *Picture This: How Pictures Work.* Chronicle Books, 2000.

Bernstein, Debra, and Kevin Crowley. "Searching for Signs of Intelligent Life: An Investigation of Young Children's Beliefs about Robot Intelligence." *Journal of the Learning Sciences,* vol. 17, no. 2, 2008, pp. 225–47.

Bernstein, Robin. *Racial Innocence: Performing American Childhood from Slavery to Civil Rights.* NYUP, 2011.

"Books by and/or about Black, Indigenous and People of Color (All Years)." *Cooperative Children's Book Center, School of Education, University of Wisconsin-Madison.* 27 October 2020. <https: //ccbc.education.wisc.edu/literature-resources/ccbc-diversity -statistics/books-by-about-poc-fnn/>. Accessed 27 January 2021.

Brouillette, Yann. "Comic Book Chemistry: Teaching Science Using Super Heroes." *CIRCE Magazine STEAM Edition,* vol. 1, 2019, pp. 47–58.

Brown, Alan S., and Brittany Logan. "How Fiction Puts the Science in Engineering." *Mechanical Engineering,* vol. 32, 2015, pp. 1–8.

Brown, Peter. Personal interview. 30 March 2016.

Cain, Kate, Jane Oakhill, Marcia Barnes, and Peter E. Bryant. "Comprehension Skill, Inference Making Ability, and the Relation to Knowledge." *Memory & Cognition,* vol. 29, no. 6, 2001, pp. 850–59.

Card, Orson Scott. *How to Write Science Fiction & Fantasy.* Writers Digest Books, 1990.

Clark, Christina. *Linking School Libraries and Literacy.* National Literacy Trust, 2010.

Clark, Christina, and Lucy Hawkins. *Public Libraries and Literacy.* National Literacy Trust, 2011.

Clute, John. "Children's SF." *The Encyclopedia of Science Fiction.* Edited by Peter Nicholls, John Clute, David Langford, and Graham Sleight, 2020. <http: //www.sf-encyclopedia.com>.

Clute, John, and Peter Nicholls. "Golden Age of SF." *The Encyclopedia of Science Fiction,* edited by Peter Nicholls and John Clute, Orbit, 1993, pp. 506–7.

Creekmur, Corey K. "Comics." *The Oxford Handbook of Science Fiction,* edited by Rob Latham, Oxford UP, 2014, pp. 212–25.

Csicsery-Ronay, Istvan, Jr. *The Seven Beauties of Science Fiction.* Wesleyan UP, 2008.

Dare, Emily. *Understanding Middle School Students' Perceptions of Physics Using Girl-friendly and Integrated STEM Strategies: A Gender Study.* 2015. U of Minnesota.

Delany, Samuel R. *Starboard Wine: More Notes on the Language of Science Fiction.* Wesleyan, 2012.

Dery, Mark. "Black to the Future: Interviews with Samuel R. Delany, Greg Tate, and Tricia Rose." *Flame Wars: The Discourse of Cyberculture*, edited by Mark Dery, Duke UP, 1994, pp. 179–222.

Dillon, Deborah, David O'Brien, and Elizabeth E. Heilman. "Literacy Research in the 21st Century: From Paradigms to Pragmatism and Practicality." *Theoretical Models and Processes of Reading*, edited by Donna E. Alvermann, Norman J. Unrau, and Robert B. Ruddell, International Reading Association, 2013, pp. 1104–32.

Dillon, Grace L. "Introduction: Imagining Indigenous Futurisms." *Walking the Clouds: An Anthology of Indigenous Science Fiction*, edited by Grace L. Dillon, U of Arizona P, 2012, pp. 1–14.

Dillon, Grace L. "Introduction: Indigenous Futurisms, Bimaashi Biidaas Mose, Flying and Walking towards You." *Extrapolation*, vol. 57, no. 1–2, 2016, pp. 1–6.

Dillon, Grace L. "Symposium on Science Fiction and Globalization: Global Indigenous Science Fiction." *Science Fiction Studies*, vol. 39, no. 3, 2012, pp. 374–84.

Ehrlich, Hannah. "The Diversity Gap in Children's Publishing." *The Open Book*, 30 March 2017, Lee & Low Books, blog.leeandlow.com/2017/03/30/the-diversity-gap-in-childrens-book-publishing-2017/. Accessed 30 November 2018.

Fichtelberg, Susan. *Encountering Enchantment: A Guide to Speculative Fiction for Teens.* Libraries Unlimited, 2006.

Fleischmann, Kenneth R., and Thomas Clay Templeton. "Past Futures and Technoscientific Innovation: The Mutual Shaping of Science Fiction and Science Fact." *Proceedings of the American Society for Information Science and Technology*, vol. 45, no. 1, 2008, pp. 1–11.

Flynn, Richard. "What Are We Talking about When We Talk about Agency?" *Jeunesse*, vol. 8, no. 1, 2016, pp. 254–65.

Foote, Bud. "Getting Things in the Right Order: Stephen King's *The Shining, The Stand*, and *It*." *Nursery Realms: Children in the Worlds of Science Fiction, Fantasy, and Horror*, edited by Gary Westfahl and George Slusser, U of Georgia P, 1999, pp. 200–209.

Fortunati, Leopoldina, Anna Esposito, Mauro Sarrica, and Giovanni Ferrin. "Children's Knowledge and Imaginary about Robots." *International Journal of Social Robotics*, vol. 7, no. 5, 2015, pp. 685–95.

Freire, Paulo. *Pedagogy of the Oppressed.* 1970. Continuum, 2000.

Gaiman, Neil. "What We Talk about When We Talk about Science Fiction." In Robert A. Heinlein, *Stranger in a Strange Land*. Penguin, 2016, pp. ix–xxii.

Galda, Lee, Lawrence Sipe, Lauren A. Liang, and Bernice E. Cullinan. *Literature and the Child.* Cengage Learning, 2013.

Gavaler, Chris, and Dan R. Johnson. "The Genre Effect: A Science Fiction (vs. Realism) Manipulation Decreases Inference Effort, Reading Comprehension, and Perceptions of Literary Merit." *Scientific Study of Literature*, vol. 7, no. 1, 2017, pp. 79–108.

Gibson, Mel. "Picturebooks, Comics and Graphic Novels." *The Routledge Companion to Children's Literature*, edited by David Rudd, Routledge, 2010, pp. 100–111.

Goldsmith, Francisca. *The Readers' Advisory to Graphic Novels.* ALA, 2010.

Gordon, Joan. "Literary Science Fiction." *The Oxford Handbook of Science Fiction*, edited by Rob Latham, Oxford UP, 2014, pp. 1–8.

Groensteen, Thierry. *The System of Comics*. 1999. UP of Mississippi, 2007.

Gubar, Marah. *Artful Dodgers: Reconceiving the Golden Age of Children's Literature*. Oxford UP, 2009.

Gubar, Marah. "The Hermeneutics of Recuperation: What a Kinship-Model Approach to Children's Agency Could Do for Children's Literature and Childhood Studies." *Jeunesse*, vol. 8, no. 1, 2016, pp. 291–310.

Gubar, Marah. "On Not Defining Children's Literature." *PMLA*, vol. 126, no. 1, 2011, pp. 209–16.

Gubar, Marah. "Risky Business: Talking about Children in Children's Literature Criticism." *Children's Literature Association Quarterly*, vol. 38, no. 4, 2013, pp. 450–57.

Gunn, James. "The Protocols of Science Fiction." *Gunn Center for the Study of Science Fiction*, University of Kansas, www.sfcenter.ku.edu/protocol.htm. Accessed 20 November 2018.

Hade, Daniel, and Laura Anne Hudock. "Redefining the Early Reader in an Era of Multiliteracies: Visual Language of Mo Willems' Elephant and Piggie Series." *The Early Reader in Children's Literature and Culture: Theorizing Books for Beginning Readers*, edited by Annette Wannamaker and Jennifer M. Miskec, Routledge, 2016, pp. 88–99.

Hartwell, David G. "The Golden Age of Science Fiction Is Twelve." *Visions of Wonder: The Science Fiction Research Association Anthology*, edited by David G. Hartwell and Milton T. Wolf, Tor Books, 1996, pp. 81–96.

Hastings, A. Waller. "Science Fiction." *Keywords for Children's Literature*, edited by Philip Nel and Lissa Paul, New York UP, 2011, pp. 202–7.

Hatfield, Charles. "Graphic Novel." *Keywords for Children's Literature*, edited by Philip Nel and Lissa Paul, New York UP, 2011, pp. 100–105.

Haynes, Carol, and Donald J. Richgels. "Fourth Graders' Literature Preferences." *The Journal of Educational Research*, vol. 85, no. 4, 1992, pp. 208–19.

Higgins, David. "Survivance in Indigenous Science Fictions: Vizenor, Silko, Glancy, and the Rejection of Imperial Victimry." *Extrapolation*, vol. 57, no. 1–2, 2016, pp. 51–72.

Hollinger, Veronica. "Genre vs. Mode." *Oxford Handbook of Science Fiction*, edited by Rob Latham, Oxford UP, 2014, pp. 1–10.

Horning, K. T. "I See White People." *CCBlogC*, 11 July 2013, Cooperative Children's Book Center, ccblogc.blogspot.com/2013/07/i-see-white-people.html. Accessed 28 January 2017.

Ioannou, Andri, Emily Andreou, and Maria Christofi. "Pre-Schoolers' Interest and Caring Behaviour around a Humanoid Robot." *TechTrends: Linking Research and Practice to Improve Learning*, vol. 59, no. 2, 2015, pp. 23–26.

Jipson, Jennifer L., and Susan A. Gelman. "Robots and Rodents: Children's Inferences about Living and Nonliving Kinds." *Child Development*, vol. 78, no. 6, 2007, pp. 1675–88.

Joseph, Michael. "Seeing the Visible Book: How Graphic Novels Resist Reading." *Children's Literature Association Quarterly*, vol. 37, no. 4, 2012, pp. 454–67.

Kilgore, De Witt Douglas. "Afrofuturism." *The Oxford Handbook of Science Fiction*, Oxford UP, 2014, pp. 1–9.

Landon, Brooks. "Extrapolation and Speculation." *The Oxford Handbook of Science Fiction*, edited by Rob Latham, Oxford UP, 2014, pp. 1–9.

Larrick, Nancy. "The All-White World of Children's Books." *The Saturday Review*, 11 September 1965, pp. 63–65.

Lavender, Isiah III. "Ethnoscapes: Environment and Language in Ishmael Reed's *Mumbo Jumbo*, Colson Whitehead's *The Intuitionist*, and Samuel R. Delany's *Babel-17*." *Science Fiction Studies*, vol. 32, no. 2, 2007, pp. 187–200.

Lenz, Millicent. "Raymond Briggs's *When the Wind Blows*: Toward an Ecology of the Mind for Young Readers." *Science Fiction for Young Readers*, edited by C. W. Sullivan III, Praeger, 1993, pp. 197–204.

Lesnik-Oberstein, Karín. *Children's Literature: Criticism and the Fictional Child*. Clarendon Press, 1994.

Levy, Michael. "*The Inter-Galactic Playground: A Critical Study of Children's and Teen's* [sic] *Science Fiction* (review)." *Children's Literature Association Quarterly*, vol. 34, no. 4, 2009, pp. 407–11.

Levy, Michael. "Science Fiction." *Oxford Encyclopedia of Children's Literature*, edited by Jack Zipes, Oxford UP, 2006, pp. 417–22.

Levy, Sharona T., and David Mioduser. "Does It 'Want' or 'Was It Programmed to . . .'? Kindergarten Children's Explanations of an Autonomous Robot's Adaptive Functioning." *International Journal of Technology and Design Education*, vol. 18, no. 4, 2008, pp. 337–59.

Mack, Elizabeth, Helen Augare, Linda Different Cloud-Jones, Dominique Davíd, Helene Quiver Gaddie, Rose E. Honey, Angayuqaq O. Kawagley, Melissa Little Plume-Weatherwax, Lisa Lone Fight, Gene Meier, Tachini Pete, James Rattling Leaf, Elvin Returns From Scout, Bonnie Sachatello-Sawyer, Hi'ilani Shibata, Shelly Valdez, and Rachel Wippert. "Effective Practices for Creating Transformative Informal Science Education Programs Grounded in Native Ways of Knowing." *Cultural Studies of Science Education*, vol. 7, 2012, pp. 49–70.

Mandler, Jean, and Nancy Johnson. "Remembrance of Things Parsed: Story Structure and Recall." *Cognitive Psychology*, vol. 9, 1977, pp. 111–51.

Mantzicopoulos, Panayota, and Helen Patrick. "Reading Picture Books and Learning Science: Engaging Young Children with Informational Text." *Theory into Practice*, vol. 50, 2011, pp. 269–76.

Matuk, Camillia, Talia Hurwich, and Anna Amato. "How Science Fiction Worldbuilding Supports Students' Scientific Explanation." *Proceedings of FabLearn 2019: 9th Annual Conference on Creativity and Fabrication in Education*, 2019.

McCabe, Janice, Emily Fairchild, Liz Grauerholz, Bernice A. Pescosolido, and Daniel Tope. "Gender in Twentieth-Century Children's Books: Patterns of Disparity in Titles and Central Characters." *Gender and Society*, vol. 25, no. 2, 2011, pp. 197–226.

McCloud, Scott. *Understanding Comics: The Invisible Art*. HarperPerennial, 1994.

McGregor, Tanny. *Comprehension Connections: Bridges to Strategic Reading*. Heinemann, 2007.

Mendlesohn, Farah. *The Intergalactic Playground: A Critical Study of Children's and Teens' Science Fiction*. McFarland, 2009.

Mendlesohn, Farah. "Is There Any Such Thing as Children's Science Fiction? : A Position Piece." *The Lion and the Unicorn*, vol. 28, no. 2, 2004, pp. 284–313.

Merla-Watson, Cathryn Josefina. "The Altermundos of Latin@futurism." *Alluvium*, vol. 6, no. 1, 2017.

Midkiff, Emily, and Bonnie Laabs. "Inspired Inquiry: Crafting K-5 STEM Lessons with Science Fiction." *K-12 STEM Education*, vol. 4, no. 1, 2018, pp. 289–96.

Milner, Andrew. *Locating Science Fiction*. Liverpool UP, 2012.

Moebius, William. "Introduction to Picturebook Codes." *Word & Image*, vol. 2, no. 2, 1986, pp. 141–51. In *Children's Literature: The Development of Criticism*, edited by Peter Hunt, Routledge, 1990, pp. 131–47.

Moebius, William. "Picture Book." *Keywords for Children's Literature*, edited by Philip Nel and Lissa Paul, New York UP, 2011, pp. 169–73.

Mohr, Kathleen A. J. "Children's Choices for Recreational Reading: A Three-Part Investigation of Selection Preferences, Rationales, and Processes." *Journal of Literacy Research*, vol. 38, no. 1, 2006, pp. 81–104.

Moss, Barbara, and Evangeline Newton. "An Examination of the Informational Text Genre in Basal Readers." *Reading Psychology*, vol. 23, 2002, pp. 1–13.

Moss, Gemma, and John W. McDonald. "The Borrowers: Library Records as Unobtrusive Measures of Children's Reading Preferences." *Journal of Research in Reading*, vol. 27, no. 4, 2004, pp. 401–12.

Nicholls, Peter. "Golden Age of SF." *The Encyclopedia of Science Fiction*, edited by Peter Nicholls and John Clute, Doubleday, 1979, pp. 258.

Nicholls, Peter. "Golden Age of SF." *The Encyclopedia of Science Fiction*, edited by John Clute, David Langford, Peter Nicholls, and Graham Sleight, Gollancz, 2011.

Nicholls, Peter. "Science Fantasy." *The Encyclopedia of Science Fiction*, edited by John Clute, David Langford, Peter Nicholls, and Graham Sleight, Gollancz, 2015.

Nikolajeva, Maria, and Carole Scott. *How Picturebooks Work*. Garland, 2001.

Nodelman, Perry. *The Hidden Adult: Defining Children's Literature*. Johns Hopkins UP, 2008.

Nodelman, Perry. "The Other: Orientalism, Colonialism, and Children's Literature." *Children's Literature Association Quarterly*, vol. 17, no. 1, 1992, pp. 29–35.

Nodelman, Perry. "Out There in Children's Science Fiction: Forward into the Past." *Science Fiction Studies*, vol. 12, no. 3, 2015, pp. 285–96.

Nodelman, Perry. *Words about Pictures: The Narrative Art of Children's Picture Books*. U of Georgia P, 1989.

Noh, Sueen. "Science, Technology, and Women Represented in Korean Sci-Fi Girls' Comics." *International Journal of Comic Art*, vol. 10, no. 2, 2008, pp. 209–34.

Onion, Rebecca. *Innocent Experiments: Childhood and the Culture of Popular Science in the United States*. UNC Press Books, 2016.

Orthia, Linda A. "How Does Science Fiction Television Shape Fans' Relationships to Science? Results from a Survey of 575 *Doctor Who* Viewers." *Journal of Science Communication*, vol. 18, no. 4, 2019, pp. 1–17.

Palumbo, Donald. "Science Fiction in Comic Books: Science Fiction Colonizes a Fantasy Medium." *Young Adult Science Fiction*, edited by C. W. Sullivan III, Greenwood Press, 1999.

Papazian, Gretchen. "Reading in the Early Reader: Mindset, Emotion, and Power." *The Early Reader in Children's Literature and Culture: Theorizing Books for Beginning Readers*, edited by Annette Wannamaker and Jennifer M. Miskec, Routledge, 2016, pp. 71–87.

Reese, Debbie. "The True Meaning of Smekday, by Adam Rex." *American Indians in Children's Literature*, 12 February 2015, americanindiansinchildrensliterature.blogspot. com/2015/02/the-true-meaning-of-smekday-by-adam-rex.html. Accessed 29 June 2018.

Richardson, Alan. *Literature, Education, and Romanticism: Reading as Social Practice, 1780–1832*. Cambridge UP, 2004.

Rose, Jacqueline. *The Case of Peter Pan, or, The Impossibility of Children's Fiction*. Palgrave Macmillan, 1984.

Rosenblatt, Louise. *The Reader, the Text, the Poem: The Transactional Theory of the Literary Work*. SIU Press, 1978.

Rosenbloom, Perry. "Best 15 Fantasy & Sci-Fi Graphic Novels for Kids (and the Whole Family)." *Geeks Raising Geeks*. 3 August 2013. https://www.geeksraisinggeeks.com/scifi -fantasy-graphic-novels-for-kids/. Accessed 15 September 2019.

Rousseau, Jean-Jacques. *Émile; or, Concerning Education; Extracts*. 1762, edited by Jules
    Steeg, translated by Eleanor Worthington, Project Gutenberg, 2009.
Sánchez-Eppler, Karen. *The Child's Part in Nineteenth-Century American Culture*. U of
    Chicago P, 2005.
Sanders, Joe Sutliff. "Chaperoning Words: Meaning-Making in Comics and Picture Books."
    Children's Literature, vol. 41, 2013, pp. 57–90.
Sands, Karen, and Marietta Frank. *Back in the Spaceship Again: Juvenile Science Fiction
    Series since 1945*. Praeger, 1999.
Saul, E. Wendy, and Donna Dieckman. "Choosing and Using Information Trade Books."
    Reading Research Quarterly, vol. 40, 2005, pp. 502–13.
Saylor, Megan M., Mark Somanader, Daniel Levin, and Kazuhiko Kawamura. "How Do
    Young Children Deal with Hybrids of Living and Non-Living Things: The Case of
    Humanoid Robots." *British Journal of Developmental Psychology*, vol. 28, no. 4, 2010, pp.
    835–51.
Scott, Colin. "Science for the West, Myth for the Rest?" *The Postcolonial Science and
    Technology Studies Reader*, edited by Sandra Harding, Duke UP, 2011, pp. 175–97.
Sipe, Lawrence R. *Storytime: Young Children's Literary Understanding in the Classroom*.
    Teacher's College Press, 2008.
Sipe, Lawrence R., and Anne E. Brightman. "Young Children's Interpretations of Page
    Breaks in Contemporary Picture Storybooks." *Journal of Literacy Research*, vol. 41, no. 1,
    2009, pp. 68–103.
Skolnick, Deena, and Paul Bloom. "What Does Batman Think about SpongeBob? Children's
    Understanding of the Fantasy/Fantasy Distinction." *Cognition*, vol. 101, no. 1, 2006, pp.
    B9–18.
Smith, Victoria Ford. *Between Generations: Collaborative Authorship in the Golden Age of
    Children's Literature*. UP of Mississippi, 2017.
Somanader, Mark C., Megan M. Saylor, and Daniel T. Levin. "Remote Control and
    Children's Understanding of Robots." *Journal of Experimental Child Psychology*, vol. 109,
    no. 2, 2011, pp. 239–47.
Spektor-Precel, Karen, and David Mioduser. "The Influence of Constructing Robot's
    Behavior on the Development of Theory of Mind (ToM) and Theory of Artificial
    Mind (ToAM) in Young Children." *Proceedings of the 14th International Conference on
    Interaction Design and Children—IDC '15*, vol. 11, 2015, pp. 311–14.
Spiers, Miriam Brown. "Reimagining Resistance: Achieving Sovereignty in Indigenous
    Science Fiction." *Transmotion*, vol. 2, no. 1–2, 2016, pp. 52–75.
Stein, Nancy, and Christine Glenn. "An Analysis of Story Comprehension in Elementary
    School Children." *Advances in Discourse Processes*, edited by R. D. Freedle, Albex, 1979,
    pp. 53–119.
Subramaniam, Mega, June Ahn, Amanda Waugh, and Allison Druin. "Sci-fi, Storytelling,
    and New Media Literacy." *Knowledge Quest*, vol. 41, no. 1, 2012, pp. 23–27.
Suvin, Darko. *Metamorphoses of Science Fiction: On the Poetics and History of a Literary
    Genre*. Yale UP, 1979.
Tan, Shaun. "The Accidental Graphic Novelist." *Bookbird*, vol. 49, no. 4, 2011, pp. 1–9.
Tandoi, Eve. "Hybrid Novels for Children and Young Adults." *The Edinburgh Companion to
    Children's Literature*, edited by Clémentine Beauvais and Maria Nikolajeva, Edinburgh
    UP, 2017, pp. 329–35.
Telotte, J. P. *Animating the Science Fiction Imagination*. Oxford UP, 2018.

Thomas, Ebony Elizabeth. *The Dark Fantastic: Race and the Imagination from Harry Potter to the Hunger Games*. New York UP, 2019.

Thomas, Sheree Renée, editor. *Dark Matter: A Century of Speculative Fiction from the African Diaspora*. Aspect-Warner Books, 2000.

Tolkien, J. R. R. "On Fairy-Stories." 1947. *Tree and Leaf*. George Allen and Unwin, 1964, pp. 109–61.

Turkle, Sherry. "What Are We Thinking about When We Are Thinking about Computers?" In *The Science Studies Reader*, Routledge, 1999, pp. 543–52.

Vizenor, Gerald. *Fugitive Poses: Native American Indian Scenes of Absence and Presence*. First Bison Books, 1998.

Walsh, Maureen. "'Reading' Pictures: What Do They Reveal? Young Children's Reading of Visual Texts." *Reading: Literacy and Language*, vol. 37, no. 3, 2003, pp. 123–31.

Wannamaker, Annette, and Jennifer M. Miskec, editors. *The Early Reader in Children's Literature and Culture: Theorizing Books for Beginning Readers*. Routledge, 2016.

Westcott, Kathryn. "Are 'Geek' and 'Nerd' Now Positive Terms?" *BBC News Magazine*, 16 November 2012, https://www.bbc.com/news/magazine-20325517. Accessed 2 February 2017.

Westfahl, Gary, Brian W. Aldiss, and Peter Nicholls. "Illustration." *The Encyclopedia of Science Fiction*, edited by John Clute, David Langford, Peter Nicholls, and Graham Sleight, Gollancz, 2018.

Westfahl, Gary, and George Slusser. "Introduction: Return to Innocence." *Nursery Realms: Children in the Worlds of Science Fiction, Fantasy, and Horror*, U of Georgia P, 1999, pp. ix–xiii.

Yannicopoulou, Angela. "Visual Aspects of Written Texts: Preschoolers View Comics." *L1– Educational Studies in Language and Literature*, vol. 4, no. 2, 2004, pp. 169–81.

Yaszek, Lisa. "Feminism." *The Oxford Handbook of Science Fiction*, edited by Rob Latham, Oxford UP, 2014, pp. 1–9.

Ybarra-Frausto, Tomás. "Latinopia Art Tomás Ybarra-Frausto 'Rasquachismo.'" *Vimeo*, Barrio Dog Productions Inc. , 15 August 2011, vimeo.com/27727487. Accessed 28 March 2017.

Yolen, Jane. "Letter to Jim." Jane Yolen Papers. The Kerlan Collection, University of Minnesota, 22 January 1979. Archived Material. Accessed 26 September 2016.

Young, Heather D., and Christian Z. Goering. "Teachers' Increased Use of Informational Text: A Phenomenological Study of Five Primary Classrooms." *Educational Considerations*, vol. 44, no. 1, 2018, pp. 1–19.

Young, Kevin L., and Charli Carpenter. "Does Science Fiction Affect Political Fact? Yes and No: A Survey Experiment on 'Killer Robots.'" *International Studies Quarterly*, vol. 62, no. 3, 2018, pp. 562–76.

INDEX

Page numbers in *italics* indicate an illustration.

ABOUT THE AUTHOR

Credit: Fabiola Photography

Emily Midkiff is an instructor at the University of North Dakota, where she teaches children's literature and literacy instruction. She spent nine years performing fantasy stories alongside children for an improv children's theater group, and now studies children's fantasy and science fiction stories with attention to what children have to say. She received her PhD from the University of Minnesota and her MA from Kansas State University.

CPSIA information can be obtained
at www.ICGtesting.com
Printed in the USA
BVHW082000220322
631905BV00003B/10